Petr Charvát

# The Birth of the State

Ancient Egypt, Mesopotamia, India
and China

Charles University in Prague
Karolinum Press
Prague 2013

Reviewed by: Prof. PhDr. Jan Bouzek, DrSc.
　　　　　　　Prof. PhDr. Jaroslav Malina, DrSc.

KATALOGIZACE V KNIZE – NÁRODNÍ KNIHOVNA ČR

Charvát, Petr
　The birth of the state : Ancient Egypt, Mesopotamia, India
and China / Petr Charvát; [translated by Daniel Morgan].
– 1st English ed. – Prague : Karolinum Press, 2013
Published by: Charles University in Prague
ISBN 978-80-246-2214-9

321.01 * 316.722(3) * (32) * (358) * (34) * (315)
– State, The – Ancient Egypt
– State, The – Mesopotamia
– State, The – Ancient India
– State, The – Ancient China
– ancient civilization – history
– monographs
930 – History of Ancient World to ca. 499 [8]

# CONTENTS

## HOW THEN IS A STATE BORN?

# PREFACE

This book features much of my research on the state and on statehood in the ancient Near East. Although I focused mainly on prehistoric and ancient Near East, I always made sure that my findings and observations also took into consideration the development of all other early state centers.

I gradually amassed considerable findings on the creation and development of early statehood in Egypt – for which I still feel an affection, as it was in this area that I had commenced my career as a researcher – in the Near East, in India and in China. This body of knowledge helped me in preparing introductory university courses on the history and culture of civilizations predating antiquity that I have taught since 1993 at universities in Prague and Plzeň.

I was also given the chance by the LIBRI publishing house to write on earlier periods of the ancient development of the centers of civilization in an encyclopedia-type series. All those readers understanding Czech are therefore welcome to delve into these books as well.[1]

The creation of the book that lies before you was not, however, that easy. Following the publication of my previous book[2] by the Karolinum publishing house, its director, Jaroslav Jirsa, invited my to present the results of my more broadly focused research to the public and kindly showed interest in publishing this work. I am sincerely grateful to him for this. In time, I realized that it really would be beneficial for my students and other readers to be presented with this kind of treatise, so I decided to begin writing it.

---

[1]  Petr Charvát, Václav Marek, Pavel Oliva: Encyklopedie dìjin starovìku (Encyclopaedia of ancient history, in Czech), Prague: LIBRI 2008.

[2]  Petr Charvát, The Iconography of Pristine Statehood – Painted Pottery and Seal Impressions from Susa, Southwestern Iran, Prague: Karolinum Press 2005.

Those leafing through this book might feel that the writing is dry and tedious, full of archaeological information, descriptions of objects and excavations. I am afraid that this is how it works with modern historical sciences and archaeology in particular. Yet my interpretation has two objectives: Above all, I hope to present a summarized account of present-day knowledge and understanding of the oldest statehood of the Old World, but also of that which preceded it. Achieving this requires nothing less than a laborious analysis of the pages and "strange volumes of this age-old and precious science," of the folios of archeological reports. On the other hand, there is clearly a need for a comprehensive assessment of the finds presented and for a review of the social process that led to the creation of the state in all its complexities. I attempt this in the fifth chapter, where I include passages from ancient texts, whose authors attested to everything that afflicted them and their nations in times of trouble.

I cannot conceal the fact that, especially in those areas that are not found within my own expertise as a cuneiformist and archaeologist, I relied on the advice and assistance of treasured friends, who provided me with significant help at various points in my research. I am extremely indebted to them for this.

Until now, most of my professional work has been conducted in two institutions of the Czechoslovak Academy of Sciences, which later became the Academy of Sciences of the Czech Republic: the Institute of Archaeology and the Oriental Institute. The Institute of Archaeology provided me with a position at the very beginning of my research career, and I am grateful for the many suggestions and role models in the creative and friendly atmosphere that prevailed there. I also benefited from advice, information, assistance and support from many people at the Oriental Institute.

I should also mention my *alma mater*, which prepared me for my research work – Charles University in Prague. My research career began in the university's Institute of Egyptology and the memories from these years will never fade.

I would often travel to Brno University for guidance, assistance and friendly advice. I am indebted to its staff, especially to my colleague Inna Mateiciucová.

A great deal of gratitude is owed to my colleagues and friends from various foreign institutions. Worthy of special recognition are Jean-Louis Huot and his dear wife, Serge Cleuziou, Jean-Marie Durand, Béatrice André-Salvini and Françoise Demange, Jean-Daniel Forest, Régis Vallet, Jean-Jacques Glassner and his kind wife, my long-time friend Erle Leichty, Barry Eichler, Steve Tinney and Philip Jones, Holly Pittman, Gregory Possehl, Mitchell Rothman, Shannon White, Richard Zettler, Charles Maisels, Dieter Schlingloff and especially Walther Sallaberger.

I acknowledge my debt of gratitude to my learned colleagues Svetoslav Kostič, Jiří Prosecký and Břetislav Vachala for help with English-language editions of the ancient texts.

This book would certainly never have been written without the full support and help of my family. My wife, Kateřina Charvátová, deserves my utmost gratitude for her understanding and support, and a special thanks goes to Jan, Lenka, Ondřej and Eva. Little Toníček Charvát has brought great joy into my life. If it were not for all of you, my dear family, this book would not have been written.

# ACKNOWLEDGEMENTS

This research for this book was made possible by the generous support of a few munificent sponsors of scientific research. In 2003–2004, I received a Fulbright grant for a residency in Philadelphia, Pennsylvania. In 2005, the American Philosophical Society, also based in Philadelphia (Franklin Grant 2005), awarded me with a research grant. In 2008, my residency in Paris was supported by the *Section des Sciences Historiques et Philologiques* of the *Ecole Pratique des Hautes Etudes*. It was thanks to the efforts of my learned friend and colleague Ludvik Kalus that I received this grant. My research has also been supported by the grant agency of the Academy of Sciences of the Czech Republic, which previously awarded me grant no. A8021401, and in 2008–2010 assisted my research with grant no. A8000 20804.

Prague, 20th of July 2013                                    Petr Charvát

# ANCIENT EGYPT

# THE NATURAL ENVIRONMENT

A key geographic factor contributing to the historical complexion of Egypt is the Nile River, which over the millions of years of its existence has carved out its riverbed in the North African bedrock. Totaling 6,695 km in length, its upper part consists of two tributaries – the Blue Nile and White Nile. While the Blue Nile's source is Lake Tana in Ethiopia, the White Nile originates with Lake Victoria and Lake Albert in Uganda. The Nile Valley cuts south to north through Egypt, stretching 1,360 km from the first cataract (cascades, rapids) near the city of Aswan. There are six cataracts in the Nile riverbed: the first near Aswan and, moving southward, the last near the Sudanese city of Khartoum. From Aswan to the mouth at the sea, the Nile Valley's gradient is 85 meters. The river runs to the Mediterranean Sea through a vast delta now demarcated by two main distributaries, the Rosetta (west) and Damietta (east). In ancient times, the Nile Delta had one more main distributary, meaning that there were three distributaries at the time.

The Nile Valley possesses a surprisingly diverse topography. Ten kilometers wide on average, it spans a maximum width of 17 kilometers at the segment south of the Faiyum Oasis. Including its delta, the Nile Valley covers a total area of 37,540 km². The river's bottom is composed of sand and rock sediment covered by layers of clay deposits.

The rock terraces over the Nile Valley previously provided quality types of building stone, lime, sandstone, granite and basalt. To both the west and the east of the river, these terraces gradually turn into a plain now covered by desert. In ancient times, the edges of the valley consisted of a grassy steppe that contained metal deposits (including copper and gold) as well as gemstones – agate, amethyst, carnelian, chalcedony, almandine, jasper, onyx, crystal and the legendary turquoise from the Sinai Peninsula.

Yet there is more to Egypt than just the Nile. Vast oases, of which the Faiyum basin is the largest, extend west of the river. This low ground covers a total area of 12,000 km$^2$ with an altitude of −44 m with Lake Birket Qarun (in ancient times it was called Moeris) forming its center. We also find the Siwa, Bahariya, Farafra, Dakhla and Kharga oases in the western desert. Furthest west by the Libyan border lies the Kufra Oasis. With its annual flooding, the Nile ensured the fertility of Egyptian fields up until the first Aswan Dam was built in 1907. The floods usually began in early June and culminated in mid August. The optimum rise in the Nile's water level was considered 16 cubits (8.36 m). With the water level beginning to drop in September, field work could be commenced in October.

The Egyptian climate is characterized by four seasons: winter (December–February), spring (March–May), summer (June–August) and autumn (September–November). It usually rains in Egypt from November to April with most of the precipitation coming in December and January. Plowing and cereal sowing usually began in October after the Nile stopped flooding. We do not know for sure to what extent, if at all, Egyptian farmers cultivated spring cereals.

The original flora and fauna were much more abundant than they are today. Various species of palm, sycamore, fig and willow trees, as well as acacia and tamarisk grew in the river valley, whose banks were covered with reeds. The Nile's banks were once frequented by elephants, rhinoceros, giraffes, lions, leopards, hippos and crocodiles. Herds of antelopes and gazelles grazed in the steppe above the river valley. The waters of the Nile were brimming with fish and various species of birds nested there.

# THE ROOTS AND ORIGIN OF ALL THINGS:
# THE PRODUCTIVE ECONOMY IN EGYPT
## (Neolithic Age, ca. 5500–4500 BC)[3]

The people of prehistoric Egypt farmed arable soil whose total area is estimated at 34,440 km² [1].[4]

The onset of a productive economy and the people's own food production came about in quite specific terms in prehistoric Egypt. Archeologists have always admired two unique traits of Egypt during the Neolithic Age: First and foremost, the Neolithic Age in the land above the Nile is relatively recent, probably not dating back earlier than 5500 BC. This differs significantly from the Near East, whose Neolithic dawn is thought to have occurred around 10,000 BC. Secondly, the "Black Land" has produced a surprisingly low number of sites yielding Neolithic findings. These essentially consist of Faiyum, Merimda Beni Salama, El Omari and Maadi in the northern part of the country, predominantly in the Nile Delta region.

What is the reason for this? We probably need to seek the cause in Egypt's distinctive natural conditions. Over the last ten thousand years of human history, the Sahara Desert was far more hospitable than it is today. It was teeming with springs, enjoyed a favorable precipitation cycle and featured abundant flora and, consequently, bountiful fauna. It therefore can be assumed that its human inhabitants, who left behind monuments of ancient art (recently brought to the general

---

[3] Unless otherwise mentioned, my main source of information in further interpretation is the publication Dossiers d'Archéologie No. 307, octobre 2005: L'Egypte prédynastique, Dijon, Editions Faton S. A. S. 2005, with contributions by Béatrix Midant-Reynes, Yann Tristrant, Krzysztof Cialowicz, Sylvie Duchesne, Luc Staniaszek, Eric Crubézy, Nathalie Baduel, Dominique Farout, Renée Friedman, Marcell Campagn and Stan Hendricks. Another source is David Wengrow's The Archaeology of Early Egypt – Social Transformations in North-East Africa, 10,000 to 2650 BC, Cambridge – New York – Melbourne – Madrid – Cape Town – Singapore – Sao Paulo, Cambridge University Press 2006. I am grateful to my colleagues Petra Maříková and Jana Mynářová for the helpful passages from this book.

[4] Charles K. Maisels, Early Civilizations of the Old World, London and New York, Routledge – Taylor and Francis Group 2001, p. 186.

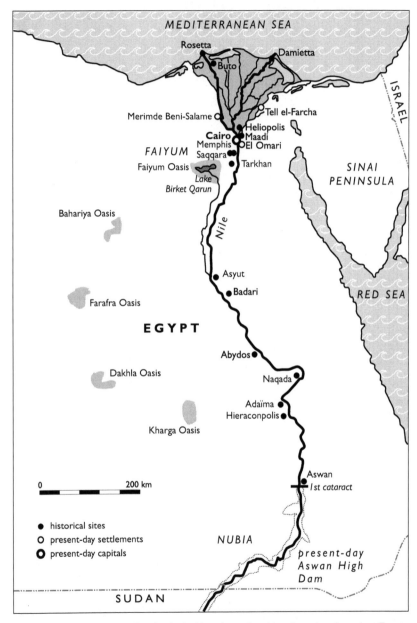

**Fig. 1** Primary historical and archeological locations of prehistoric and early ancient Egypt.

public's attention by the film *The English Patient*), led the kind of life that could be called "clustered and scattered". At the more perilous times of the year – most likely during the hot and exhaustive summer – they probably moved in smaller groups to protected and shaded position next to running water, where they could better survive the summer heat.

When the climate was more hospitable – probably mainly in winter – they concentrated on the open steppe in camps numbering dozens and often even hundreds. There, on the migration paths of animals moving from summer to winter grazing lands, they hunted the weaker stragglers from the passing herds. In Egypt, we could examine the traces around the settlement of smallish sub-groups that wandered here, weighed down with the kill from winter hunts, so that in tolerable climate conditions they could harvest occasional crops from lands watered predominantly by the regularly flooding Nile.

As far as agriculture is concerned, Neolithic Egypt in no way differed from the Neolithic farming of other cultures and continents. Crop farming mainly consisted here of the cultivation of cereals, mainly barley and wheat, but also flax. Knowledge of garden and orchard farming still had not been developed; this was primarily due to the regular migration of groups subsisting on shifting cultivation. Egyptian livestock farmers, just as those from other lands, raised herds of sheep, goats and cattle, as well as lithe and nimble pigs. Domesticated dogs apparently helped them in their work, and donkeys may have also been used as beasts of burden. The hunting of game remained a constant subsistence custom for the people of the Neolithic Age in Egypt. Such game included large animals such as elephants, hippos, crocodiles, antelope and cervids. The sea, the Nile and some lakes were fished, and gathering techniques were used for other game (e.g. turtles).

Prehistoric Egyptians mastered working with natural materials without much difficulty. In addition to everyday domestic necessities, they used clay to created handmade pottery, painting the surfaces shades of red, brown or black. Pottery adorned with engraved patterns has been found at other sites. Stones were used for smaller cutting tasks and served as common household tools – blades, sickle blades, knives, peelers, chisels, arrowheads and the likes – as well as for making heavier and cruder grinding tools such as plant and vegetable grinders, sharp-edged axes and even hoes. Owing to its abundance and fissility, bone was often used in tools such as spikes, bodkins, needles and harpoons. Larger bones could also be used as trowels, forming tools or spatulas. Seashells or ostrich eggshells were used in a similar manner to make spoons and other utensils. Galenite finds indicated that they may have already at that time attempted to use metals. Organic materials were used to make a broad spectrum of objects during the Neolithic Age in Egypt. Wood was used to make dwellings and functional parts of tools (e.g. scythe handles were made out of tamarisk), as well as flails for threshing grains. Tanned hides were used to make clothes (shoes) accessories and for coverings and carrying aids (bags, sacks, pouches, packs). Delicate linen was woven from harvested flax, while sheep wool was used to make coarser cloth. Plant tissue of all kinds – from reeds or twigs – served a wide range of purposes: It could be used for light structures or shelters, but was also undoubtedly used for bed matting, for packaging goods and for making all kinds of baskets. Prehistoric Egyptians clearly used organic materials to build canoe-like vessels with upright bows and sterns used to navigate the Nile.

Only faint traces were left of the settlements of Egypt's Neolithic people. They probably lived in light, above-ground dwellings made from woven sticks, packed clay and timber poles that were easily built and could be freely abandoned without much loss. We know nothing of their furniture, of which there was probably very little. The settlements featured fireplaces and open-air furnaces offering better visibility for work. There were also a number of pits or large containers and baskets set into holes dug out of the ground that probably served as storage, depositories or caches. It is interesting that these pits were generally concentrated in a single place or within one confined area in the settlement. This leads us to believe that every family did not have its own pantry; instead, the entire community kept its reserves together in one place. This attests to the rather strong group solitary of these early Egyptians, who most likely arrived here already organized into communities bound by blood or quasi-blood relations. Some finds provide testimony of dwellings on elevated places, among which the aforementioned supply pits were concentrated at less elevated sites.

In most cases, these were seasonal settlements occupied at the end of spring and early summer.

The negligible number of burial sites is a striking feature of Egyptian Neolithic cultures. This may, however, be given by the fact that the deceased were sometimes simply laid to rest in the ruins of abandoned settlements. Though it is evident that the communality of the Neolithic Age in this area was not overly strong, obligatory burial rituals already begin to appear at some sites: The dead generally lie crouched on their right side with their heads pointing south; they are wrapped in a blanket or pelt and accompanied by pottery vessels or shells, cosmetic palettes, or even small trinkets such as beads made from ostrich eggshells, and any funerary objects they may have received for their final voyage. However, Neolithic Egyptians probably had yet to lay claim to the "Black Land" in the form of large and permanent burial grounds – an act characteristic of communality in its defined and deliberate spatial action ("this land is ours because our ancestors are buried here").

It is extremely difficult to attempt a description of the spiritual profile of Egyptian society in the Neolithic Age. The clay figurines of

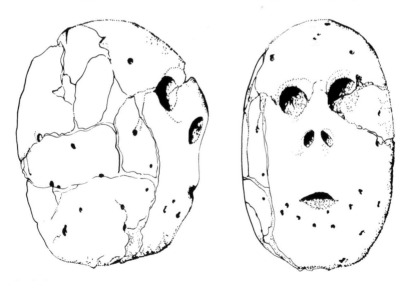

**Fig. 2** Clay rendering of a human head. Merimda Beni Salama, Neolithic Age.

horned cattle bring to mind the customs of Neolithic cultures in Asia from a settlement context. The form of a human head, found at the Merimda Beni Salama settlement site [2] and most likely originally featuring hair and a beard made from organic material, evokes the idea of cults not exceeding the traditional standards of an egalitarian society, whose main criteria consist of age, sex and acquired status. Yet we lack more detailed information on this.

# THE CHALCOLITHIC AGE OR BUILDING INEQUALITY: THE BADARI CULTURE (4500–3800 BC)

At first glance, the Egyptian prehistoric culture referred to as the Badari in the northern part of Upper Egypt does not overly differ from its Neolithic predecessors. This is, however, merely an illusion.

Generally speaking, the culture's *habitus* did not change all that much. Curiously, in addition to wheat, barleys, millet and legumes, the seeds of wild growing (and most likely gathered) plants reappear. The raising of sheep, goats, cattle, pigs and geese[5] was supplemented by fishing, sometimes conducted seasonally during the fish passages[6] and gazelle hunting.[7] The presence of metals, especially that of copper, used for ornament, weapons and tools in the Badari culture is worth noting. Relatively inconspicuous, though extremely meaningful changes indicating social development were occurring.

Highly significant among the finds are stone palettes used to hold coloring agents applied to the face and body. These were not merely cosmetic aids. Given that cosmetic palettes would later become an extremely important indicator of a prominent social position (and thus a badge of the Egyptian elite) and conveyors of a message of considerable spiritual content, they signify the first distinction of individuals still performing perhaps more of a specific cult role, i.e. that of a prehistoric shaman of sorts.

Another striking aspect is that these first cosmetic palettes were made from a single type of mineral: greywacke (metapelite). This attests to a sufficiently detailed knowledge of the geology of Egyptian

---

[5]   Cyril Aldred, Egypt to the End of the Old Kingdom, London, Thames and Hudson 1965, p. 25.

[6]   Kateřina Postupová, Počátky kontaktu Egypta a Předního Východu (Early contact Between Egypt and the Near East), B.A. thesis, Plzeň, West Bohemian University in Plzeň, Faculty of Arts 2007, p. 12.

[7]   Charles K. Maisels, Early Civilizations of the Old World, London and New York, Routledge – Taylor and Francis Group 2001, pp. 45–46.

minerals and also to the domestic nature of the Badari culture; it seems that its people no longer roamed great distances to the future Sahara Desert, but probably moved within the "Black Land."

They also lived here in circular abodes made of clay or poles and wattle. Fireplaces and storage pits supplemented these dwellings.

The Badari were already at this point burying their dead in large burial grounds with a greater abundance of funerary objects than before. In addition to elegant red vessels with black edges, the deceased received for their final voyage numerous jewels, shells, objects made from bone, ivory or ostrich eggshells, spoons, combs, cups, stone vessels, weapons and tools. We also find here cosmetic palettes and shells from the Red Sea, and even copper trinkets. Exactly what was used to carve the female figurines of bone and ivory for the Badari's deceased is still a mystery.

Yet a major change in the burial ritual is evident. For the first time ever, the Egyptian dead are positioned according to uniform rules: in a curled position on a north-south axis with their heads to the south and generally facing west. Although it is remarkable that even in Egypt's historic culture the burial grounds are located in the west, of even greater importance is the finding that the burial of the dead is, for the first time ever, subject to strictly set rules. We therefore need to scrutinize the creation of the first world view imposed upon the survivors to provide the deceased with an eternal repose in accordance with already spatially fixed notions regarding the arrangement of the visible and invisible world. Early social distinction evidently assumed a symbolic nature and manifested itself in the spiritual sphere through a clearer idea about the arrangement of the worlds accessible and inaccessible to our senses. At the same time, those individuals entrusted with communicating with the supernatural also began to use their external appearance to distinguish themselves from others in their community.

# EMBRYONIC SIGNS OF THE STATE:
# NAQADA I, II AND III (4000 BC)

## Economy

Excavation of the settlements revealed that the culture's overall *habitus* remained the same – hunting, fishing and gathering. Wheat, barleys and legumes continued to be grown, while livestock consisted of sheep, goats and pigs. The gathering of wild crops, fishing and the gathering of bivalves in the waters of the Nile were other forms of subsistence.[8] The first artificial materials, faience vessels, appeared in the manufacturing sphere.[9]

It is not until 4000 BC that we see the series of changes that led to the birth and establishment of statehood in the society of prehistoric and ancient Egypt.

First of all, there occurred here a fundamental change in farming and the notorious "disappearance of settlements." It has been alleged that a large number of settlements simply disappeared from the horizon of Egyptian archeology and that around 4000 BC their population dropped to 40% of its number prior to that.[10]

This is obviously an optical illusion: the settlements in Egypt did not disappear; their archeological traces have simply not been preserved. The reason for this can probably be found in the location of these settle-

[8]  Charles K. Maisels, Early Civilizations of the Old World, London and New York, Routledge – Taylor and Francis Group 2001, p. 49.

[9]  Kateřina Postupová, Počátky kontaktu Egypta a Předního Východu (Early contact between Egypt and the Near East), B.A. thesis, Plzeň, West Bohemian University in Plzeň, Faculty of Arts 2007, p. 10.

[10]  Lech Krzyzaniak, Trends in the Socio-Economic Development of Egyptian Predynastic Societies, in: Acts of the First International Congress of Egyptology, Cairo, October 2–10, 1976, Berlin, Akademie-Verlag 1979, pp. 407–412, on pp. 409–410; further literature given by David Wengrow, The Archaeology of Early Egypt – Social Transformations in North-East Africa, 10,000 to 2650 BC, Cambridge – New York – Melbourne – Madrid – Cape Town – Singapore – Sao Paulo, Cambridge University Press 2006, p. 82, note 13.

ments: While in the Neolithic and Chalcolithic ages they were located, among other places, on rock plateaus above the Nile Valley, in 4000 BC they were more prone to being built directly in the river valley and to occupy advantageous positions within the Nile's flood plain. Their disappearance from the archeological picture can be accounted for by the fact that the Nile's fluvial plain was repeatedly flooded each year by many meters of sludge. In this light, any archeological discovery of remnants of these settlements is much more a case of incredible luck than anything else.

Yet if during the 4th millenium BC the regular settlement descended into the Nile's flood plain, this would represent proof of an extremely important social process, i.e. a mass transition to settled agriculture (in contrast to the migratory agriculture of the preceding period) carried out directly in the most advantageous locations: in the arable land of the Nile Valley regularly revitalized by the river's repeated flooding. A settled agricultural population offers state agencies other advantages as well: it is very productive and, therefore, taxes can be imposed in higher amounts. Settlements in fixed places are also controllable and governable.

A model of a hut, previously discovered at one of the burial grounds from around the same period, offers us an idea of what settlements looked like at that time. The small structure is oblong with walls of wattle, most likely plastered with clay and protruding in the upper part into a round roof. The jamb casing was most likely made from wooden beams.[11]

Yet the transition to settled agriculture did not mean that other subsistence activities came to a halt. Graves from that period reveal harpoons, fishing tackle, knives and quivers, clearly demonstrating the importance of hunting, fishing and gathering activities on the unfarmed land.

---

[11] Cyril Aldred, Egypt to the End of the Old Kingdom, London, Thames and Hudson 1965, p. 34, fig. 22 Charles K. Maisels, Early Civilizations of the Old World, London and New York, Routledge – Taylor and Francis Group 2001, pp. 48–49.

## The embryos of cities

Another social process reflected in archeological finds was occurring at this point in time in Upper Egypt and possibly elsewhere: the creation and development of extraordinary settlements – the first cities of sorts. Hieraconpolis, (Nekhen in Ancient Egyptian) the original capital of Upper Egypt with the temple of the hawk deity Horus of Nekhen, was one such settlement. A reverence for "the Spirits *(bau)* of Nekhen" attests to the sacredness of the place at this time. These spirits were deities with jackal heads, considered to be companions of the reigning pharaoh and representatives of the deceased kings of Upper Egypt.[12] Even though Hieraconpolis had already been settled in the Badari period (ca. 4500 BC), its rise to unrivalled importance occurred in 3800–3500 BC.

By roughly the mid 4th millenium BC a rectangular area of 2.5 × 3.5 km had been settled. Excavation of the settlement site also revealed spatial differentiations in the residential quarter, manufacturing quarter and cult and burial areas. Crafts working with fire (and therefore dangerous), such as pottery shops, were located on the city's perimeter. Numerous finds of various kinds of ovens and furnaces support this. An especially popular location was the valley's cliffs that cut Hieraconpolis roughly in half from north to south. Not only did the locations of pyrotechnic workplaces keep them at a safe distance from the densely built residential quarters, they were also positioned to better avail themselves of the open air currents that provided a better draft for the furnaces. Excavation of the city's perimeter revealed a potter's dwelling with a workshop that burned down during prehistoric times and thus provided us with access to a very interesting sample of original Egyptian architecture with roof beams and walls made of large poles. Another find from Hieraconpolis offers a clear picture of this kind of dwelling. Its recessed part measured 4 × 3.5 m and was 0.45–0.80 m deep in the ground. The dwelling's internal walls were plastered with

---

[12] Jiří Janák, Chapter 105 of Kniha mrtvých v období Nové říše – Staroegyptské pojetí vzkříšení (The book of the dead during the New Empire – the Ancient Egyptian concept of resurrection), doctorate dissertation, Prague, Charles University in Prague, the Hussite Theological Faculty, Religious Studies Department 2002, p. 25.

clay and there was at least one adobe wall. The roof was held up by eight wooden posts, of which two were positioned at the structure's axis. It was entered from the eastern side and the interior was equipped with an oven, a storage vessel and a ceramic block, perhaps to regulate the heat flow.[13] Another settlement on the city's periphery, apparently belonging at one time to a cattle farmer, was built as a farmstead surrounded by a palisade with buildings, fireplaces, large storage vessels and kitchen areas. A similar periphery location possesses another type of pyrotechnical workplace, presently linked to the brewing of beer. Experts estimate the capacity of one of these with eight boiling vats to be a respectable hectoliter of beer per person, which was to cover the daily consumption of 300 people. This can be seen as the first signs of the existence of a redistributive economy, quite clearly an indication of the path to statehood in still ancient Egypt. We will ascertain to what extent the centralized supply of beer was also accompanied by the mass distribution of cone-shaped loaves of bread baked in special ceramic "tube pans" once we are able to fully confirm that these "tube pans" were really used to bake bread.[14]

Visitors of ancient Hieraconpolis would enter a central temple located in the middle of the city. Worshippers passed through an oval 40 × 13 m courtyard in front of the building itself. This courtyard was first surrounded by a fence of reeds plastered with clay, later by adobe walls. Near the longer, northern side of the complex there stood at least five rectangular structures, some of which served as chipped-stone industry workshops for silex and carnelian beads. The temple's facade on the opposing, southern side of the courtyard featured four massive posts with the largest 1–1.5 m in diameter, perhaps whole trunks of imported Lebanon cedars. A pit to secure a single large pole, perhaps for a flag or symbol of the deity, was located across from the entrance.[15]

---

[13]  Charles K. Maisels, Early Civilizations of the Old World, London and New York, Routledge – Taylor and Francis Group 2001, p. 49.

[14]  David Wengrow, The Archaeology of Early Egypt – Social Transformations in North-East Africa, 10,000 to 2650 BC, Cambridge – New York – Melbourne – Madrid – Cape Town – Singapore – Sao Paulo, Cambridge University Press 2006, pp. 94–97, depiction of bread "tube pans" also on p. 88, Fig. 4.4 below.

[15]  Charles K. Maisels, Early Civilizations of the Old World, London and New York, Routledge – Taylor and Francis Group 2001, p. 69.

The temple stood for about 500 years and was reconstructed several times over the period of its existence. A large number of black oval-shaped vessels and red bottle-shaped vessels come from the waste pits beyond the surrounding wall. These might have been aids for performing fertilization rituals, in which the red vessels represented the parched and barren bottom of the Nile Valley before the flooding, while the black represented the fertile earth brought to the Egyptian field by the floods. Along with vessel fragments, the bones of possible sacrificial animals – crocodiles, hippos, gazelles and wild goats – were also found here. The liturgy of the temple thus referred not only to the people of the Nile's waters and river valley, but also to the creatures freely roaming the steppe and desert on the vast areas of the rock plains, into which the Nile had carved out its riverbed over the course of millions of years. A fragment with an engraved image of the fertility goddess Bat and with a picture of a female captive dominated by a symbol of royal power was found in the temple. A close link is thus already evident in the prehistoric period between the fertility of the "Black Land" and Egypt's highest ruling office.

The burial grounds in ancient Hieraconpolis will be analyzed later in the book.

It was therefore more than just a quantitative increase in the area of the settlement that occurred here; a deliberate and calculated determination of the structure of the settled area was also carried out. This can unquestionably be considered early urbanism.

## Social differentiation: the elite and the others

Differences within society continued to deepen here [3]. Exceptional movable and immovable assets indicating the prominent position of some individuals began to appear. Although the aforementioned cosmetic palettes continued to be found in burial grounds, sometimes in distinct groups of graves, they were also found in sacred areas, cult centers and temples.

Individuals of authority possessed magnificent objects bearing emblems, frequently weapons such as flint knives with engraved or

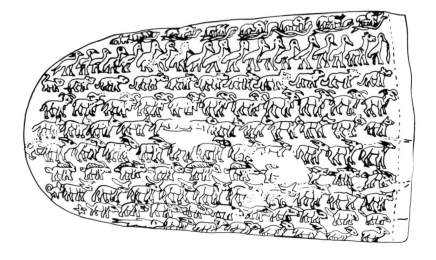

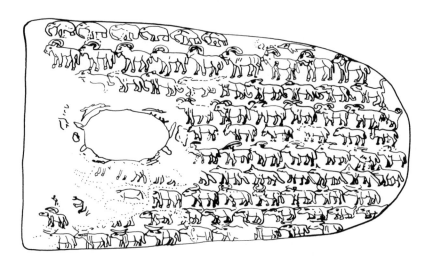

**Fig. 3** The Brooklyn Museum knife handle, ivory, early Naqada III period, ca. 3400 BC.

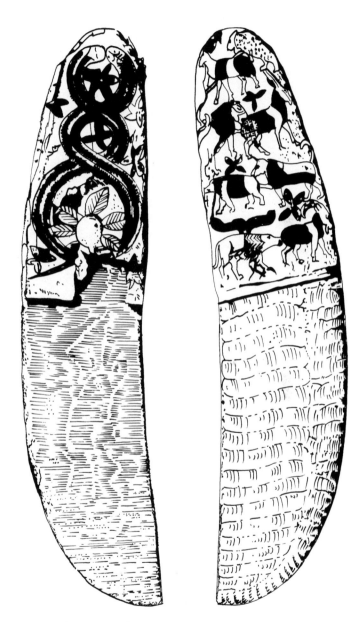

**Fig. 4** Knife from Gebel el-Tarif with gold-leaf handle. End of Naqada II period 3600–3500 BC.

**Fig. 5** Ivory knife handle from Gebel el-Arak. End of Naqada II period 3600–3500 BC.

otherwise adorned handles from precious materials such as gold or ivory [4, 5]. They would tend to their appearance with luxurious ivory combs and use their cherished cosmetic palettes. We find here the first monumental graves, in which the deceased were laid to rest with an abundance of funerary objects and whose interiors were sometimes also adorned with artistic decoration (e.g. frescoes).

In some cases we even find evidence of power structures that existed prior to the creation of a united Egyptian state. Symbols of a scorpion, fish, bull's head and bird appear on inscriptions from the Tomb U-j at Abydos. All of these are considered to be names of early leaders of some of the Egyptian lands.[16]

---

[16] Literature cited by Jane A. Hill, Cylinder Seal Glyptic in Predynastic Egypt and Neighboring Regions, Oxford, Archaeopress 2004, on p. 15.

Over time we find mounting proof of society's division into the ruling and the ruled. Telling signs of this are the cosmetic palettes, gradually changing from mere beauty aids into relics of art that were most likely kept in the land's prominent temples. These were originally meant as appearance-refinement aids, or to be used in a similar way but for another purpose (e.g. making "masks" for participation in a magical or ritual act). Coloring agents found from this period and used for cosmetic purposes include green malachite (copper ore), black galena (lead ore) and the color red. Some skulls have even revealed traces of complete make-up coverage of eye and nose areas in green and other parts of the face in red. A piece of green malachite, placed in children's graves under the head of the buried child, and sometimes alternating

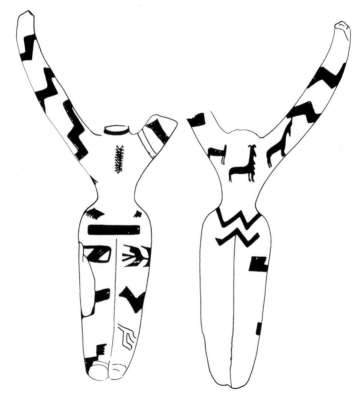

**Fig. 6** Clay figure of dancer with tattoo or paint. Naqada II period.

in this position with an amulet in the form of a cow head, encourages us to interpret make-up in terms of the general symbolism of fertility power. The paint on mainly female sculptures (most likely referring to fertility themes) from that time has revealed that paint was applied not only to the face, but to the entire body and that this was done on occasions that called for dancing [6]. Painting on male sculptures instead emphasized aspects of grandeur and authority.[17] In some cases, medicinal effects could be attributed to painting or the application of coloring agents.

In the early Naqada period, cosmetic palettes were still of a simple, diamond shape. Only from the end of the first and during the second Naqada period (ca. 3600–3200 BC) did they take on the form of turtles, birds, fish and various quadrupeds. In contrast to those of simple geometric shapes, these figurative palettes were equipped with a hole for hanging. Although they are found in graves, and mainly at the head of the deceased, they also appear in settlements [7], as demonstrated by the excavation of a residential site from the pre-state period at Adaïma in Upper Egypt. At the end of the pre-dynastic period, only two forms of cosmetic palettes remained – simple rectangular models and those in the form of a shield, often bearing opulent artistic decoration.

Cosmetic palettes disappear from archeological finds after the Egyptian state is established.

Unlike the green coloring agent found quite frequently in graves, the palettes appear to accompany final resting places for a smaller number of deceased – most likely for those who held an elite social position. A black coloring agent appears in closed sectors of burial grounds and may therefore indicate the geographic or biologic origin of the buried.

The relief ornamentation of these palettes often depicts the memorable deeds (victory over an enemy or over a wild animal) of those who gave them. On other finds we see ancient rulers of the Egyptian lands as they perform religious ceremonies. At a certain point in this period, the first forms of crown jewels were also created. These at one time rested on the head of the rulers of a united Egypt – the White Crown of Upper Egypt and the Red Crown of Lower Egypt.

---

[17] Adeptly described by Tatjana A. Šerkova, "Oko Chora": simvolika glaza v dodinastičeskom Jegipete, "Vestnik drevnej istorii" 1996/4, pp. 96–115.

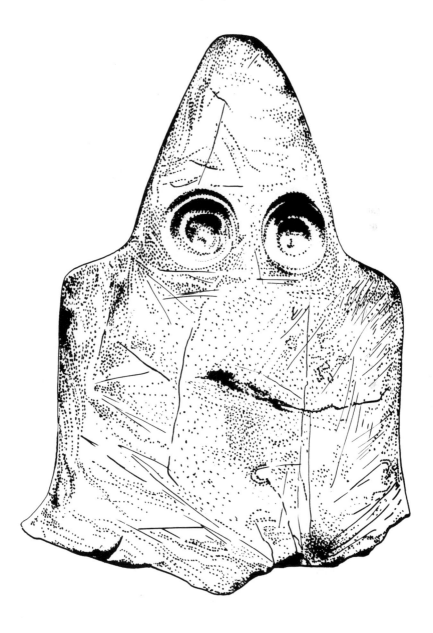

**Fig. 7** A fragment of a cosmetic palette in the form of a turtle from the Adaïma settlement.

## Egyptian society of the pre-state period in burial rituals

The Adaïma site in Upper Egypt provides us with an example of the early stratification of ancient Egyptian society. Of the two burial grounds at this site, the western one dates back to prehistoric times (ca. 3700–3300 BC). The eastern burial ground is linked to the slightly more recent period of 3200–2800 BC. The earliest grave of the western burial site is that of six deceased at the top of a sandy mound near a settlement from the same period. A group of double graves are positioned around this burial, possibly "marking" the burial ground at a set distance from the earliest grave. Other graves of those possessing a high social stature are located between the zone of the double-graves and the earliest mass grave on top of the mound. Yet the entire burial ground ends with an "external lining" of non-elite graves surrounding the central burial area. We do not know where the elite from the 34th and 33rd century BC disappeared to.

It is quite remarkable that the oldest, southern part of the eastern burial ground, established ca. 3300 BC, holds exclusively the remains of children. Except for its northern sector, which dates back to the dawn of Egyptian history, this burial site reveals a normal breakdown of ages of the deceased buried there. Separated burial of the deceased by age and sex indicates, from today's archeological perspective, the society's relatively low degree of social stratification. Signs of differences in the social position of the buried children are, nevertheless, betrayed by found cosmetic palettes, an abundance of funerary objects and the use of exotic imported materials in some graves.

The method of laying the deceased to rest in a crouched position on their left side with their heads pointing south and facing west, regardless of age and sex, still prevailed at this point at the Adaïma burial site. The corpse was sometimes buried in a grave lined with reed matting or animal skins. Sometimes in the western burial site a wooden "coffin" served this purpose; in the northern part of the eastern burial site we come across "coffins" made from baked clay. Some excavations have revealed the deceased laid to rest in boxes made from wattle held together by clay.

Another noteworthy trait of the western cemetery is the removal of the heads of the deceased long after their death. This was documented in two cases and could have something to do with a belief in the immortality of one of the human being's parts and with the desire to preserve the deceased's presence among the living. A fitting analogy, although remote in time and space, is provided by information from a Pyrenean village in what is now the Provence region of southern France from around the turn of the 14th century AD. When a venerable patriarch from a family of one of the leading homes of the town of Montaillou died, a family member would cut a lock of hair from his head the morning before the funeral and immure it in the home so that his "lucky star would not leave." We also have proof at the same burial site of a secondary burial of already deteriorated, yet intentionally dismembered human remnants in a clay "coffin." A severed right hand placed in the grave in a non-anatomical position, however, evokes the idea of posthumous punishment carried out on the deceased for a misdeed either he or one of his relatives did. The question lingers to what extent we can interpret traces of cut necks, observed in three cases in the western burial ground and in one in the eastern burial ground (while alive or post-mortem?), as the sacrificing of the individuals in question.

We hope further research will clarify the extent to which similar customs are derived from some of the earliest known forms of the Egyptian myth of the murdered, dismembered and magically reassembled god Usiris (Osiris).

Adaïma's deceased were often buried with household objects, usually consisting of personal ornaments, cosmetic necessities, dishes, tools and weapons. The pair of sandals made from painted stucco that accompanied one of the deceased in the western cemetery is undoubtedly emblematic of a higher social status. The placement of ornaments in the graves of very small children, who were unable to wear them for long, reveals an attempt to use legitimate means to incorporate the children into one of the groups of the adult population. These groups were represented by jewelry that was worn on the body for an extended period so that the personality of the wearer penetrated these decorations. The jewelry thus became part of the wearer's "narrower social persona," indicating his social rank. The presence of cosmetic pallets, which we have already mentioned and will talk more about later, represents an especially noteworthy feature. Judging the social position of the deceased based on a lack of funerary objects should certainly not be taken as an exact science, and this is emphasized by the fact that traces of green malachite have been found preserved on the eye brows of skulls of some of the dead, who were laid to rest without accompanying objects. Such an attribute would indicate that they were among the Egyptians of higher status.

An interesting side note is provided by an archeological find in an adjacent settlement from the pre-state period, within a context that can be dated to roughly 3500 BC: the remnants of matting containing the facial part of a human skull together with three cattle tailbones. This is evidently an expression of white magic in which the force and energy of the deceased in question, indicated by a bull tail, was to remain in the home even after the individual's death and be passed on to its occupant. The immuring of skulls into clay benches in dwellings of the Euphratean site of Mureybit in Syria in phase II of this Neolithic settlement presents a clear analogy here.[18] It is still not known the extent to which the image on the vessel from grave U-239 at the burial ground in Abydos, depicting a figure with a hairy (?) tail, hair adorned with feathers and armed with a club, tyrannizing smaller human figures – perhaps captives – is related to this.

At this point, a fact of a more general nature should be noted: Beginning in the Naqada II period, the deceased would take with them to the next world not only opulent table pottery, but also simple kitchen utensils – in increasingly larger quantities. We are left here with the impression that in this period the Egyptian dead began to depart for the next world fully equipped: with both a simple bowl for cooking and magnificent table serving sets.[19]

---

[18]  Information on Asian sites and life and institutions can be found in the publication of Eric M. Meyers (ed.), The Oxford Encyclopaedia of Archeology in the Near East I–IV, Oxford etc., Oxford University Press 1996.

[19]  David Wengrow, The Archaeology of Early Egypt – Social Transformations in North-East Africa, 10,000 to 2650 BC, Cambridge – New York – Melbourne – Madrid – Cape Town – Singapore – Sao Paulo, Cambridge University Press 2006, p. 94.

# LOWER EGYPT: BETWEEN THE PHARAOH
## AND THE RED SEA

Remarkable testimony on the contact maintained between Upper and Lower Egypt, indicating a fairly high level of social organization, should be mentioned with regard to the relations between the two regions. Central Egypt, the Nile foreshore running about 250 km between Fayum and Asyut, has yet to provide any evidence of settlement during the pre-state period of ancient Egypt. This leads us to believe that the people of both of these lands considered this to be a kind of "no man's land," separating the two parts of the Egyptian ecumene and assigning specific spheres of authority to them. This then indicates a high level of centralized management of social activities in both pre-state formations of ancient Egypt.

## Economy

Archeological finds in Lower Egypt (the area of the Nile's lower part and delta) dating back to the 4th millenium BC depict a well-formed culture that originated here, while demonstrating clear contact with continental Asia. These people's livelihood consisted mainly of the cultivation of cereals and other crops – wheat, barley, flax and legumes. Livestock included sheep, goats, cattle and pigs, while domesticated dogs helped them tend to these animals. The people of Lower Egypt did supplement their diet by hunting and gathering in the wilderness. Evidence of this is provided by finds of hippopotamus, bird (even peacock) and fish bone, turtle shells and shells from the Nile.

Lower Egyptian master craftsmen worked their pottery on a slowly turning potter's wheel, actually a potter's bench, on which the potter would create a vessel in the traditional way from pieces or strips of clay, turning the base on which the vessel was created so that they did not have to run around the object being worked on. In the final phase of the work, they could perfectly center the vessel by rapidly spinning the slow wheel, or by slowly turning the wheel they could decorate the still soft surface of the vessel with imprints or engravings of straight or wavy lines. The Lower Egyptians made all kinds of tools and weapons from stone, particularly fissile varieties such as silex (flint) or hornstone. An especially distinctive material worked with by Lower Egyptian craftsmen was copper, creating decoration as well as tools from it: sticks, spatulas, hatchets and fishing hooks. Copper appeared relatively suddenly and in large quantities; this can be viewed as a deliberately driven technological progress. Although copper artifacts from Lower Egypt and Asia have much in common with regard to shape and form, this probably was not a direct import from the continent. Asian hatchets, for instance, are different in appearance. Chemical analysis tells us that Lower Egyptian craftsmen worked with copper that was originally from the Sinai Peninsula, where miners and metallurgists most likely processed extracted ore in the ingot of raw metal of a surprisingly constant weight (ca. 825 g) which was then exported to consumers.

One surprising find was the remains of a domesticated donkey from a Maadi site; this clearly attests to the focus of the Lower Egyptian culture on remote contact, since this pack animal does not belong to the spectrum of farm animals expected to be found with settled farmers. Nile fish bones found in Palestine indicated that there was even long-distance trade with the food products of Lower Egypt. We can also assume that pottery and stone vessels were exported, as well as cutting instruments, shells from the Nile and even pork. In return, Lower Egyptians received from their continental trading partners goods imported in containers of Levantine origin or raw materials for manufacturing cutting utensils out of rock. They also received vessels made from basalt, copper ingot from the Sinai Peninsula, shells from the Red Sea, dyes, resin, oil, cedar wood and tar.

Starting around the late 4th millenium BC, the Upper Egyptian culture began to penetrate the distinctive milieu of the Lower Egyptian regions. To date, the finds attesting to this are extremely rare: pieces of cosmetic palettes, ivory combs, cone-shaped club heads and even some stone vessels. Some of the first finds come from the site of a storage center in Tell el-Farkha. The delta site of Buto sheds light on the further development of these relations after 3300 BC. Here artifacts of a southern origin begin to be accompanied by architecture inspired by Upper Egyptian models. We still do not know if this expansion occurred by way of a peaceful entry into the population or if it is proof of forced occupation.

## Settlements

The people of the Maadi settlement, spread out over an area of a little more than one hectare, lived in three types of dwellings. The huts were of an oval shape built from posts covered with mat or other organic wattle, perhaps like an Indian tee-pee. These abodes were entered from the North, the direction from which the Mediterranean Sea's refreshing breeze blew. Another type of post dwelling possessed either an oval or rectangular shape and its walls were sunk into a shallow foundation trough. This may have served as a modest enclosure for livestock as well. Four homes of the third and least common type were found in the western part of the site. These consisted of oval dwellings with lengths of three and five meters, sunk into up to 3 meters of bedrock. They were entered by a descending corridor similar to the entrances of medieval sunken-floored dwellings equipped with stairs cut into the rock. The builders made their walls out of stone or, in one case, out of adobe. A structure lodged into post holes in the floor evidently supported the roof. The presence of fire pits, storage containers and a communal waste dump – of tools or animal bones and the remnants of vegetable aliment – convincingly attest to the residential nature of such structures. Living in these abodes probably was not overly healthy. Linguists have pointed out to experts on such structures from medieval Europe the shared origin of the words "dung" and "dungeon."

Women cooked here over fire pits that were either sheltered or in the open air. The massive furnaces up to two meters long were most likely used for firing pottery. The settlements were also equipped with wells and large storage containers dug into the ground. Other sites have revealed dug-out hollows used for storing pottery and pits up to two meters deep serving as storage areas or even as workshops.

The Tell el-Farkha site opened a whole new world to us. In ca. 3300 BC there appeared large rectangular buildings positioned with their corners at the cardinal points – a novelty in the Lower Egyptian milieu. As in prehistoric Mesopotamia, this positioning should probably be linked with the prevalence of a premeditated and clearly formulated world view that held the practical necessity of incorporating human habitations into the universe's order and adapting to it their external parameters exactly aligned with the cardinal points. The novelty and unusualness of these buildings is probably illustrated by the fact that they were repeatedly destroyed by the Nile's flooding and were, contrary to all logic, rebuilt on the same place. Archeologists found the remnants of several stages of an ancient brewery in the middle of one of these buildings. These finds have provided us with proof that a crucial form of the socially managed movement of material goods, i.e. redistribution, was at this time introduced. This concerned the central distribution of foodstuffs, though redistribution also meant taxes, allowances and payments of all kinds – a decisive step toward building the first state. We will ascertain to what extent the centralized supply of beer was also accompanied by the mass distribution of cone-shaped loaves of bread baked in special ceramic "tube pans" (cf. p. 28) once we are able to fully confirm that these "tube pans" were really used to bake bread.[20]

This milieu also provided us with significant proof of social differentiation: A sunken-featured dwelling with massive stone walls was found at Maadi site in the Nile Delta.

## Burials

The people of the pre-state Lower Egyptian culture buried their dead in special burial grounds. Constant social stratification is demonstrated

---

[20] David Wengrow, The Archaeology of Early Egypt – Social Transformations in North-East Africa, 10,000 to 2650 BC, Cambridge – New York – Melbourne – Madrid – Cape Town – Singapore – Sao Paulo, Cambridge University Press 2006, p. 94–97, picture of bread pans; ibid, p. 88, Fig. 4.4.

by the finding that some children had been up to this point buried under the floors of people's dwellings in coffin-like enclosures. Archeologists interpret the burial of children, women and men separately as the mark of an egalitarian society. The bodies of the deceased were first arranged in a position with heads pointing north. A change in position gradually came about so that the heads of the interred pointed south and they faced east, not west – the direction in which ancient Egyptians believed the empire of the dead to exist and which those laid to rest in Upper Egyptian burial grounds faced. A crouched position on the right side (and sometimes on the left) also slowly became the norm. This left/right positioning depended on regional specifics, not on differences in the sexes as was the case in Mesopotamia at this time (men were laid to rest on their right sides, women on their left). With their heads resting on charred stones from fire pits, the dead were wrapped in a blanket or a pelt to protect them on their final journey. In contrast to the Upper Egyptian culture from the same period, the Lower Egyptian deceased were only minimally equipped for the next world, receiving a pottery vessel or two, some shells from the Nile (perhaps used as spoons), but hardly any personal ornaments and only rarely was an ivory comb or stone pottery found. It is only from this point that we gradually begin to find cosmetic palettes, simple tools from chipped rock and even quartered animals, which were most likely provided as food for the final journey. In some cases, simple shelters made of wood, perhaps of tree branches, shaded the grave sites.

The burial of animals – including dogs, goats and sheep – alongside people attests to a solid integration into nature's order and the notion of the basic equality of all creatures. A remarkable find was that at one burial ground (Heliopolis near Cairo) the goats were laid to rest in exactly the same position as their owners – crouched on their right side with their heads pointing south and snouts to the east, wrapped in a blanket or pelt and accompanied by pottery. These discoveries were made among the most affluent graves of the burial ground. Dogs, accompanying people on the eternal hunt, were found buried next to their masters throughout the cemetery.

## Beyond everyday borders: contact with Asia

From the beginning of the 4th century we find pottery of Asian origin at the Buto site in the Nile Delta. This was pottery typical of the Palestinian culture of Ghassul and made on potter's wheels in Egypt. However, Egyptian potters gradually adopted it as their own pottery style and even stopped using a potter's wheel for it.[21]

The unique ornamentation on painted bowls from an undetermined Egyptian location also confirms that there was contact in this early period, maybe even earlier. These are among the white cross-lined ware (also called c-ware) and feature the decoration of vertical combs facing each other with hunting scenes accompanied by shaded triangles.[22] Similarities with the decoration on pottery from Susa in western Iran from level A (the transition period of the Ubaid and Uruk culture, ca. 4000 BC) are so clear that we must assume that contact was established.[23]

One other very surprising group of finds comes from Abydos graves of a later period. The imprints of cylinder seals in clay were found in a number of large mausoleums. In inventing the cylinder seal (ca 3700–3600 BC), the Sumerians were able to magically control the time and space around them. This was mostly used to seal the packaging of goods or (later) the doors of storage spaces. The rotating cylinder with the negative of the ornament or scene carved into it was pressed into the damp clay or other soft material, leaving the impression in positive. The people of ancient Egypt buried in Abydos graves used cylinder seals in the same way. Evidence of the arrival of this new administrative tool from Asia is represented by one of the Abydos imprints (from grave U-153), presenting the cuneiform sign NAGAR.[24]

---

[21] Kateřina Postupová, Počátky kontaktu Egypta a Předního Východu (Early contact between Egypt and the Near East), B.A. thesis, Plzeň, West Bohemian University in Plzeň, Faculty of Arts 2007, p. 33–34.

[22] David Wengrow, The Archaeology of Early Egypt – Social Transformations in North-East Africa, 10,000 to 2650 BC, Cambridge – New York – Melbourne – Madrid – Cape Town – Singapore – Sao Paulo, Cambridge University Press 2006, pp. 107–108, depiction of bread "tube pans" also on p. 88, Fig. 5.5 on p. 108.

[23] Petr Charvát, The Iconography of Pristine Statehood – Painted Pottery and Seal Impressions from Susa, southwestern Iran, Prague, Karolinum Press 2005, e.g. p. 255, No. 1 (Coll. 3223).

[24] Petr Charvát, review of Jane A. Hill, Cylinder Seal Glyptic in Predynastic Egypt and

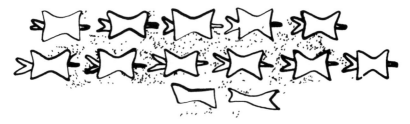

**Fig. 8** A seal from grave U-153 in Abydos with the repeating cuneiform sign NAGAR. Late Naqada II period, 36th–35th century BC.

This cuneiform sign gives the name of a Sumerian city in northern Syria whose ruins are today covered by the hillock of Tell Brak [8]. Other Abydos seals also bear traces of the influence of Sumerian art, specimens of which must have arrived in Egypt even before 3500 BC. In Egypt, however, technology coming from abroad was very quickly adopted, and Egyptian artists had soon adorned their cylinder seals with exclusively domestic ornamentation and scenes. Cylinder seals spread to such an extent throughout the lands of the Nile that we even find imprints in the Nubian region of Egypt.

The impressions of cylinder seals found at the En Besor site in Sinai represent a unique case in which this originally Sumerian discovery was re-imported from Egypt back to Asia. It was here, next to a building full of brewing equipment for beer production, that a total of 99 cylinder seal imprints of Egyptian origin (the seals bear hieroglyphic writing), but from local clay, were found. The cylinders are clearly carved in an Egyptian style. The place obviously served as a wayside and supply station on the road from Egypt to the part of Palestine they had conquered, but also as a toll for tributes from subjugated lands.

The fact that Egyptian cylinders were used to stamp seals on goods of local origin can only mean that this was the place that the Palestinians' taxes and allowances were delivered to. These payments were affixed with the seals of the individuals entitled to a portion of the taxes levied by pharaonic rule of the northern provinces. En Besor apparently served as a meeting and exchange point where officials from the

Neighboring Regions, Oxford, Archaeopress 2004, in "Bibliotheca Orientalis" LXIII/5–6, September–December 2006, pp. 519–522, on p. 520.

northern provinces of Egypt delivered tributes marked with the seals of those they were designated for and where procurators took possession of the relevant goods from these Egyptian agents. These procurators evidently broke the seals here, disposed of the original seals and took possession of the goods individually on behalf of their masters, who had sent them here for this purpose.

Egyptians were extremely interested in Palestine at this time and began to invade the land after 3400 BC. Finds of Asian pottery from the U-j grave in Abydos, which we will further examine, provided significant information on the extent of mutual contact. Originally, there were some 700 Levantine bottles with wine containing terebinth resin and chopped spiced figs. The total amount of intoxicating drink accompanying the deceased elite to the next world was about 4,500 liters.[25] We know that, in addition to staging posts like En Besor, temporary Egyptian posts also operated near larger settlements in Palestine. "Dual" sites where both Egyptians and Palestinians lived together were also discovered here, as were larger centers where people of Egyptian and native origin evidently resided together. The Egyptians' main imports from Palestine were wine, oil, resin and honey.[26] Other imports included beans, asphalt from the Dead Sea, wood and goods manufactured from it, turquoise and cupriferous ore. Obsidian from Anatolia was imported as goods in transit.[27] These trade relations carried on even after the establishment of the ancient Egyptian state.[28]

---

[25] David Wengrow, The Archaeology of Early Egypt – Social Transformations in North-East Africa, 10,000 to 2650 BC, Cambridge – New York – Melbourne – Madrid – Cape Town – Singapore – Sao Paulo, Cambridge University Press 2006, p. 202.

[26] An analysis of residue in pottery attributed to the pharaoh Djer of the 1st dynasty of ancient Egypt provided concrete evidence: David Wengrow, The Archaeology of Early Egypt – Social Transformations in North-East Africa, 10,000 to 2650 BC, Cambridge – New York – Melbourne – Madrid – Cape Town – Singapore – Sao Paulo, Cambridge University Press 2006, p. 148, note 17.

[27] Marc Lebeau, Thierry de Puter: Un fragment de vase en pierre égyptien vraisemblablement d'époque protodynastique découvert á Tell Beydar, Syrie, in: Baghdader Mitteilungen 37, 2006, pp. 279–294, on p. 285.

[28] Marc Lebeau, Thierry de Puter: Un fragment de vase en pierre égyptien vraisemblablement d'époque protodynastique découvert a Tell Beydar, Syrie, in: Baghdader Mitteilungen 37, 2006, pp. 279–294, on the discovery of pottery probably dating from the I/II Egyptian dynasty made of metagabbro from the Eastern Desert in Egypt in secondary storage at Tell Beydar IIIb (ca. 2450–2400 BC).

# CONFRONTING THE ENEMY: NUBIA

Nubian culture closely resembled Egyptian culture at this time. Nubians farmed the land, utilizing the Nile's flooding, and raised livestock. Burial grounds located in the vicinity of the Nile have provided us with information on their culture. Those buried here took with them on their final journey ornaments made of stone, ivory and nacre, as well as cosmetic necessities, including palettes similar to those previously described. These, however, were made of quartzite and not of greywacke as in Egypt. Pottery and tools were also found here. Metal appeared rarely and, if so, it was imported.

An increasing number of objects imported from Egypt appeared in Nubia. Even symbols and emblems suggesting the close proximity of the emergence of the first Egyptian and Nubian states were found in some of the elite burial grounds. At a certain point it was not clear who had borrowed from whom with regards to these symbols and emblems. The Nubians were intensive trading partners with the Egyptians. It appears that they mainly supplied the Black Land with foodstuffs and raw materials, livestock, fruit, tropical woods such as the renowned ebony, pelts and, in particular, gold, which was extremely abundant in Nubia.[29]

Nevertheless, the Egyptians soon began to send military expeditions from their bases in the southern part of Upper Egypt. If the Nubian chiefs did not voluntarily submit and did not promise to pay tributes to Egypt, the Egyptian soldiers would attack the Nubians, enslave them and take their crops, livestock and valuables. Sometime around 2700 BC, Lower Nubia became part of the Egyptian state as its frontier zone.

---

[29] Cyril Aldred, Egypt to the End of the Old Kingdom, London, Thames and Hudson 1965, p. 61, fig. 50, fragment of an ebony seat from a grave in Saqqara dating to 3000 BC.

# THE BURIAL OF THE FAMOUS AND POWERFUL IN THE NORTHERN PART OF UPPER EGYPT: ABYDOS

The burial ground excavated at the Abydos site in Upper Egypt provided exceptional information on early Egyptian statehood. This was the sister site of Hieraconpolis, though it is not known whether the city also claimed a sovereign position in politics or whether their citizens were satisfied with its spiritual status.

The Abydos burial ground dates back to roughly the first two phases of Naqada culture, i.e. to 4000–3300 BC. In addition to the common pits dug in sand or clay that held the bodies of the deceased, the famous and powerful were also memorialized here with burial edifices made of brick – actual mausoleums. The famous U-j tomb was, for instance, 9.1 × 7.3 m in size and 1.55 m deep. They were usually rectangular and normally contained a large burial tomb in the ground where the deceased would lie with their most valuable funerary objects. The tomb was usually located in the central part of the entire rectangular structure that was composed of a series of rooms for storing the most numerous part of the funerary objects – food in pottery, wooden and other materials and textile supplies. The entire surface of the tomb was usually made of brick, though builders often used wood, too. Although originally the bodies of the deceased were wrapped in reed blankets, this custom slowly disappeared from large and prominent graves starting around 3400 BC.

A substantial finding here is that a number of these graves are situated with their corners aligned with the cardinal points. We must therefore assume that the deceased were laid to rest in posthumous dwellings that were built in accordance with the universe's order and with the principles of the visible and invisible world.

The Abydos tombs were not spared the destructive march of time or the prying hands of thieves. In excavating them, therefore, archeologists generally only found mere remnants of the original, grandiose and opulent funerary objects. Yet even these lamentable bits have provided us with ideas of the wealth of the ancient deceased, of the social practices of their age and of what they brought with them to the next world. The opulent objects attesting to the high social position of the Abydos people included frequent finds of an abundance of jewels, weapons, textiles and pottery. The most commonly found jewels were necklace beads made from imported minerals, e.g. from the famed lapis lazuli that regularly appeared at this time in Egypt in great quantities.[30] Weapons most frequently found consisted of daggers chipped from flint (silex) and equipped with handles made from precious materials (usually ivory). Not much fabric was preserved, but archeologists interpret the small chips of bone, ivory or wood with hieroglyphic symbols that appeared in the above-ground structures of the Abydos tombs as lists of the rolls of material stored in the tomb. Along with the luxurious vessels made of precious metals or choice stone, the Abydos dead took with them dozens and sometimes hundreds of pottery vessels. It is generally believed that the survivors of the deceased filled these vessels with supplies for the journey to the next world and for life in it. These vessels, probably originally containing oil, beer, milk, fats and similar edibles, were usually made in Egypt. However, merchants brought a substantial number of these vessels, filled with an extremely rare and valued drink – grape wine, from the Palestinians lands. For instance, the aforementioned U-j tomb contained in its three rooms 700 supply vessels with a total of 4,500 liters of wine.[31] We do not know if ancient Egyptians also knew how to make palm wine as the Sumerians did.

Board games, remnants of which were also found in Abydos tombs, assumedly accompanied the dead for leisure purposes.

Emblems of power, such as an ivory scepter, were also among the secular objects found here. Also found in Abydos tombs were ivory carvings depicting the transport of various goods by throngs of people

---

[30]  Kateřina Postupová, Počátky kontaktu Egypta a Předního Východu (Early contact between Egypt and the Near East), B.A. thesis, Plzeň, West Bohemian University in Plzeň – Faculty of Arts 2007, p. 46.

[31]  Kateřina Postupová, Počátky kontaktu Egypta a Předního Východu (Early contact between Egypt and the Near East), B.A. thesis, Plzeň, West Bohemian University in Plzeň – Faculty of Arts 2007, p. 42.

and animals and the viewing of prisoners. The deceased in Abydos also took with them emblems of sacral power such as sacred objects and sometimes even entire shrines carved out of wood. These are clearly the objects of individuals whose authority overlapped into both lay administration and religious areas. This is especially apparent in some of the objects that survivors buried with the deceased: Clay imitations of agricultural products, such as garlic, onion and poppy head were found in the Abydos tombs. Obviously, the intention was to supply the deceased for the next world with everything they could have possibly needed for their earthly life. It therefore seems that ancient Egyptian religion described to its people an afterlife that was more or less a picture of their life on earth.

# BURIAL GROUNDS OF THE SOUTHERN KINGDOM
# OF UPPER EGYPT: AN ELITE BURIAL SITE
# IN HIERACONPOLIS

As early as ca. 3800–3600 BC the remains of leading figures were buried in a special cemetery that was separated from the final resting place of the population's non-elite classes. For their final journey they generally received ivory and stone objects, a large supply of pottery, jewels, cosmetic palettes and weapons made of silex. In some cases, we already find here the deceased wrapped in long strips of linen and their faces covered with funerary masks made from baked clay.

One of the largest tombs here (no. 23) has a burial tomb 5.5 × 3.1 m in size with a depth originally exceeding 1.2 m. The burial tomb is bordered on each side by eight post holes that originally supported the top part of the tomb made from wood and reeds. On the eastern part of the tomb the double row of post holes attest to an additional top structure, probably a shrine venerating the dead or a funeral chapel. The entire complex was surrounded by a post fence that was 16 × 9 m in size with a northwest entrance. According to the pottery discovered, this mausoleum dates back to roughly 3500 BC.

Another very surprising discovery was made in close proximity to this tomb. An oval burial pit, perhaps also with an above-ground wooden structure, held the remains of a young elephant, roughly ten years old, wrapped in linen strips and accompanied by funerary objects.

Similar discoveries were made in other places of the burial ground for the elite of Hieraconpolis. Aurochs *(Bos primigenius)*, related to today's bison, another elephant and a large ram were buried here. Other graves revealed baboons, wildcats, hippos, a domesticated bull and a lamb. Discoveries of silex figures of animals from the funeral chapel of tomb no. 23 raises the question of whether this was an attempt to magically secure for themselves in the next world access to the powers of nature represented by these animals, whose depiction was intended to forever provide this privilege to the deceased in tomb no. 23 [9].

Although tomb no. 23 had been repeatedly dug up, archeologists have made a significant number of discoveries there in both the 20th and 21st centuries.

According to the funerary masks, there were at least two people buried here, although the burial tomb also contained the remains of four human bodies positioned without uniform orientation, without blankets of reeds or animal pelts and without funerary objects. Over 600 fragments of a life-size human sculpture from limestone were found in the vicinity of the above-ground entrance structure, which was probably a kind of funeral chapel. Several animal sculptures painstakingly

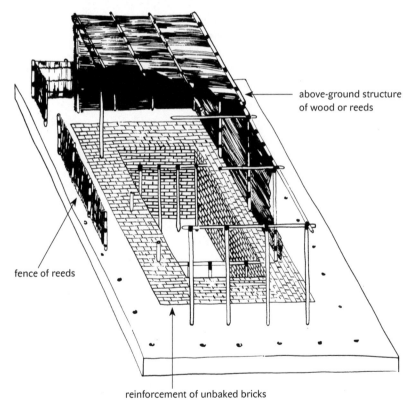

above-ground structure
of wood or reeds

fence of reeds

reinforcement of unbaked bricks

**Fig. 9** A reconstruction of a prehistoric Egyptian tomb resembling tomb 23 from Hieraconpolis.

cut from silex were found in the charred layer in this structure. We might legitimately ask if this is proof of a form of ritual "made timeless," familiar to us from other sites and from buried animals in other elite parts of burial sites (Heliopolis in Lower Egypt). Other finds here included the top of an ivory club, arrowheads and a human neck bone with a deep cut.

It seems that this primary burial site of the Hieraconpolis elite was not left in peace. The wooden above-ground structure of tomb no. 23 caught on fire and the sculpture, possibly belonging to the deceased laid to rest in it, was intentionally broken into tiny pieces.

Later, sometime after 3300 BC, the Egyptian elite began using vast brick tombs in the southern part of the site. Dozens of vessels holding supplies for the deceased's afterlife were found in these tombs. Here we find renowned tomb no. 100 (5.85 × 2.85 × 1.50 meters) decorated with murals depicting ships, hunting scenes, a battle scene and victory in it – all of which were subjects that the pharaonic administration later adopted for its symbolism. Weapons, jewelry, objects made from precious metals and imported lithic raw materials were also found in the tomb. At that time, the facades of the brick structures served to divide in regular spatial intervals the niches that would later become a permanent feature of Egyptian architecture. This development ended with the advent of large funeral structures, hundreds of meters in size, consisting of the tomb's own space and a rectangular courtyard where commemorative ceremonies were held. It is entirely possible that animals and even people were sacrificed here, though these events were becoming scarcer at the end of the rule of the First Dynasty of Ancient Egypt.

Sometime during this period similar funerary architecture returned to the original elite burial grounds. This was most likely done intentionally to establish a bond with the momentous funerary structures of their predecessors. It seems that Hieraconpolis was not the only place where this occurred. The intentional link to the customs of ancient predecessors went so far that they began to make red pottery with black borders and ancient animal themes reappeared in art. The pre-dynastic Hieraconpolis temple, already standing in the desert at that time, was reconstructed. The Hieraconpolis of the Egyptian pharaohs was moved under the Nile's steep rocky cliffs, to the fluvial plain.

In addition to these burial grounds of the Egyptian elite, excavations have revealed a large number of buried Egyptians clearly not belonging to the ruling class [10]. Prehistoric Hieraconpolis has provided us with several such burial sites. The remains of the deceased are buried here in a crouched position with their heads pointing to the south and facing west. Their bodies were often wrapped in linen, a reed blanket or a goat or gazelle pelt. They were also protected by slabs made of hard materials such as baked clay. The deceased here were buried with ornaments, tools, weapons and vessels – sometimes they were even laid to rest in large containers used as coffins. The vessels often contained food provisions for the final journey – bread, beer, gruel or fruit. Impressive red pottery with a black border was found here along with weapons made of flint or metal, metal tools (e.g. needles or fishing tackle), cosmetics, such as the aforementioned make-up palettes, and ivory objects. The deceased received sea shells and steatite beads as ornaments, as well as ground malachite green used as make-up. Flint knives and daggers were also found, sometimes attached to wooden handles and kept in leather sheathes. Excavations also revealed objects made of bone, horn, ivory or of hard or rare types of stone. It is worth pointing out that women of advanced age usually received the most valuable funerary objects. In Hieraconpolis, one of these matrons was buried with four vessels, bird-shaped greywacke cosmetic palettes, a "toilet bag" of sorts, a basket with stone amulets, a comb and needles made of bone, make-up and scented fabrics. Wrapping the body in linen filled with resin may have come from the need to preserve the human body as long as possible and probably represented the first step toward mummification. We also find here the aforementioned evidence of a cut neck or decapitation. The remains of some twenty bodies of men and women ranging in age

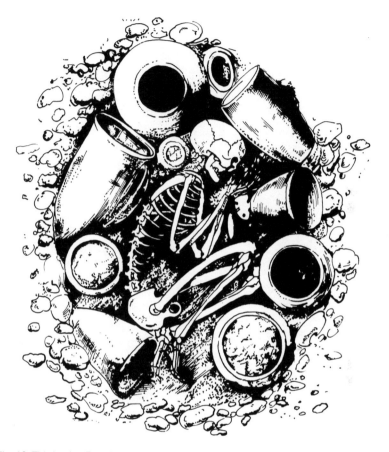

**Fig. 10** This is what Egyptian graves looked like during the period immediately preceding the creation of the state: a grave from the El-Amra, Naqada II period (latter third of the 4th millenium BC).

from 16 to 65 years were found at the Hieraconpolis burial site with 470 graves.

Among them were the bodies of five young men whose skulls bear subtle cuts as if from scalping. As mentioned above, we will decide here between the testimonies of some of the earliest forms of the Osiris myth or the desire to preserve the place of the human being's immortal component among the living. The find of a row of bones and skulls in tomb T5 at the Naqada burial site points to the considerable significance ascribed to the human collective.[32] This clearly evokes the idea of human solidarity enduring in a mythical, enlightened "afterlife" just as it did during the individual's earthly life. Community members using the burial ground here were, therefore, as in Neolithic Asia, a collective both of living people and of those who had already departed for the afterlife.

---

[32] Kateřina Postupová, Počátky kontaktu Egypta a Předního Východu (Early contact between Egypt and the Near East), B.A. thesis, Plzeň, West Bohemian University in Plzeň – Faculty of Arts 2007, p. 16.

# THE DAWN
## OF THE EGYPTIAN WRITING SYSTEM[33]

Ancient Egyptians created a writing system composed of figural symbols written in rows or columns. The writing generally reads from right to left, but monumental inscriptions might read from left to right. The direction of the writing is always given by the fact that the figurative symbols look in the direction of the text's starting point. The writing could essentially run in any direction, just not up and down. The system is based on an association of graphic symbols and of sounds of the spoken language joined on the principle of rebus and charades. The image of a goose, pronounced *sa* in Egyptian, sounds the same as the expression for son, *sa*. This is why the term "son" is written in hieroglyphics as a symbol depicting a goose.

The oldest Egyptian writing possesses a relatively transparent nature of image-coded information, yielding relevant information through a mix of icons, indexes and symbols, providing in unclear cases sound (or image) references on the principle of rebus and charades. For example, a square with the name of a pharaoh designated AB has human hands and holds a club in one of them. The pharaoh clubs a bound captive, who is designated XY [11]. Interpretation: pharaoh AB is victorious over the land XY.

Hieroglyphs are divided into two categories: those carrying meaning and those carrying sound. Originally, the individual symbols most likely stood for whole words and were read as such. Later, however, most of the signs represented sounds with a single consonant (and

---

[33] See Christopher Eyre and John Baines, Interactions between Orality and Literacy in Ancient Egypt, in: K. Schousboe and M. T. Larsen (ed.), Literacy and Society, Center for Research in the Humanities, Copenhagen University, Ko/benhavn, Akademisk Forlag 1989, p. 91–119. Also see David Wengrow, The Archaeology of Early Egypt – Social Transformations in North-East Africa, 10,000 to 2650 BC, Cambridge – New York – Melbourne – Madrid – Cape Town – Singapore – Sao Paulo, Cambridge University Press 2006, pp. 198–207.

probably also a vowel, but those were not written). In some cases, signs stood for sounds with two or even three vowels.

This writing system is sometimes supplemented by phonetic complements that can provide, for clarity's sake, a sound that contains a read word and thereby determines which word is meant.

Hieroglyphs also feature ideograms, pictographic symbols determining the conceptual sphere that the word belongs to. A picture of a person indicates that the concept relates to a human being; a picture of a circular enclosure inscribed with a cruciform signifies that a city is being spoken of; a picture of a pyramid on a plinth tell us that the writ-

**Fig. 11** Ivory tag with depiction of the Pharaoh Narmer's victory over his enemies. One of the signs with which the pharaoh's name is written wields a club and clutches the hair of a kneeling captive. On the right part of the upper row of the tag we see the pharaoh's name in a small frame representing the front of the royal palace (serech). 3200–3100 BC.

ing has to do with a pyramid complex. A single sound (homophone) can be written with different symbols, while a single symbol can be used to capture different sounds (polyphones). Hieroglyphic script as such is extremely heterogeneous. One and the same symbol can either represent an entire word or, instead, can act as a phonetic component in writing by using symbols capturing speech sounds. This writing system apparently emerged over the course of the 4th millenium BC, as indicated by symbols cut into pottery of the first and second Naqada periods (ca. 3800–3200 BC). Further examination is needed to determine the extent to which this was inspired by the primitive cuneiform script noticed on the stamp from tomb U-153 in Abydos (NAGAR site, Tell Brak in Syria).

One of the oldest samples of Egyptian script comes from Abydos tombs, dating back to ca. 3300 BC. Vessels from the U-j tomb there bear ink writing most likely indicating names of the estates from which supplies of goods stored in the vessels originated.[34] These are probably different locations within the Abydos surroundings.

Writing on papyrus has not been preserved from the most ancient times; it has only been found on pottery and on pieces of wood, bone, ivory, stone and clay. Palettes, club heads and weights have also been found to have writing on them. Writing from this period has been discovered on stone vessels and cylinder seals, while the oldest writing was found inscribed on rock faces exposed to the elements.

Egyptian script evolved into the first meaningful messages created at around the establishment of a united state shortly before 3000 BC. A combination of direct depictions of an act or event, its symbolic expression (e.g. clubbing an opponent as a symbol of victory) and actual written messages points here to the mixed nature of a system of graphic symbols that still cannot fully rely on a system of fixed characters with set phonetic values. The entire writing system did, however, stabilize at the very beginning of the Old Kingdom, ca. 2700–2600 BC. The Egyptians themselves called their script the "words of the gods" and its symbols "pictures." The same word was used to refer to a scribe and artist.

---

[34] See Jane A. Hill, Cylinder Seal Glyptic in Predynastic Egypt and Neighboring Regions, Oxford, Archaeopress 2004, p. 15.

During the New Kingdom some 800 hieroglyphic symbols were used, while 24 phonetic-like symbols were available. The multivalence of this script, suiting its esoteric nature and utilized by the tight circle of rulers, was maintained until the very end of the script's existence in Late Antiquity. Egyptian scribes then developed at the dawn of the 3rd millenium a simplified, cursive script called hieratic (priestly) for the common needs of everyday registration records.

The even freer Demotic ("popular") script emerged in the 7th century BC. In the Hellenistic period, the Egyptian language began to use Greek upper-case characters supplemented by seven symbols adopted from Demotic script. This resulted in the creation of the Coptic script, which is still used today.

Most of Egypt's ancient documents are official notices written by pharaohs who used them to record facts relevant to their rule. More often than not, they were of a religious nature. In many cases, not only have sacred writings to honor the gods been preserved, records on royal military campaigns and sometimes even a form of "ethnographic report" on newly discovered lands have survived. Given the binding nature of the royal titulature's wording and of the phraseology of inscriptions, the writing on Egypt's monuments possesses a high level of consistency and repetition. Ninety percent of all Egyptian texts allegedly adhere to a standard formula. The widespread Egyptian custom to remove the names of individuals who had committed some offence, or whose remembrance had simply become undesirable, attests to the active use of such monuments for cult purposes. Such cases of *damnatio memoriae* most frequently appear in connection with the "Heretic Pharaoh" Akhenaten, worshipper of the sun god Aten (1353–1335 BC). Yet this appeared in many cases, both before and after.

The Egyptian historian and priest Manethon (or Manetho, lived under the Hellenistic rulers during the Ptolemaic dynasty, 321–246 BC) can also be mentioned within Egyptian culture He promoted the cult of the syncretic divinity of the Dionysian and healing nature of Serapis, but is remembered mostly as the author of a work on the history of Egypt written in Greek. This work drew heavily on original Egyptian records and he divided the rulers of Egypt into thirty dynasties – a classification still used today.

# THE BIRTH OF THE EGYPTIAN STATE

In contrast to the other centers of early statehood, Egypt offers us a unique monument of art that practically captures the very instance of this key moment in history. This is the famous Narmer Palette found in the late 19th century in the Main Deposit of the Temple of Horus in Hieraconpolis and probably stored there sometime in 1400 BC [12].

This monument dates back to the times of the Egyptian state's establishment by the pharaoh Narmer, also called Menes or even Hor-Aha, around 3000 BC. Narmer, standing victorious over rows of decapitated corpses, is presented here as the one responsible for the ritual massacre of his enemies. Assuming the form of a bull, he blasts through the fortification of the enemy's city, while his servants tame two mythical animals with the bodies and heads of lions and the necks of snakes – perhaps symbols of hostile chaos.

The god Horus personally takes part in the scene of the massacre and, on the other side, the goddess Hathor observes another scene of the enemy's destruction. Here an unknown ancient Egyptian writer presents the pharaoh's basic duties with regards to honoring the gods, ritual and war.

The Main Deposit from the Temple of Horus at Hieraconpolis also revealed a more peaceful role of the royal office, perhaps linked to the king's responsibility for the fecundity and fertility of the land and its people. In addition to the Narmer Palette and the club head of King Narmer's club, the deposit also held the club head of King Scorpion (derived from the symbol used to write his name). This club head features a picture of the king performing what is probably an agricultural ritual.[35]

---

[35] Kateřina Postupová, Počátky kontaktu Egypta a Předního Východu (Early contact between Egypt and the Near East), B.A. thesis, Plzeň, West Bohemian University in Plzeň, Faculty of Arts 2007, p. 19.

From today's research perspective, however, the Narmer Palette is not a preface, but an epilogue to the construction of the ancient Egyptian state. Inscriptions with Narmer's name are found all over Egypt and in Palestine. It seems that the ideas for statehood came from Upper Egypt, and that Lower Egypt, a typical "buffer zone" wedged between the ambitions of Upper Egypt and continental rulers, had no choice but to join in. Abydos, Hieraconpolis and perhaps even Naqada were most likely the earliest centers of Upper Egypt that the pharaohs' dominion arose from. We will probably never know what their mutual relations were like and whether they indeed divvied up "spheres of influence" and expansion directions – Abydos to the north and Hieraconpolis to the south. The extent to which the painted decoration of tomb No. 100 from Abydos dated to this period – a flotilla of ships, people with emblems of power (a staff and whip), battle, hunting and ritual scenes – truly depicts the ideology of the conquering forces of Lower Egypt's rulers is still unclear. Monuments from some of the Abydos tombs indeed depict throngs of captives, the transport

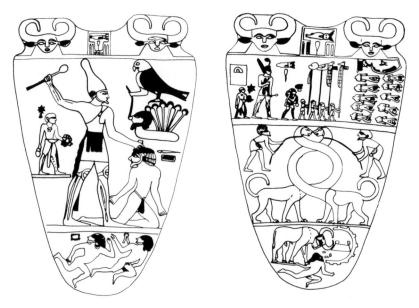

**Fig. 12** The Narmer Palette.

of goods and herding of livestock. The "seepage" of Upper Egyptian-Naqada culture northward, to Lower Egypt, starting in the latter third of the 4th millennium BC, also remains a question: Was this a matter of colonization or occupation? Or did it have something to do with cultural assimilation and the ensuing absorption? Many questions arise and few have been answered. It seems that, to a certain extent, Lower Egypt followed the pace of Upper Egypt's social development: Even before King Narmer's times, rulers with animal names appeared in the delta lands. Inscriptions of a king named Crocodile found in Tarkhan offer an example of this.

In any case, the important thing is that at the dawn of the united Egyptian state's history a new capital city also arose in Lower Egypt. At the time it was called *Inebou Hedjou* (translated as "the white walls"), later acquiring the name Memphis. It was situated at present-day Sakkara, south of Cairo.[36]

The pharaoh did not own land at the dawn of Egyptian history. He and his court lived off the taxes paid by the population and, in particular, off the livestock tax levied every two years.[37]

The Egyptian pharaoh was, above all, a spiritual and religious official. In performing rituals, he essentially connected with the gods and became a god himself. In doing so, he was able to summon the essential moments of creation and of the universe's configuration, and over time became one with the sun god.[38]

Egypt's ruler took over from his predecessor and father, the creator god (most often the falcon-god Horus), the obligation to take care of the world and maintain its life and order [13]. Given his origin, he shared the "divine spirit," the power to revitalize all beings in the name of *ka*, and was thus "consubstantial" with divine beings, but also with the generations of previous rulers. He was then worthy of divine reverence, since he performed his duty in bringing together individual

---

[36] Kateřina Postupová, Počátky kontaktu Egypta a Předního Východu (Early contact between Egypt and the Near East), B.A. thesis, Plzeň, West Bohemian University in Plzeň, Faculty of Arts 2007, p. 21.

[37] Charles K. Maisels, Early Civilizations of the Old World, London and New York, Routledge – Taylor and Francis Group 2001, p. 72.

[38] Charles K. Maisels, Early Civilizations of the Old World, London and New York, Routledge – Taylor and Francis Group 2001, p. 59.

**Fig. 13** Stela of the pharaoh of the 1st dynasty of Djet (2900–2800 BC). Above: a representation of the royal palace, over which a serpent indicated the ruler's name. The sculptor depicted the god Horus in his falcon form.

human beings and creating a community of them. He was responsible for their lives and was nothing less than the *ka* of his people.[39] The royal *ka* carried enormous significance in Egypt. He was responsible for the fertility of the soil, animals and people, for the people's lives and for the way the world was.[40]

The sense and meaning of the myth of Egyptian society, i.e. the story of righteous Osiris, loyal Isis, the treacherous Set and the brave Horus are evidently based on this idea. Osiris, the ruler of Egypt, was murdered by his evil brother Set, who cut up the latter's body into pieces so that Osiris could never return to this world. Set thus unjustly stripped his brother of and took over his royal *ka*.

Yet Osiris' wife, the loyal Isis, gathered up all the pieces of her husband and magically brought him back to life, and they then conceived their son Horus. The mother was able to raise her son, who grew into a brave man and revenged his father by killing Set in a fight. In doing so, he assumed possession of the royal *ka* that had originally belonged to Osiris and had subsequently been stolen by Set. He thus gave his father the gift of life and became the rightful ruler and, consequently, the source of life, fertility and bliss for Egyptians.[41]

These myths evidently formed the ideological basis of the pharaoh's power and social position in the public life of ancient Egypt.

---

[39] Jiří Janák, Chapter 105 of Kniha mrtvých v období Nové říše – Staroegyptské pojetí vzkříšení (The book of the dead during the New Empire – the Ancient Egyptian concept of resurrection), doctoral dissertation, Prague, Charles University in Prague, the Hussite Theological Faculty, Religious Studies Department 2002, p. 33., p. 36.

[40] Ibid, p. 37.

[41] Ibid, p. 38 and p. 178.

# STABILIZATION
## OF THE EARLY EGYPTIAN STATE


Altogether fundamental – and irrevocable – changes for the history of the land occurred quickly after that, during the so-called archaic or early dynastic period (ca. 2920–2575 BC). It was then that the rulers of a united Egypt, the pharaohs, achieved economic independence, lording over numerous "state estates," agricultural operations scattered throughout the land that delivered their crop to the ruler.

In the political sphere, the pharaohs rid themselves of "significant" competitors, individuals of higher social status whom we know little about and with whom they still had to share public support in the period around 3000 BC.[42] It is probably at this time that we find proof of the division of Egypt into administrative territories – nomes – with 20 and 22 in Lower and Upper Egypt, respectively.

Finally, it is in the spiritual sphere that creators of that period attributed to the pharaohs a fundamental importance in this world. The gods were believed to have created a sacred order in creating the world (*maat* in ancient Egyptian), preconceiving the proper and just arrangement of things of the visible world. The pharaoh, who according to Egyptian doctrine was in the individual parts of his being "consubstantial" both with the gods and his people, came to this world to carry out this divine order and to stifle the forces of evil and chaos. Nobody was to oppose him since he had been invested with authority from the highest places. All of these changes probably came to an end the moment the architect Imhotep built the first known step pyramid for his master, the pharaoh Djoser (2630–2611 BC), in present-day Saqqara.

---

[42] Peter Kaplony, "Rollsiegel", in: Lexikon der Egyptologie, vol. V, Wiesbaden, Harrassowitz 1983, pp. 294–300, mainly pp. 294–295.

# CHARACTERISTICS
# OF THE EARLY EGYPTIAN STATE

Let us now briefly take a look at the information available on how early Egyptian state administration was run at this time.[43]

Egypt's ruling structure consisted of three basic pillars – the pharaoh and his court, the state's economic administration and governance of the nomes.

It was around this time that the private property of the pharaoh and of his family was separated from the strictly state property that formed an economic requisite for the pharaoh's office. Among the pharaoh's personal property were craft shops (stonecutters) and sources of mineral resources (stone quarries for the manufacturing of vessels). The royal court, the first public institution in the land, was from the mid-2nd Dynasty managed by an official, often translated as a "vizier," on orders of the ruler. The vizier organized the work of experts in precisely defined areas and that of individuals with more generally defined authorities. They were primarily "courtiers" in the broader sense of the word, or valets. We know that one of them took part in supplying a certain temple and, therefore, had administrative duties involving redistribution. Also belonging to this group were "those in the court (palace)," masters of ceremonies tending to the sacred royal insignia, crowns, robes and the king's personal jewelry. Records were found from this period on the existence of a "solar barge," a boat for the deceased pharaoh to use on his journey to the heavens.

---

[43] I am drawing here from Petra Vlčková's study Kamenné nádoby s nápisy – Prameny k poznání správního systému Raně Dynastického Egypta (Stone vessels with inscriptions – Sources for understanding the administrative system of Early Dynastic Egypt), in: Ľubica Obuchová, Petr Charvát (edd.), Stát a státnost ve starém orientu (The state and statehood in the ancient Orient), a set of studies by the group "Man and the Landscape in History," Prague, The Czech Oriental Society 2006, pp. 8–25.

The main source of income from the pharaoh's court consisted of revenue from the royal domains (larger farming complexes) and the individual estates. Along with their production functions, they also served as fiscal bodies since the taxes and contributions levied by the ruler on the subjects were concentrated in them. All the royal authority's income was delivered by the payers to the pharaoh's treasury, a kind of "ministry of finance."

The central treasury could also have had regional branches. Part of the treasury consisted of a supply division, perhaps an executive agency in charge of redistributing certain contributions.

Egypt's ruling administration was also subject to judicial proceedings carried out by tribunals and specially designated officials.

Much of the executive power was in the hands of the governors of Upper and Lower Egypt and of the administrators of the various regions (nomes). Lands beyond Egypt's borders that were subject to the pharaoh's rule were governed by "foreign-land protectors."

We find the situation regarding religious cult institutions and their relations to pharaonic rule to be somewhat chaotic. Besides state-wide cults, there were local (or regional) cults, which, however, we have less information on. It was apparently the royal workshops that supplied the liturgical furnishings or at least some of its components to the temples. The pharaoh's warehouses also supplied sanctuaries, their personnel and even their stockrooms with foodstuffs. We also know of the "domains" of the various deities, without having to answer the question whether this was property obtained independently by the temple or assigned to it for use by the ruling administration. Cult personnel included, above all, priests carrying out funeral ceremonies and dealing with the pharaoh's mortuary cult. There were other clergy members whom we know only by title. Important temples were led by high priests.

# ANCIENT MESOPOTAMIA

# THE NATURAL ENVIRONMENT

Mesopotamia, literally "Between the Rivers" is the Greek name for the land between the Euphrates and Tigris rivers [14]. In ancient times, this term was most likely only applied to describe the region of the Eastern Anatolian foothills between the places from which both rivers originate. Today we use the term to designate the entire area (especially the lowlands) around both rivers demarcated by the Iranian and Eastern Anatolian foothills, the Persian Gulf and the steppes and deserts of Syria and Arabia. Mesopotamia did not possess an overly favorable natural environment: The alluvial activity of both rivers created a vast plain between the massifs of the Taurus and Anti-Taurus mountains (in Anatolia) and of the Zagros Mountains (in Iran). Here a massive coat of alluvial clay covered the bedrock. Geologically speaking, Mesopotamia is practically completely void of any mineral resources. An exception to this are the bitumen deposits in the middle section of the Euphrates, as well as a few outcrops of low quality limestone poking through the thick layer of sediment deposits of the alluvial plains. Both rivers – the Euphrates and the Tigris – originate in the Eastern Anatolian Mountains. The Euphrates arcs westward and then curves across the Syrian-Mesopotamian lowlands. In Syria it takes on two tributaries – the Balikh and Khabur rivers. The Tigris flows in more of a straight line from its spring area in the mountains, follows a more direct route to the alluvial plain and its path to the sea is shorter than the Euphrates. The Tigris takes on the Zab and Diyala tributaries. The Euphrates is generally considered to be more navigable, while the Tigris is wilder with a less predictable current. Today the two rivers flow into a confluence, the Shatt al-Arab River, which receives the Karun and Karkheh tributaries and then empties into the Persian Gulf. Originally, however, the Tigris and Euphrates followed separate paths to the sea. Both rivers regularly flood their littoral plains. This generally

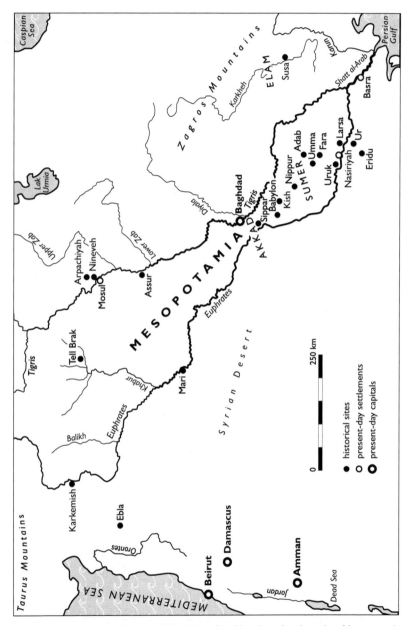

**Fig. 14** Primary historic and archeological sites of prehistoric and early ancient Mesopotamia.

occurs in April and May following the thawing of the winter snow in the Anatolian Mountains. Yet the timing and intensity of their flooding is difficult to predict, and both rivers' floods are therefore a blessing that often turns tragic. Farmers are unable to use these floods to their advantage since they come at a time when the winter wheat, watered by the winter rains, has already come up. Spring wheat, for which the conditions are generally unfavorable in the Near East, is rarely planted.

The unpredictability of the flooding has also forced Mesopotamia's hydraulic engineers since ancient times to build both irrigation canals utilizing flooding and floodwater retention reservoirs to store excess water for later use. Both rivers also possess an extremely low gradient (angle of drop in the riverbed) in traversing the Mesopotamia plains. This means that they flow very slowly and that their water is filled with mineral salts from their riverbeds. Measures must therefore be taken to properly rinse out the mineral salts from the irrigated soil. In southern Mesopotamia, with little rainfall, there is practically no other useable source of moisture for farming. If these salts are left to degrade the arable soil, crops will cease to grow and the soil must then lie fallow for 5 to 10 years to recover its fertility. Another result of the low gradient of both rivers is their relative instability and a propensity to suddenly change their courses. We can imagine the result of a change in the hydrologic regime for a large city for which the river represents the most important transport artery, energy source and sewer facilities. Although the Mesopotamian soil is clayey and dry, it is extremely fertile when irrigated. It is estimated that a harvest of eight fold the sowing rate that was typical for the highest quality soil of pre-industrial Bohemia represents the lowest possible harvest capacity for Mesopotamia. In other words, the maximum yield of arable soil in Bohemia approximated the minimum in Mesopotamia.

The Mesopotamian climate essentially consists of two seasons – winter and summer, with an interval in April and October. Winters are usually mild, raw and rainy with temperatures around 10 °C, but which can drop to freezing. Summers are dry and extremely hot with temperatures capable of rising to between 40 and 50 °C. Most of southern Mesopotamia receives under 200 mm of annual rainfall. This is considered the minimal limit for farming without irrigation.

This central arid area is bordered by a curved "fertile crescent" at the base of the Iranian, Anatolian and Syro-Palestinian Mountains whose average rainfall exceeds 200 mm annually (although not by much). The climate has maintained its current state for the past six thousand years. Before that, following the recession of the most recent ice age around 18,000 BC, there was a gradual improvement of the climate with the most favorable conditions present in the regions during ca. 12,000–7000 BC. The vegetation in southern Mesopotamia is characterized by an adaptation to the arid climate. The low gradient of the riverbeds at the lower parts of the Euphrates and Tigris rivers causes overflowing and creates wetlands with a particular abundance of reeds. The herb and shrub layer is composed of resilient species with deeply penetrating roots (various species of wormwood, thorny shrubs). Willows, tamarisk, acacia and poplar were among the trees that originally grew here. Northern Mesopotamia is characterized by Mediterranean-type vegetation with its forests featuring oak and pistachio trees and an elaborate shrub and herb layer, including grapevines. Animal species include wild sheep and goat (in mountainous regions), gazelle and onager, wild ass (in the open steppe), Bos primigenius (similar to today's European bison), deer, fox, bear and boar (in wooded areas). Small rodents provide a welcome food supply for reptiles and there are even poisonous arthropods (scorpions).

# THE DAWN OF A MORE ADVANCED
## SOCIAL STRUCTURE
### (the Halaf culture, 6000–5000 BC)

We've previously noted that the people of prehistoric and ancient Mesopotamia farmed an estimated 65,000 km² of arable land.[44]

It is deep in the prehistory of the land of the Euphrates and Tigris that we find the very first glimmers of the idea that would later lead to the social and spiritual principles of ancient Mesopotamia.

Splendidly painted Halaf pottery of the first more progressively organized settlement of prehistoric Mesopotamia reveals patterns that anticipate later substantiated components of the Mesopotamian spiritual world.[45] It is the color composition of the Halaf culture's colorful pottery that is mostly responsible for such overtones here. A color chord of white, red and black, prominent in its final phase, characterizes an important milieu of Halaf culture during that period at Tell Arpachiya in today's city of Mosul in northern Iraq. The residents of a large rectangular home uncovered at the site in layer TT6 ate from luxurious tableware decorated with patterns in these three colors, wore jewelry with a combination of the same colors and possessed reserves of mineral dyes in the same color chord. Even the handstones used to pulverize the larger clumps of dye in preparing polychromatic composition composed of the same colors were made of rocks of these three shades.

The Arpachiyan people of the Halaf culture most likely wore these three colors on their bodies, ate from them and probably used them to decorate the interiors of their homes or to embellish their personal appearance.

---

[44] Charles K. Maisels, Early Civilizations of the Old World, London and New York, Routledge – Taylor and Francis Group 2001, p. 186.

[45] Conventional dating to 5500–4000 BC; today there is a prevailing tendency to date the culture's beginnings to ca. 6000 BC or even earlier. For more on Mesopotamia's prehistory see Petr Charvát, Mesopotamia Before History, London and New York, Routledge, Taylor and Francis Group 2002.

**Fig. 15** Mosaic decoration from colored stone cone tops driven into a layer of mud plaster. Southeast façade of the Pillared Hall (Pfeilerhalle). Uruk, late Uruk period (3500–3200 BC).

Given that the site was visited by numerous people and that their movement must have been facilitated by at least two paved paths leading up to the top of the "sacred mound," this place must have possessed extraordinary significance in the Halaf culture. This leads us to view this as a central point, probably of a sacral nature, where crowds of worshippers came to take for their efforts valuable goods that were unavailable elsewhere. These highly sought "goods" might have included exceptionally beautiful painted pottery. Yet it is also possible that visitors took goods of a non-material nature, such as various forms of "divine blessings."

It should be noted in this light that the white-red-black color chord survived the extinction of the Halaf culture, was part of the Ubaid culture and even lasted into early Sumerian history. It was this very color combination that adorned the walls and various architecturally emphasized elements (such as niches) of early temples in the city of Uruk that were built in the later phase of Uruk culture (3500–3200 BC) [15]. In historical cuneiform literature, these three colors characterize the material from which are made the highest heavens: the seat of the most ancient and majestic Sumerian god Anu.[46]

---

[46] Wayne Horowitz, Mesopotamian Cosmic Geography, Winona Lake, Indiana, Eisenbrauns 1998, pp. 9–11.

Yet the patterns themselves on Halaf pottery also provide information that can today be deciphered and interpreted. One type of
recurring ornamentation on Halaf pottery is the checkered pattern
appearing in different forms on various shapes of vessels. Sumerian
mathematicians used the checkered pattern in the proto-cuneiform
period as a symbol of unbelievably high numbers that were more of a
theoretical nature.[47] We also have at our disposal, on one of the seals
found in the refuse of administrative materials from the archaic layers
of the city of Ur (ca. 28th century BC), the picture of a man and woman
engaging in sexual intercourse (a scene of obvious fertility connotations), above whom shines a sun with a checkered pattern.

It is probably not a far stretch to suggest that the checkered pattern
symbolizes fertility and the general fertile powers of people and nature.
The pattern itself directly invites such an interpretation: Once even
its smallest nucleus has been constructed, it can be expanded in any
arbitrary direction for any given distance and length of time.

However, Halaf pottery has other patterns that can also be interpreted in referring to later written and pictorial (iconographic) sources
of ancient Mesopotamia. These patterns are a rosette, usually eight-
pointed, and a four-pointed star [16].

Both patterns are so similar that we could consider them as variations of one and the same graphic element, though I feel that this is
not exactly the case. In later images on seals from the proto-cuneiform
age the (eight-pointed) rosette is a graphic symbol of divine substances
contained in the plant world. The fact that the ornament maintained its
importance/meaning even in a later period is attested to by the eight-
point star's symbolization of Ishtar, the goddess of female fertility, in
the art of ancient Mesopotamia.[48]

Though the four-pointed star can be interpreted as a simplified
version of the rosette, I think that it more likely refers to a different
conceptual structure generally prevalent in the human consciousness:
the idea of the four cardinal points. A symbol of all by people of the
inhabited and therefore humanized and "tamed" world appears in this

---

[47]  They continued to use this marking for the later phase of the Uruk culture, a period in
which writing was discovered and introduced and of state organization (3500–3200 BC).
[48]  I am indebted to my learned friend and colleague Jiří Prosecký for this information.

**Fig. 16** A painted bowl from the Halaf culture with rosette and checkered motifs (ca. 5500–4000 BC).

form in a number of cultures and civilizations of our world. Its appearance in Halaf pottery can thus express the intention to relate magical acts, represented by the accompanying ornamentation and carried out using the relevant painted pottery, to the entire world inhabited by people of the same culture.

Special attention should be devoted to a bowl from the Halaf culture bearing the depiction of two combs positioned with their teeth

**Fig. 17** A painted bowl from the Halaf culture with the motif of two combs (ca. 5500–4000 BC).

facing each other.[49] Since the image of the comb will play an extremely important role in further interpretation, it is not too early to consider this essential information for the interpretation [17].

In a number of cultures and civilizations the comb evokes the idea of head and body hair as a symbol of a person's inner most character. Head and body hair, growing from the inside of the human body, is "rooted" in the unique character of each of our personalities and, therefore, outwardly expresses the individuality of each person. This individual characteristic is conveyed in two aspects: it symbolizes the real individual nature of its person and also represents each individual

---

[49] Petr Charvát, Mesopotamia before history, London and New York, Routledge 2002, p. 62 Fig. 4.13.

human personality in expressing the role that society designates to each individual.

The first aspect is most markedly evident in status changes accompanying the individual development of each of us. This includes the cutting or shaving off of one's hair to signify a status change: since a "new person" is created from a change in social position, this change should be visibly reflected in the removal of the old hair. That which is new within, must be new outwardly as well. Hence, the symbolic importance of cutting one's hair accompanies important occasions in life – both for religious rituals, and for more prosaic occasions such as beginning military service. This is most distinctly demonstrated during the coronation ceremonies of the ruler of one of the clans of the Igbo tribe in Nigeria: before being enthroned, the future ruler's hair is ceremoniously cut off, whereupon, accompanied by the oldest member of his extended family and the priest of ancestral veneration, he leaves for the ancestral shrine in the forest. There he offers his cut hair to the ancestral altar, while placing his loincloth in a termitary, considered to be an entrance way to the empire of his ancestors. He can now sit on the throne as a new man: the king.

An even clearer case can be found in the funeral rituals of the Central American speakers of the Nahuatl language. There they cut a lock of the infant's hair and save it. After the individual matures, grows old and dies, the descendents also cut a lock from the deceased's head. Then the body is burned and stored in a wooden, human-shaped box where the two locks of hair are added to the deceased's ashes. Thus the deceased, whose earthly life and deeds are inscribed in the coordinate system of these two locks, crosses over to the world of his ancestors and begins his or her new existence there.

The second aspect, often as a wish for good fortune and success, points out the various defining moments in a person's life. As part of a beautiful wedding ceremony, Russian wedding guests comb the bride's hair in a manner symbolizing the plowing of a field. Again, the fertility connotation is obvious. Sometimes the bride's hair is even treated with milk or honey so that the act symbolizes moisture falling on the furrows of a freshly plowed field and activating the vitalizing fertility power. We have reason to believe that bearers of the cuneiform culture of ancient Mesopotamia were also familiar with this aspect in this form.

In brief, we can therefore draw the conclusion that the image of the comb can be seen as a symbol of that which this unique and unrepeatable human being essentially is – or that which it should be according to its society. This bowl, featuring two combs from the Tell Halaf site in Syria, thus depicts the shared dining of two human beings. The first idea to come to mind is that it was a "wedding dish." Unfortunately, we will never know if, in fact, the Halaf wedding guests cared for the brides' hair just as gently and thoroughly as Russians later did.

An attempted interpretation can be made of at least some of the ornamentation on Halaf pottery: Various individuals are referred to here, as are fertility forces, the divine aspect of the plant kingdom or the four cardinal points as the symbol of the world inhabited by all people known to the user's culture. Yet how are we to imagine the magical effect of pottery decorated in this manner?

In interpreting this, we would work with ideas documented in researching pre-state and pre-literate communities, beginning at the level of shifting agriculture. The notion of wresting a living from unfarmed land as an insertion of man into the events of nature is repeatedly documented in this kind of milieu. The farmer, capable of providing his family with enough food, is viewed here as a human being of such superb qualities that nature's fertile potential is activated simply by his involvement with unfarmed land. Nature, in turn, reacts positively to its ennoblement through the virtues of a good person by providing him with sufficiency, and even abundance and surplus. The community of this kind of farmer, and especially its less successful members, can then wish to share in the excellent qualities of his personality "objectified" in the return on his endeavors in that they accept his hospitality and eat the food that he provides to them and that is nothing more than a hypostasis of his own personality, inserted into nature and multiplied by it. A very important social role is thus assigned to the successful farmer as a giver of prosperity and a source of abundance who, if he so wishes, can "recharge" the members of his community – or those dining at his table – with the positive potential of his personality based on the results of his work. This probably has something to do with one of the sources of ancient social differentiation and society's division into more and less esteemed and valued individuals.

We now also understand the extremely important role of lavishly painted pottery of the prehistoric Near East and of the Halaf culture in particular. It is not known if those considered important Arpachiyan figures actually dined with this luxuriously painted tableware. Nevertheless, the message that these goods carry today is clear: "may the divine element of the plant world contained in the food that I eat from this bowl fill me with fertile power" (rosette bordered by checkered pattern), "may the food that I eat from this bowl make fertile my entire world" (four-pointed star bordered by checkered pattern), "may the two human beings who eat from this bowl live in harmony" (two symmetrically positioned combs).

# EARLY HISTORIOGRAPHY:
## SUSA at the Close of the 5th Millenium BC

Let us now direct our attention to the late 5th millenium BC when one of the focal points of the Near East's further historical development clearly emerges. This is the city of Susa in present-day southwest Iran that is positioned on a plain between the Karun and Karkhenh rivers that very much resemble that alluvial plain of the Euphrates and Tigris rivers in ancient Mesopotamia. Archeological finds from the city of Susa have provided us with invaluable source material on the birth of statehood in the Near East.

## Mausoleum of Susa

At the very end of the 5th millenium, a final resting place was established for the deceased of Susa and of the lands around the city, which would later become the ancient Iranian state of Elam. Hitherto barren land slightly sloping toward the banks of the Shaur River was chosen as the site. We are unsure exactly how the deceased were laid to rest here, since published reports of archeological research concerning this site differ. It was originally assumed that the excavation below a huge tell settlement – roughly 25 meters high – uncovered the remnants of a burial ground. Later, however, the excavators revised this, claiming that it most likely was a giant burial mound with a 12-meter diameter and a preserved height of approximately 3 meters. The burial mound consisted of both brick tombs for the individual elite and graves between these structures. This appears to have been a kind of "central" burial ground, since the deceased were apparently transferred here following an interval after their death. The non-anatomical positioning of their remains attest to this: some graves apparently contained, instead of whole bodies, merely bones. The deceased received here a wide range of objects for their final journey, including personal decorations, toiletries such as round mirrors made from carefully polished copper, tools and weapons.

However, the following pages will deal with splendidly painted pottery that was among the most frequent funerary objects buried with the Susa deceased. The authors of the research originally assumed that there were approximately 2,000 graves in Susa. Roughly 400 graves can be ascertained from the available documentation, and we currently have a total of 246 painted vessels from them. That in itself is a sufficiently large sample of the works of one of the most conspicuous "painting schools" of the ancient Far East for us to attempt an interpretation as to what purpose this pottery served and what exactly the message was hidden in these often extremely elegant and aesthetically pleasing ornamentation that adorned it.

Susa pottery represents a version of the luxurious tableware that we are familiar with from the preceding Halaf culture. This usually consisted of bowls, dishes, taller vase-like vessels, pitchers and cups; a legged bowl is even documented. A prehistoric potter made them from finely prepared beige- or ochre-colored clay dough in his hands (not yet on the wheel). After finishing the surface of the vessel, he carefully smoothed it and probably passed it on to the painter, who painted the vessel with mostly darker shades. We will now examine these motifs painted on Susa pottery.

In analyzing in detail the various elements the decorative compositions featured on Susa pottery, we should note that some of them repeat and that together they form compositions with a deliberate order. Assuming that the patterns on Susa pottery carry a message or statement from our ancient ancestors, let us now try to decipher some of these images.

Careful examination of the artistic elements of Susa pottery seems to invite a categorization of three large groups. The first group features pictorial symbols behind which the bearers of the Susa archeological culture are most likely concealed. The second group then represents "reports" of their activities, while the third group addresses in symbolic form some of the deities whom the inhabitants of this region of the Near East worshipped at this time (and later).

## Painted pottery of Susa:
## the people and their communities

The first group primarily consists of an element that we have already encountered in the pictorial repertoire of painters from the Halaf culture: the comb, probably symbolizing a single, specific human being.[50]

The image of the comb on Susa pottery probably also represents individual people – most likely those who initiated the creation of the painted pottery or those to whom the pottery was (even posthumously) given.

One not entirely common element should be mentioned here as well: a rectangle filled with parallel-running wavy lines. This image within the curvature of the ibex's horns is not a depiction of a stream or pond as was assumed in another interpretation. The representation of a pair of such rectangles, symmetrically positioned within a geometric composition that most likely depicts architecture, indicates that we have here a figure that could correspond to the later Sumerian term *gipar*[51] [18a]. In Sumerian, *gipar* has a quite unique series of meanings. It can mean a mat of reeds, but also a fresh green pasture and the residence of the entu-priestess performing fertility ceremonies in the temple – particularly the ceremony known as the "sacred marriage." Is it at all possible to surmise where all these meanings came from? The logical conclusion would be that they came from a common base: the mat as a wedding bed for the husband and wife of the house. It was from this mat which all plenitude and abundance enjoyed by the members of the household originated.[52] This would also satisfy the image of fresh pastures and the residence of the individual responsible for magically ensuring fertility. The exceptional meaning of the mat of reeds is also attested to by the archeological situation found in a later temple, named the "Stone Building" (*Steingebäude*) by its excavators, in the Sumerian

---

50  Petr Charvát, The Iconography of Pristine Statehood, Prague, Karolinum 2005, p. 271, No. 33 (Sb. 3163). Here the Coll. numbers refer to Louvre registration numbers beginning with Sb.

51  Petr Charvát, The Iconography of Pristine Statehood, Prague, Karolinum 2005, p. 277, No. 45 (Sb. 14 293).

52  Petr Charvát, The Iconography of Pristine Statehood, Prague, Karolinum 2005, p. 277, No. 46 (Sb. 3199).

**Fig. 18a** A painted vase from the first level of Susa culture from Susa (ca. 4000 BC). The ibex, perhaps symbolizing one of the mythical forces of the universe, carries in the curve of its horns an image interpreted here to be a gipar.

city of Uruk. This rectangular temple is composed of a central cell surrounded by a corridor. A podium in the position of an altar stands at the front of the cell. In analyzing the podium under a layer of rock fragments imbedded in mortar, a lower coating of thin white mortar was found in which the unknown builder had at one time impressed a total of five indentations arranged like the number five on present-day dice. Under this coating of mortar there was found the remains of a reed mat that both upper layers were resting on. We are left with the impression of a symbol of the civilized world (five indentations = the four cardinal points and its center) supported by a primary base of reeds, as described by the later Babylonian creation mythos, the *Enûma Eliš*. If we are correct in our interpretation, this rectangle with wavy lines could be a depiction of the wedding bed, and the compositions in question could work with the conceptual circle concerning marriage, or perhaps the broader theme of fertility.

The third element of the first group is a cross or a four-arm Greek cross.[53] Here we are most likely working with the concept of the entire world as "that which is inhabited by people of our culture," which the ancient Greeks used the term *ekumene* to describe. However, as we shall see, this is not the entire inhabited world, but merely one of its components: a city or settlement founded in harmony with the universe's order. Significant testimony in this regard is provided by the fact that, starting in this period, we frequently find that corners of important prehistoric buildings of the Near East are positioned to face the cardinal points. This is how important architecture is entered into the ordered structure of all that exists in the world. Once again, it is the oldest Sumerian proto-cuneiform that provides a clue here in that the cross symbol appears both in the form of the term $BAD_3$, "city firmly established," "fortification," etc., as well as the term EZEN, "festivity." What do these two terms have in common? Well, if you establish a town or city on land not yet inhabited by people, you are taking the property of spirits who had lived there until then. You must therefore compensate them for it, most likely by performing a religious ceremony with a sacrifice offering to the previous owners, who would then be appeased.

---

[53] Petr Charvát, The Iconography of Pristine Statehood, Prague, Karolinum 2005, p. 274, No. 40 (Coll. 3202).

The ancient Bohemian verb "třiebiti" (to clear), which originally meant both "to clear the forest" and "perform a pagan sacrifice" provides an excellent parallel. A similar association is offered here: If you clear the forest, you take the property of spirits, whom you must then provide with compensation in the form of a sacrifice.

The fourth and final member of the first group consists of a triangle-based composition. Although here we come up against certain difficulties in interpretation, it does seem that the ancient writing of Elam (southwestern Iran) from the period of ca. 3000 BC will provide us with a clue. In proto-Elamite script, as this writing system is called, the triangle forms the basis for the emblem of a fringed triangular standard that bears the symbol of the relevant member town of the proto-Elamite communality and appears in written documents and artistic monuments as an identification mark of the relevant social body. Perhaps the most likely hypothesis is that the triangular compositions on Susa pottery represent the idea of the "whole world," "all areas inhabited by the people of our culture."

This first group therefore features the culture bearers of early Susa: individuals, couples establishing new families, a settlement founded in harmony with the order of the universe and, finally, the entire inhabited world, which is, of course, the world of "our" culture.

## Painted pottery of Susa: the people and their work

The second group then features symbols of some of the most important activities that the inhabitants of Susa were involved in at that time. The first activity that should be mentioned here is of an agricultural nature: the cultivation of fields often represented by pictures of ears of cereal or even a triangular pile of grain, tellingly filled with a checkered pattern, which we have already interpreted as a fertility symbol [18b]. We also find here parallel-running wavy lines, most likely representing liquid elements, most commonly water or various beverages, as evident on a pitcher featuring a band of wavy ornament. In one case we even find on Susa pottery a prototype of the proto-cuneiform character RAD, which most likely meant "an intervale near a river." Perhaps this image brings

**Fig. 18b** A painted vase from the first level of Susa culture (ca. 4000 BC). Zigzag with checkered pattern and images of ears of cereals (?) possibly symbolizing the abundance of a crop from irrigated land.

to mind the work of a hydraulic engineer, who ingeniously tamed the river and forced it to serve the community.[54]

Hunting scenes appear quite frequently on Susa pottery [18c]. The hunting of game, sometimes using dogs and even trained birds of prey, is an oft repeated theme of these pictorial compositions. The question arises whether these ancient hunting scenes commemorate a "noble sport" (though, naturally, also the best peace-time training for war) that the elite of that period engaged in, or whether they represent the

[54]    Petr Charvát, The Iconography of Pristine Statehood, Prague, Karolinum 2005, p. 287, No. 66 (Sb. 14 290).

**Fig. 18c** A motif from a painted vase from the first level of Susa culture. (ca. 4000 BC). A human figure with a bow and arrow symbolizing the hunter's role or an emblem of sovereignty.

symbolic aspect of hunting.[55] Indeed, it seems as if the hunting of wild game represented in later historical periods in the Near East an activity of the most elevated members of society – the king himself took part – that also had a civilizational dimension. In killing dangerous animals the noble hunter imposed human solidarity on the wild, untamed, unhumanized and uncivilized land, thereby expanding the borders of the human world and protecting it from its natural enemies. There are indications that the elite of the ancient Near East were familiar with this symbolic aspect of hunting.

Yet the obligations of Susa's leaders consisted of more than just defending their community from wild beasts. They also had to confront

[55] Petr Charvát, The Iconography of Pristine Statehood, Prague, Karolinum 2005, p. 255, No. 1 (Sb. 3223).

the plots and intrigues of human enemies. This is represented in depictions of all kinds of weapons on their painted pottery.

We have reason to believe that in these cases it was a triumphal symbol used by warriors to celebrate victorious returns from battle. The repeating images of spears or quivers full of arrows certainly indicate something of this nature.[56]

Analysis of the final motif appearing in this group borders on guessing. A unique shape, perhaps best compared to a crescent or curved bread roll, appearing on some cups could have something to do with the proto-cuneiform symbol RU, denoting "giving," "surrendering" or even "sacrificing." The images on these cups lead us to speculate that it could be a symbol depicting a religious activity such as the libation that is to be discussed in the following section.

The people of early Susa also left records on their painted pottery reflecting activities that they considered to be the most important: farming, hunting expeditions into the wilderness, war campaigns and their veneration of the gods.

## Painted pottery of Susa: deities

Lastly, we find in the third group of Susa motifs symbols that we believe represent the deities of that place and time. Since most ancient cultures shared a certain unwillingness to depict their gods directly, it is no surprise that the people of Susa preferred emblems over direct depiction.

The symbol of a sun was among the most prevalent of these appearing on Susa pottery. We have reason to believe that this depiction concerned the daily light and the passage of time, and that the final recipient of this sign of respect was most likely the sky-god and lord of constellations known to Sumerians as An. We have already entertained the idea that if the trichromatism in the Halaf and Ubaid culture really refers to An, it can be assumed that the veneration of this god has endured since the earliest historical period.

---

[56] Petr Charvát, The Iconography of Pristine Statehood, Prague, Karolinum 2005, p. 269, No. 30 (Sb. 3137).

One piece of Susa pottery features a rectangle whose interior is filled with a checkered pattern and whose outer edge consists of networks of straight lines intersecting at right angles.[57] This icon was most likely intended to evoke the name of the deity of atmospheric phenomena and of everything between heaven and earth. The Sumerians called him Enlil. This checkered pattern refers to the proto-cuneiform writing of Emil's name involving this type of ornament and possibly even interwoven in a reed mat.

A lingering question is whether – and to what extent – the depiction of wavy lines on Susa pottery refer to Enki, the deity of water and later also of wisdom.

A unique case of Susa pottery decoration consists of the motif of two equilateral triangles positioned so that their points touch in a kind of "hourglass" or "butterfly" design. This pattern repeatedly appears in images that could be interpreted as mountain landscapes, but that are also linked to fertility-themed pictures. It might be accompanied by figures of wild animals and we also find them on the familiar picture of the "bridal chamber" with a double bed.

These testimonies identify the symbol as a reference to the fertility goddess known to Sumerians as Ninhursag, the "Lady of the Foothills" as Dutch cuneiformist Frans Wiggermann humorously calls her.

So it is possible that Susa pottery features paintings of four of the later most important deities of the Near East's pantheons – the god of the heavens, atmosphere and even of the water, and the goddess of female fertility.

The results of the new scientific analysis of this beautiful pottery should be considered important in studying the social context of this painted pottery of Susa at the close of the 5th millenium BC. Analyses geared toward observing the origin of pottery dough using a typical composition of trace elements ascertained two phases in the development of the pottery style of Susa. In the initial phase, the pottery with such paintings was made only from clay of a single raw material source. In the second phase, however, while maintaining a uniform style, the pottery was made from different raw material sources. This allows us

---

[57] Petr Charvát, The Iconography of Pristine Statehood, Prague, Karolinum 2005, p. 301, No. 93 (Sb. 14 281).

to draw the important conclusion that the artistic motifs and compositions on the pottery of Susa represent a system of symbols apparently shared and understood by multiple communities.

## Painted pottery of Susa: Why?

We should now attempt to determine the significance and meaning of paintings on the pottery of Susa, though I admit that an unproven hypothesis is all I can offer for the time being. There are two basic facts that we have to grapple with. This first and foremost concerns pottery's role in the funeral ritual. As explained above, I am working with the assumption that the patterns and compositions on Susa pottery represent a uniform set of symbols referring to facts that are important from the perspective of survivors of the deceased laid to rest in the mausoleum in Susa.

Ethnographic analogies tell us that legitimizing society's highest administrative positions and determining the rules for succession in such positions are fundamental problems that a number of pre-state and pre-literate societies had to deal with. In most cases, we come across the principle of legitimization through a relationship to the spiritual world. A link to the world of deceased ancestors, often to the world of otherworldly beings, is frequently a factor. The customs of some Pacific chieftaincies are very characteristic of this. During the new chief's inaugural ceremony on the Tonga islands the most important moment of transferring supreme power occurs when the successor chief drinks from a cup holding a special drink, thereby mystically joining with all his ancestors and, through them, with the supreme being – the sky goddess.

In connection with such customs and traditions, the mausoleum in Susa could be considered a massive means of legitimization, in front of which the ceremonial inauguration of new leaders of the Susa community was held. A relatively similar ceremony is known to have taken place in Ebla of present-day Syria, as described in writing dating back to roughly 2300 BC (ARET 11). Apparently, on the day the queen was to be married, the bride and groom would retire to the royal family's mausoleum and await the sunrise. As soon as the sun rose, music began and, before the start of the main sacrificial ceremony and all festivities, a special messenger recited: *Nintu renewed Shura, she renewed Barama, she renewed the ruler and the mistress.*[58] This ceremony can be seen as an apt analogy to that which took place in front of the mausoleum of Susa.

If, as part of the enthronement ceremony, each newly anointed ruler of the Susa community also mystically connected with all his ancestors laid to rest in this "burial mound," this ritual may very well have occurred *in illo tempore* over the course of the ancestors' lives, accompanying all ceremonious acts. If it did in fact happen this way, a record would exist on these acts undertaken by the ancestors.

This could be the reason why in Susa survivors of the deceased placed such superbly painted ceramics in their graves. This may also have been due to the belief that the deceased maintain their social status in the next world, thereby legitimizing the prevailing social order in the world of the living. We have learned that the painted pottery of the Halaf culture, apparently through a mystical infusion of the host's positive characteristics into a tangible form, served to legitimize the social position of those organizing such feasts. The leaders of Susa society would then further elaborate this role of painted pottery. The impressively painted pottery therefore not only represented their social position, but was a means of obtaining a certain level of immortality. A record of their life and deeds, replayed again and again during the inaugural ceremonies of their descendents, would bring them back to life in a mythical time. We are touching here on a primary impulse that might have precipitated the need to use graphic symbols of a more enduring nature to depict a record of human deeds – the creation of the first *rerum gestarum*, of an early chronicle of people's lives and deeds.

---

[58] Walther Sallaberger, Nachrichten an den Palast von Ebla: Eine Deutung von níg-mul (-an), in: Semitic and Assyriological Studies Presented to Pelio Fronzaroli by Pupils and Colleagues, Wiesbaden, Harrassowitz Verlag 2003, p. 600–625, on p. 610.

## SUSA AT THE DAWN OF THE URUK PERIOD: FIRST REPORTS FROM THE CREATION OF THE STATE   (early 4th millenium BC)

Fundamental changes occurred in Elam's capital city in the early 4th millenium BC following the abandonment of the mausoleum in Susa.

The people here built a monumental terraced structure from clay bricks not far from the ancient burial grounds. Archeologists excavating this edifice called it the High Terrace *(haute terasse)*. It was at least 8 meters high and the measurable length of one of its preserved sides was at least 80 meters. Later excavation verified the existence of a total of three building complexes at the top of the Terrace. A structure bearing a resemblance to later temples is the main feature here. We also find architecture that is more of a residential nature, most likely a home for Susa's elite at that time. The complex also included spaces that were most likely used for storage purposes [19]. The Terrace only lasted for a limited time as its maintenance was gradually neglected. Its front side first began to slump and eventually collapsed onto buildings that careless tenants had built directly underneath it. The people of Susa had twice attempted to repair the front of the dilapidated building, but were unable to prevent it from falling down. People then stopped using the Terrace and it became an abandoned ruin.

Our interest is, however, focused on the buildings atop the terrace. The storage complex might have been used to supply both the "temple" and the "palace" – and possibly both institutions at once. The quotation marks are necessary here, since we are obviously unable to support the interpretation of the temple and palace without written records. The duality of this most ancient center of Susa's rulers is indeed remarkable: In contrast to ancient Egypt, where only one person – the pharaoh – ruled the state from the very beginning, the Susa community of the early 4 millenium BC may had two from the start. Now let us see if documented proof exists that would provide information on this.

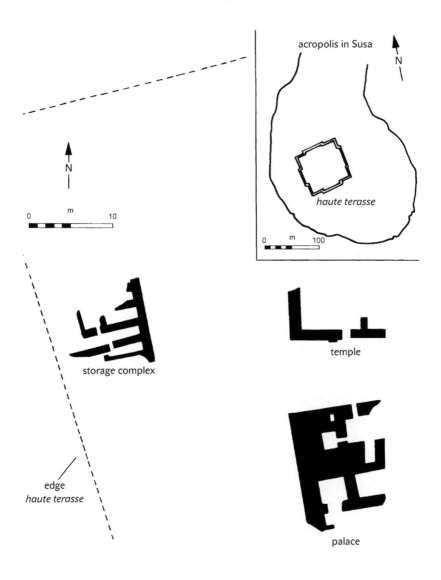

acropolis in Susa

N

haute terasse

0   m   100

0   m   10

N

storage complex

temple

edge
haute terasse

palace

**Fig. 19** Ground plans of buildings found at the top of the *haute terasse* in Susa.
3900–3800 BC. Palace (?) at lower right, temple at right center, storage complex at left.

Although we still do not know of any exclusive painted pottery from this period, excavations here have provided us with other substantial finds. These consist of the oldest Susa seal impressions pressed from matrices or dry seals cut from organic materials, wood or bone into clay.

Unfortunately, the excavators of Susa did not leave behind detailed documentation on their finds that would give us an idea of the archeological context of the discoveries of these seals.

An examination of their "reverse sides" yields the important finding that they mostly come from packaging – baskets, sacks, containers, packages, etc. The fact that suppliers sealed the packaging of their goods means that there was movement of the goods in question between three places: the place of the sender who supplied and sealed the goods, the delivery path of the package to the recipient and the residence of the recipient who received the package, broke the seal and consumed the goods. (Unfortunately, archeological sources do not inform us what the end consumers provided to the senders as payment). We must therefore assume that these early seals point to the first, hitherto undifferentiated process of a socially driven exchange of material goods, known in ethnological parlance as *reciprocity*. This was not yet a case of *redistribution*, in which a center uses its receptors to gather goods from manufacturers and redistributes them to consumers who are not the same as the original manufacturers. While reciprocity is compatible with a wide range of social organizations of pre-state communities, the existence of redistribution points to a more developed, organic organization of society – to a chieftaincy or even an early state.

The meager archeological information shedding light on the circumstances under which the early Susa seals were discovered mostly tells of their origin in the settlement's layers, most likely created by dumped rubbish. These are objects that were simply discarded after they fulfilled their social function.

In one case, an excavator recorded the occurrence of a larger number of seals accompanied by what were probably storage containers. This could have been a place where foodstuffs and possibly beverages were supplied for mass consumption, perhaps for a ceremonial feast of some kind.

## The sacral face of the age: activating fertility powers

In the first group of seals from Susa, featuring depictions of human and animal figures, we find the form of an important individual holding a cup or bowl in a highly raised hand.[59] It appears that this member of lower nobility is performing a libation. In undertaking this ritual, documented in later written sources of the cuneiform civilization, we are quite certain that he is worshipping some of the deities of that age. The nobleman is dressed in special attire.

Although the entire picture was not preserved, we do know that he wore a long flowing robe and that his head was adorned with a special cylindrical tiara, from whose edges hung a kind of fringed decoration. The nobleman's face is depicted on such a small space and with such caricature-like hyperbole that we are unsure whether he is performing the ritual with his uncovered face or if he is wearing a mask. The figure of the assistant standing next to the nobleman increases the ritual's importance.

Are we able to figure out the reason behind the nobleman's libation? Maybe. We are familiar with seals from this period found in both Susa and at other archeological sites of the Near East that bear pictures referred to as the "tamer" or "animal master" in professional literature. This is an axially designed human figure holding a quadruped in each hand – in discernible cases the animal is most likely a big cat or other beast. The animal is standing on its rear legs and is resting its front claws on the "tamer's" shoulders. Until now, experts have interpreted this figure as a heroic warrior using his unbridled force to tame wild animals, and thus protecting those around him. Yet some depictions on the seals found in Susa offer information indicating a somewhat different explanation. The "tamer's" attire here is quite complex, composed of a belted robe with two straps crossing at the chest (we are almost tempted to compare it to the "sacred threads" of India's Brahmins). His face is concealed by a mask and, although his hand is raised in a friendly gesture, he does not hold the animals. Instead, the animals

59 Petr Charvát, The Iconography of Pristine Statehood, Prague, Karolinum 2005, pp. 321 and 322, Nos. 133 (Sb. 2265) and 134 (Sb. 2265).

approach him by themselves [20a]. There is also a more recent finding regarding this motif on a piece of older painted Susa-style pottery in which the "tamer" is placing his hands on the snouts of animals approaching him from both sides.

These scenes suggest that we do not have before us a heroic act of fighting, but religious activities instead. The tamer does not subdue the animals, but gives them something. We are then tempted to link this scene with the above-described image of the libation performed by the nobleman and to draw the conclusion that he is in this way requesting that the gods activate the forces of fertility. Here he dispenses the fertility power not only to people – for this there were other ceremonies – but also to the wild beasts of nature that certainly benefited human communities by providing an abundance of food.

**Fig. 20a** A seal from the second level of Susa culture from Susa 3900–3700 BC. The "tamer" wearing a mask with arms outstretched in a protective gesture over wild beasts.

Therefore, the first representative of an elite class that we come across in Susa of the early 4th millenium BC is a priest, an expert in effective communication with the supernatural. His principal task is to perform the relevant ceremony to ensure the activation of nature's fertility powers.

## The secular face of the age: building, protection, tradition

In addition to the images that we have just described, Susa seals from the early 4th millenium also provide us with other motifs that we can now try to interpret.

**Fig. 20b** A seal from the second level of Susa culture from Susa 3900–3700 BC. A composition with cross motif.

The most prominent feature observed here are the cross-like compositions previously described in the paragraphs on painted pottery from the mausoleum in Susa [20b]. These most likely also refer to communities of people, primary cities deliberately created in harmony with the universe's order. Here, too, the symbolism of the four cardinal points is relevant.

It is not clear if these are communities established according to the wishes of Susa's central administration, or contributions sent by this kind of established communality that spontaneously arose.

A scene with a second major figure found on Susa seals is also noteworthy: it features a man with a bulbous tiara on his head, stripped to the waste and wearing a long skirt with triangular patterns. It is certainly also possible that this part of the ruler's overgarment is an

**Fig. 20c** A seal from the second level of the Susa culture from Susa 3900–3700 BC. The successor places his hand beneath the underarm of the ruler transferring power.

outer jacketing, perhaps a kind of armor made from an organic mesh. Our conclusions are derived from the overall nature of the scene. The ruler-figure is accompanied by the smaller figure of a servant carrying out extremely telling activities: he takes arrows from a quiver set upright to the left of the ruler and breaks them by stepping on them.[60] We do not even have to spend much time analyzing the symbolism of the ruler's bow and arrows in the Near East to know that we have before us a scene depicting a military victory. The ruler conquered the enemy, whose weapons are destroyed by his servant.

Yet it is the third seal that represents the most interesting scene. This seal features an axial position of the same ruler with a bulbous tiara and woven skirt. This time, however, the ruler raises his left hand. A man of smaller stature approaches from the left (the beard gives away the figure's sex) and puts his hand beneath the underarm on the ruler's left side [20c].

What exactly is happening here? Why is this smaller man tickling the underarm of the larger man? We have already deduced that in ethnological societies head and body hair generally mean the inner most character of the given figure. Underarm hair is also understood to represent a specially concentrated expression of selfhood of the individual in question. If the smaller man then places his hand on the underarm hair of the larger man, the obvious conclusion is that he is assuming possession of his character or, if you will, his charisma. This is indeed a unique scene – the oldest known portrayal of the transfer of political legitimacy in history. Unfortunately, the sense in which this political sovereignty is transferred eludes us. It could either depict the transfer of power from an older brother to his younger brother or from a father to his son in accordance with the principle of succession recognized in the given communality (chronological principle). This could also be a case of empowering a representative of the ruler in a region remote from Susa's administrative center (topographical principle).

This scene is, in fact, extremely interesting for two reasons. First of all, this image is proof that Susa's secular elite found a way for the institutionalized transfer of political power at a time still preceding the

---

[60] Petr Charvát, The Iconography of Pristine Statehood, Prague, Karolinum 2005, p. 318, No. 127 (Coll. 2266).

establishment of the state, thereby ensuring one of the prerequisites for a coordination center's seamless operation in both space and time. The second reason is probably even more remarkable than the first: For the first time in history we come across testimony to the fact that an individual's human body is not in itself the target of the community's attention, but that it can be a medium of a force or message of supernatural origin. This personal charisma filling the ruler's body can even be transferred by touch. For the first time ever there is pictorial testimony that the human body is not the last link of creation, but that a person can become a loudspeaker of a greater power. The images on the painted pottery of the Susa mausoleum referred in the comb motif to individual personalities and celebrated their lives and memorable deeds. In the ensuing historical period, a seal from Susa bore the image of a person as a bearer of a higher message that enters this world through the individual as medium. The notion of the supernatural and the human relation to it thus appears for the first time ever in historical documents. As we will later see, the creators of the first ancient state in the Near East will work intensively with this idea.

# SUMER, THE SOUTHERN PART OF MESOPOTAMIA: WHILE THIS WAS HAPPENING

Regretfully, the land currently recognized as the cradle of the state and writing – that of Sumer in the southeast region of present-day Iraq, located roughly between the cities of Hilla and Nasiriyah – has fewer informative archeological monuments than the land of historical Susa, the capital city of Elam, provided us with for the early and middle phase of Uruk culture (4000–3500 BC). We must therefore rely on estimates and conclusions drawn from interpretations of records made at a later date.

## Activating the potential of fertility powers

It is important to note that the attempt to ensure the activation of nature's fertility powers, on which the survival of communities in this region ultimately depended, played a fundamental social role for Sumerians during this period. It seems, however, that they resorted to magical ceremonies that differed from the traditions of the people of Susa. As we later find, the high priest EN and high priestess NIN performed this basic magical act during the later phase of Uruk culture (ca. 3500–3200 BC) described in early written records. Together they performed the $NA_2$ ceremony, most likely a predecessor to the "Sacred Marriage." In contrast to the traditions of Susa, fertility was apparently activated by real or simulated heterosexual intercourse in an act of white magic. It cannot be ruled out that this type of ceremony was brought to Sumer and specifically to its then capital of Uruk from somewhere north of Mesopotamia. Several images from seals depicting sexual intercourse between a man and woman that could aptly portray the same ceremony were found in the XI and XIA layers at the Tepe Gawra site (middle period of the Uruk culture).[61]

---

[61] Most recently shown in: Denise Schmandt-Besserat, The Interface Between Writing

The invention sometime during this period of the first writing, whose introduction into use is presently dated to the middle phase of Uruk culture (Uruk, layer VII depth probes), was indeed of historic enormity. Although it may be considered paradoxical, the circumstances surrounding the invention of writing are aptly explained by the above-mentioned facts concerning the secular images on seals from Susa. As soon as the idea was conceived that the objects of the visible world, including the human body, could be a medium or conductor of supernatural forces, the impulse to try to manipulate these forces and use them to the benefit of the communities (including their elite) at that time probably quickly arose. It was for this very purpose that writing was most likely created. Those who invented writing endeavored to provide people with a means, by using magical operations with graphic symbols (referring to the existence of the visible and invisible worlds), to undertake acts that, by involving entities of a higher order, benefited the communities and fulfilled their wishes.

## Writing! Writing?

Most present-day reference guides state that the discovery and introduction of writing occurred in the late period of Uruk culture (3500–3200 BC) in the Sumerian city of Uruk. Although this indeed was the place of the oldest cuneiform writings in clay, we have no proof that the texts were written there, let alone invented and introduced. We do not know what the earliest cuneiform writing looked like and probably never will. This doubt arises from the fact that the oldest known cuneiform symbol for a "writing tablet" quite clearly refers to a tablet made of organic materials – wood or bone. Wax was poured on a writing area that had slanted crossing lines and the symbols were then engraved into the wax with the nib of a writing implement. This type of written record, well known from European archeological sites of Antiquity and the Middle Ages, obviously has no chance of surviving

and Art – The Seals of Tepe Gawra, in: Syria 83, 2006 (Hommage à Henri Contenson), pp. 183–193, p. 188, Fig. 4, pp. 86, 87 and 88.

in the Near East's soil conditions. We are therefore left with only indirect evidence in our research of the earliest cuneiform writing.

Symbols of the earliest cuneiform script consisted of a mixture of pictures, characters and symbols related to the realities of human life. Originally, their relation to the sounds of speech was loosely based, if it even existed at all. Later, however, symbols depicted individual syllables, or even whole Sumerian words. Still later they began to be used for the syllabic transcription of longer words. Although in some cases we find, already in the earliest period, symbols most likely representing words of spoken Sumerian, in most instances this is not the case and the earliest cuneiform script consists exclusively of its iconographic (pictorial) and symbolic values. Homophony (a single sound can be transcribed using different symbols) and polyphony (a single symbol can be used to depict different sounds) also appear here later. Ideograms, pictorial symbols determining the conceptual sphere that the word belongs to and which were part of the set cuneiform script, have been found dating back to the 27th century BC. The symbol KI indicates the names of countries, URU the names of cities, etc. The symbols of early cuneiform writing were originally written in soft clay tablets using a pointed writing implement made from a reed. Starting in roughly the 27th century BC the symbols were written in clay using sharp-edged writing implements with a flat chisel-like top. The symbols were originally read top to bottom and from right to left. In the 3rd or 2nd millenium, though we are unsure exactly when, the direction of the writing turned 90° to the right (counterclockwise), so that writing was read downward in rows and from left to right.

What was writing first used for? We have already partly answered this question. It seems that one of the main ceremonies attributed with special importance by the people of Susa consisted of the magical activation of the potential of fertility powers also involving, perhaps as an impetrative moment, libations. Some archeologically ascertained facts suggest hypotheses that the master of ceremony (the aforementioned "Cylindrical Tiara" nobleman) applied this activation to pristine nature, as well as to those areas already altered or cultivated by man. This could have been done using referents of "customer" villages – packages with their seals affixed to them and possibly even writing mediums (tablets) bearing the names of such villages. In other words, after the "Cylindrical Tiara" nobleman requested the gift of fertility from the gods, he magically transferred this gift into symbols of the villages for which he had performed the ceremony – into their seals and their written names. Although the proof we have to support this hypothesis is scanty, it does exist: some clay mediums with writing from Susa dating back to this period have been found.

## The enchantment of cylinder seals

Another invention, to which a civilizing role has been justifiably attributed to in this period, clearly represents the way of thinking of the early elite in the ancient Near East up to this point: the cylinder seal. This was a seal that was cylindrical in shape with a negative image engraved on its outer surface. Pressure was applied in rolling the cylinder in a soft substance (e.g. pugged clay), leaving the engraved pattern or scene in positive.

Most reference books hold that the Sumerians made a great contribution to human civilization with the cylinder seal. The writers of these works generally do not explain in detail why such a small and relatively insignificant artifact is so highly valued. Later phases of human communality also offer us proof of the use of a rotational seal matrix to imprint an image into a soft substance. Pottery decorated by such cylindrical seal matrices, generally known as rouletted decoration, is abundantly represented in pottery from both Antiquity and the Middle Ages. Yet the significance of early cylinder seals mainly lies in their symbolic and semantic role.

The cylinder seal perfectly embodied in its use the ideas held by the sages of this period on the primary categories of the world's existence – space and time. The cylinder seal turns when used and thus symbolizes time in its cyclical aspect, both as we are familiar with it from a Sumerian perspective and from the conceptual understanding of other ancient civilizations – especially that of Chinese spirituality. While creating the imprint, the cylinder seal moves in a specific direction and thus represents time in its linear aspect, which the ancient Sumerian civilization was also familiar with in this form. When my learned friend and colleague Jean-Jacques Glassner provided insight in his book on the famous ancient chronological guide to Sumer, *The Sumerian King List*, into how the author of this ancient manuscript understood the passage of time, it bore an uncanny resemblance to the movement of a cylinder seal in linking its cyclical and linear aspect. Moreover, by impressing the seal's image into a soft medium, not only does the cylinder seal depict the passage of time, it also magically creates a space. This space consists of a scene or ornamentation that pre-literate societies understood as being fully equivalent to three-dimensional reality. The impression can be repeated as often as the owner wishes and enables the construction of a magical correlate of reality that, in contrast to actual reality, has one enormous advantage – it can be manipulated at will. And if we understand the imprints of cylinder seals on goods delivered by supply system receptors to their centers as symbols of the supplying of such centers, the cylinder seal could represent, in addition to time and space, abundance and sufficiency as well.

Nothing then will prevent us from perceiving the owner of a cylinder seal as the master of time, space and abundance, and also, therefore, the activator of the potential of nature's fertility powers.

## "You will not be like gods"

Truth be told, the elite of ancient Near East society are depicted as men and women of arrogance and haughtiness. It would appear that, by creating the impression of supernatural powers controlling events on earth, their only work consisted of manipulating facts of the invisible world for the good of their communities, but above all for their own benefit. Yet this was not the case, and the ancient elite did not succumb to the depraved narcissism and self-centeredness of spiritual masters. The Near East's elite never became gods, and if they had indeed assigned themselves such a position over the course of the earliest ancient periods, such arrogance would have met with a well warranted punishment. Earlier cuneiform literature makes it distinctly clear that the only owners and guardians of fertility are the gods themselves. When in a Sumerian and later Akkadian epic poem the fertility goddess Inanna descends to the underworld, the punishment for her pride is death. Ereshkigal, the empress of the dead, rests her evil eyes on Inanna, and from that moment the reproduction process comes to a halt on Earth, leaving the people helpless to do anything about it. An elaborate scheme by Enki, the god of wisdom, is needed to free the fertility goddess from the clutches of darkness. Reference to the deities of the sacred bed, on which the $NA_2$ ceremony (predecessor to the aforementioned "sacred marriage") was performed, dates back to as early as 2600 BC. This tells us that the mortal participants in this ceremony were not deities and were not on the same level as the gods. If they were, there would be no need for special deities to oversee the successfully performed ceremony. The high priest and priestess are only people here, servants of their communities and their deities who do nothing more than initiate the relevant magical process.

The prehistoric elites of Susa and Sumer thus arrive on the scene as intellectuals and conjurers, but not as charlatans, and certainly not as gods. Unlike Egyptian civilization, the chasm in the Near East between the world of the people and that of the gods is unsurpassable.

# BEHOLD, CIVILIZATION:
## THE GREATER COMMUNITY OF THE LATE PERIOD
## OF URUK CULTURE (3500-3200 BC) –
## EN, NIN, NAMESHDA

Today we know that the first written documents composed in proto-cuneiform script came from Uruk, the capital of Sumer during the late period of Uruk culture. Uruk has been subject to considerable archeological research thanks to the efforts of generations of German archeologists who have been continuously active in this area – save for an interruption caused by the unfortunate events in our age – since 1912. Therefore, there is little need to go into a detailed description of the site, since numerous books offer this. A brief summary will suffice. We can focus directly on the spiritual, administrative and controlling structures of the greater community that stood at the forefront of Uruk. This greater community can most likely already be characterized as a state; at any rate, it is a very original work of human ingenuity and organizational talent.

**Uruk** – called Warka by today's inhabitants, is an archeological site in southeast Iraq, 60 km northwest of the city of Nasiriyah [21]. It is one of the major focal points of Mesopotamian cuneiform culture with evidence of settlement starting in prehistoric times (Ubaid culture) and lasting until the end of antiquity. The religious center of Uruk was composed of two sacred districts: the Eanna quarter of Inanna, the goddess of the passionate aspect of human nature (of love and war), and the Kullab quarter of the sky god Anu. Researchers first focused their attention on Eanna. Using a depth stratigraphic probe they found that the settlement consisted of 18 phases beginning in the 6th mil-lenium BC (layer XVIII provided a calibrated radiocarbon date of 5300–4575 BC). According to the latest results, the XVIII–XVII layers belong to pre-Uruk development, XVI–XIII to the proto-Uruk culture, XII–IX to the early Uruk phase, VIII–VII, to the middle Uruk level and VI–IV to the late Uruk culture (usually dated to 3500–3200 BC).

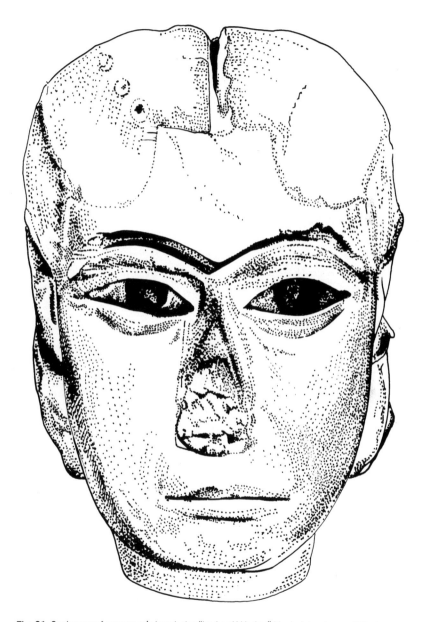

**Fig. 21** Sculpture of a woman's head, the "Lady of Warka." Uruk, late phase of Uruk culture (3500–3200 BC).

Monumental architecture begins here in layer VI with the Stone-Cone Temple (called "Steinstifttempel" by the German excavators) possessing a T-shape and a large central nave. The temple's walls were made of cast concrete and featured red-white-black ornament using stone cones. The building was surrounded by a wall whitewashed on the outside and adorned with rich mosaic decoration using blue and greenish-yellow stone cones on the inside.

The Limestone Temple (called "Kalksteintempel" by the German excavators) was found in layer V. This was a large T-shaped temple with its main area bordered by wings of rectangular chambers. The multiple entrances, extremely unusual if compared to buildings of the Ubaid culture, which were generally accessible through a single entrance, indicate the public nature of this building. The most extensive architectural components of Eanna belong to layer IV, although the relations between the individual buildings are still the subject of research. A split in the city's religious life, resulting in the older temples' facilities no longer sufficing, is demonstrated by the large collection of valuable materials stored for good in the Riemchen Building ("Riemchengebäude"). The building's foundation pit, consisting of a central rectangular chamber surrounded on all sides by corridors, was sunk into the north corner of the no longer existing Stone-Cone Temple. Stored in the corridor was a vast inventory of storage containers and food (animal bones), textiles, jewelry, weapons, furniture decorated with a black-and-white mosaic pattern, metal and stone vessels, as well as necessities for ceremonies. Fragments of a life-size human sculpture may depict the city's ruler. The entire building was later buried. The Cone-Mosaic Temple ("Stiftmosaikgebäude") complex apparently belonged to the new form of Eanna in this period (IV b-d). The building featured two triple naves enclosing a courtyard with a colonnade whose walls shone with a mosaic made from terracotta cones with red, white and black heads. The large triple naves of "temples" C, F, G and H also belong here, while building E, whose four wings enclose a rectangular courtyard with a colonnade, is interpreted as a palace. All of these buildings were destroyed though, and the final phase of layer IV (IV a) looked completely different. The only building preserved from the older period was "temple" C, augmented by new buildings: the

Great Hall ("Hallenbau"), the Pillar Hall ("Pfeilerhalle") and the monumental triple-nave temple D. The Bath Building with numerous rooms, whose floors and lower parts of the walls were treated with tar, served visitors of the local center. Due to later interventions, the heavily damaged Red Temple, named after the color of a mural, went down in history as the excavation of the oldest ever currently known written documents in human history. These were clay tablets bearing early cuneiform script. The sunken featured Great Court with two concentric rows of benches made of clay and bricks treated with tar also belong here. Excavators found here numerous other cuneiform texts, as well as seals in the clay. At the end of phase IV all of these buildings succumbed to decay and the architecture of the ensuing layer III was designed completely differently. The sole edifice worth noting among the more recent structures is a giant building made from hardpan, which King Lugal-zage-si had built as an administrative and apparently even tax collection center.

The temple district of Kullab some 400 meters southwest of Eanna acquired from the very beginning of the Uruk-type culture a temple with a triple-nave ground plan, situated on a raised rectangular terrace. This temple was rebuilt at least five times before 3000 BC and additional reconstruction projects later ensued. Its form, known as the White Temple from the close of the 4th millenium, was augmented by the Stone Building ("Steingebäude"), an open, partially underground hall perhaps used for religious purposes with an altar-like podium and equipped for libation ceremonies. The Temple of Anu was again rebuilt in the 8th century BC. During the Hellenistic age it acquired the forms of the gods Anu and Antum and was named Bit Resh and Irigal. The annual ceremonies of the "cult journey" by Anu to the sacred pavilion ushering in the new year in the northern part of the city were performed here, followed by his return to the temple. The construction of the building with a façade decorated with colorfully glazed bricks was paid for by dignitaries of the Seleucid administration of Uruk, Anu-uballit Kefalon and Anu-uballit Niarchos. Other city buildings include King Sin-kashid's palace from the 19th century BC.

Uruk's ordinary residential structures were examined randomly and unsystematically. The city walls of Uruk, built during the first and second phase of the dynastic period (3000–2600 BC) have received considerable attention. Based on the literary data available to us from the third Uruk dynasty (2112–2004), these walls are credited to the mythical ruler of the city, King Gilgamesh. Empty spaces are, however, found within the city walls, while there is evidence that people lived in areas outside the walls. Although the settled area of Uruk continued to systematically grow over the course of the $3^{rd}$ millenium BC, the number of rural settlements on the city's cadastre was gradually reduced. The migration of the rural population to the city was evidently responsible for this.

## Economy: redistribution prevails

In economic matters, the greater community of Uruk can be characterized as an extensive redistribution organism. The greater community's administrators assessed the economic potential of all of their member communities and decided how each would contribute to the general welfare. The greater community thus obliged each member community to supply goods that it had the highest know-how and experience in manufacturing. Agriculturally focused communities would provide their cultivars, while communities specializing in cattle would contribute animal husbandry products. Communities by rivers or near the sea coast would supply their catch, while towns located at outcrops of raw materials – in some cases in such areas directly established by the greater community – would introduce into circulation semi-finished products or the finished products made from them. The society's external bodies or receptors supplied the greater community with exotic goods, such as wine from grapes imported from lands in present-day Iran.

All of these contributions were amassed at the collection center or at collection points established for this purpose. The center would then coordinate the movement of these goods to those consumers with a right to them or in urgent need of them. There is evidence of at least one rescue operation in which the center came to the aid of one of the member communities that had been suddenly afflicted by an acute lack of food.

The entire circulation of these goods was complicated by the fact that administrating it required that attention be paid to not only spatial or, more precisely, topographical considerations – each product was produced in a certain region, but consumed throughout the entire greater community – but that timing factors also be taken into account. Some food sources had to be exploited depending on the times in which they were available. Sheep-milk products, for instance, were only available in February-March at winter pastures in river valleys and in June-July at summer pastures on the slopes of highlands where the sheep were herded in April in search of fresh grass, water and a more tolerable climate. A wide range of factors complicating the production and circulation of consumer goods had to be taken into consideration when exploiting natural and production resources. It is worth noting that the administrators of the greater Uruk community carried out this task honorably, and that their managerial abilities were praiseworthy.

As a side note, it should be emphasized that an old invention, that of writing, was very much made use of during the administrative process. Writing provided for a sufficient overview of the time/space context regarding the availability of food sources. With the use of writing becoming more widespread in the later period of the Uruk culture (3500–3200 BC), a whole series of new symbols were introduced for the various religious and service areas of the given communities (e.g. storage complexes), for the professional staff active in the public life of that period, for socially important events (e.g. public assemblies with decision-making powers), for various forms of material goods circulating through the vast redistribution system of the greater Uruk community and for an audio or visual "cue" in problematic readings. The linguistic relation of this early cuneiform to the various languages of the Mesopotamian communality, the Sumerian and Semitic languages in particular, is debated. This script was written in columns from top to bottom and from right to left.

The practical needs of writing obviously led to its expanded use and to a switch to script-bearing mediums of a more enduring nature, such as clay tablets, baked if necessary. Many of the tablets found in Uruk are small in size and relatively sturdy. They are about the size of a bar of soap and were certainly easily transported in their day. The notion that a piece of writing found in Uruk must have also been written in Uruk is far from true.

## Spiritual and political leaders: EN, NIN, NAMESHDA

The administrative structure of the greater community of the Uruk culture's late phase most likely consisted of a very elaborately conceived system that balanced the interests of the elite of the sacral and secular social spheres.

Let us begin by describing the relations of the spiritual elite since most of the proto-cuneiform documents that we have at our disposal (we know of roughly four thousand today) arose from the temples' activities and thus depict in greater detail the relations in the sacral sphere [22]. We still have great difficulties in reading proto-cuneiform texts. The reader certainly has already noticed that a number of terms that we use here are transcribed in capitals. This is to indicate that, even though the cuneiform symbols were later read in this manner, we are unsure whether this reading applies to the oldest phases of Sumerian script as well.

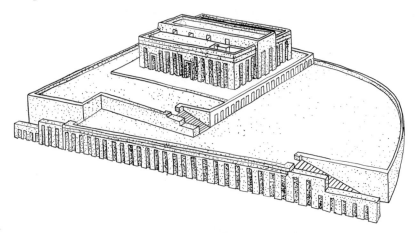

**Fig. 22** Reconstruction of a "temple" of the late Uruk period on a raised terrace (3500–3200 BC).

We have previously noted that the "pontifical pair" – the high priest EN and the high priestess NIN were referred to in the found records as the central spiritual body of the Uruk community. The high priest EN apparently served in the Uruk temple of the goddess Inanna, while the high priestess NIN performed services in the temple of the sky god Anu. In addition to other, probably very diverse religious obligations performed at these temples, they included the obligation to carry out regularly, most likely each season, a ceremony that appears in the found sources as $NA_2$, transcribed using the symbol for a bed. In the earlier cuneiform tradition this term meant "to repeatedly sleep," "to repeatedly intimately dwell with someone," "to repeatedly have sexual intercourse with someone." We therefore believe that this was a ceremony representing the predecessor of the later "Sacred Marriage" performed by the king and high priestess of one of the fertility goddesses to magically ensure the fertility of fields, of all nature and human families. The $NA_2$ required a number of cult necessities and was apparently performed in a temple that featured a sculpture or symbol of the deity expressed as ALAN. Those attending this temple then took away activated fertility potential through a process referred to in the found sources as $TAK_4$. ALAN, "the touching of a sculpture." We even have evidence of a scene in which a leading figure of the age, perhaps the high priest EN, transports a cult object on a boat, to make the activated fertility potential accessible to a broader community of "consumers." It is possible that, as payment for performing the $NA_2$ ceremony, the high priest EN and high priestess received a share of the harvest or other goods acquired as a result of nature's fertility potential being activated. EN and NIN evidently paid the operating costs of their support organization groups from these payments [23].

Unfortunately, we have hardly any information on the highest position of the Uruk greater community's secular sphere – the dignitary that probably reads NAMESHDA. It only appears in so-called lexical lists, which are essentially glossaries of terms used in cuneiform literature. NAMESHDA always occupies the top position among vocations, indicating that he is a figure of great importance. Unfortunately, it seems that the office of the NAMESHDA never kept any written protocol in proto-cuneiform form, or at least did not record it on a

**Fig. 23** Scenes depicted in relief on an Alabaster vase of the late Uruk period (3500–3200 BC) from Uruk. The high priest EN or the dignitary NAMESHDA is depicted before NIN in the top band.

medium able to survive to our day. We therefore know absolutely nothing about his office and the tasks he carried out for the greater Uruk community. Although the figure of the so-called Man in the Net Skirt (Mann im Netzrock) appearing frequently in artistic monuments of the late Uruk culture phase (sculptures or cylinder seals) has for the time being been designated as EN, an inscription is nowhere to be found and we therefore cannot rule out that it is the ruler NAMESHDA that is being portrayed.

His activities may have included some explicitly secular acts captured in the art of that age – e.g. the hunting of game and perhaps some military events, or presiding over ceremonies (feasts?) with a toast.

With their use of the term "assembly" (UKKIN), Proto-cuneiform texts attest to a certain degree of autonomy of the greater Uruk community. Ancient records provide hardly any information on them except for proof that they existed. Although Viennese cuneiformist Gebhard Selz interprets this term on the basis of later substantiated Sumerian words such as "people of work" (*UN + KIN), the symbol's form used to express this term, the picture of a pot with a spout, contradicts this. This is more of an indication that this institution originated from the ceremonial feast tradition that was already discussed in detail in the section on the prehistoric period of the Near East.

The earliest greater Uruk community thus had in its administrative-political and spiritual realm a number of specialists carrying out specialized tasks. The dual function of this administration, probably linked to precedents in Susa (EN + NIN and NAMESHDA), is remarkable.

The level of early Sumerian urbanism and defense architecture – and with it perhaps one of the spheres of activity of the dignitary NAMESHDA – clearly indicates the way the Sumerian city of later Uruk culture was fortified at the site of Habuba Kabira in present-day Syria (3500–3200 BC). Elements of the city's defense system, otherwise universal and identical with, for instance, medieval cities – an outer ward wall beyond which are located the main walls with rectangular towers, allowing for the space directly in front of the walls to be monitored, and featuring specially fortified gates – created a well-arranged system providing for effective combat activities that eliminated the threat of sieges. It is therefore apparent that the military architect that fortified the city at Habuba Kabira drew from past experiences with sieges on fortifications in creating his design. Enemy attacks of this nature are depicted on cylinder seals from the late Uruk period.

# Innovations at the dawn of the 3$^{rd}$ millenium BC: LUGAL, NIN, NAMESHDA

For unknown reasons the greater Uruk community ceased to exist as a centralized political body and further development took place in separate communities that had once been members of a larger community, but were now independent of their former obedience to Uruk (Adab, BU2+BU$_2$+NA$_2$, Eresh$_x$, Kesh$_3$, Kuara, Larsa, Nippur, Uruk, Ur, Zabala and Ummah or Akshak). Although these communities maintained a semblance of unity and solidarity with the parent political power by establishing a league of cities through a confederation of city states that evidently shared some administrative bodies (office, seal), the individual members of the league of cities began acting independently from this period.

The disintegration of the greater Uruk community's system of government posed a completely new problem for the league of cities: How were they to ensure the legitimacy of the political bodies that now headed the independent city states? It seems that the ruler with the title NAMESHDA maintained absolute political power, although his position now assumed a more symbolic nature. We have proof that NAMESHDA levied taxes in the individual member communities of the league of cities. These taxes were administrated by NAMESHDA's officials and by officials of the league of cities. We do not know, however, where his administration office was located or what its particulars entailed.

The most sweeping changes occurred within the internal life of the individual member communities of the league of cities. These communities adopted the former Uruk model of sovereignty of the "pair of high priests" in the spiritual sphere, though when applying it in their specific conditions they ran into certain difficulties. In Uruk, the nature of the highest pair was derived from the duality of the Uruk cult sphere, divided between the supreme male deity (Anu, high priestess NIN) and the supreme female deity (Inanna, high priest EN). This duality was missing, however, in most member communities of the league of cities, since the majority of Sumerian city states only worshipped a single deity. Under such circumstances, only one figure represented their highest spiritual authority: the high priest EN if the primary deity of the city was female or the high priestess EN if the city's deity was male. A problem therefore arose in properly meeting the conditions for performing the $NA_2$ ceremony: the highest priest or priestess of the city had to find for his or her partner NIN a legitimate partner approved by the divine sphere with whom NIN could perform the relevant ceremony. The high priest or priestess EN could not perform the ceremony properly since he or she was wed to the city's divinity, and joining intimately with someone else was therefore out of the question.

It was under these circumstances that a figure, who would later become extremely important, appeared on the political horizon of the Sumerian city states – a dignitary with the title LUGAL. Once during the period of the greater Uruk community this individual held the position of a higher (though certainly not highest) official. He seems to have held the office of the spokesperson for the age group of married men and heads of families in the court of the high priest EN. But then he must have had certain religious powers, since in the successor Uruk community, the archaic Ur (3000–2700 BC), we find him in a position fully corresponding to Uruk's EN. He is also a source of fertility for fields and all living creatures for the community of archaic Ur. LUGAL clearly occupied the position next to NIN that once belonged to EN and was responsible for activating the potential of nature's fertility. The high priestess EN then withdrew to the temple of the city's deity, the moon-god Nannar, and devoted herself to her religious and liturgical obligations.

Of course, the LUGAL of Ur is still beneath the level of a "king" of later Sumerian history. Instead, he is a "lord," "a giver of life" or "benefactor." The term "lord" is, in fact, appropriate here as it is taken from the old English expression *hláford,* or "bread warden."

This title also has its female counterpart, *hláfdiga,* from which the later title "lady" is derived. The community of archaic Ur evidently regarded LUGAL's main duty to be his role as the provider of fertility – and with it the people's subsistence. This information comes not only from written sources on the history of archaic Ur, but also from the existence of the famous Royal Tombs of Ur (2700 BC). Excavation of the Ur burial grounds of the 3rd millenium (ca. 2,500 graves in all)

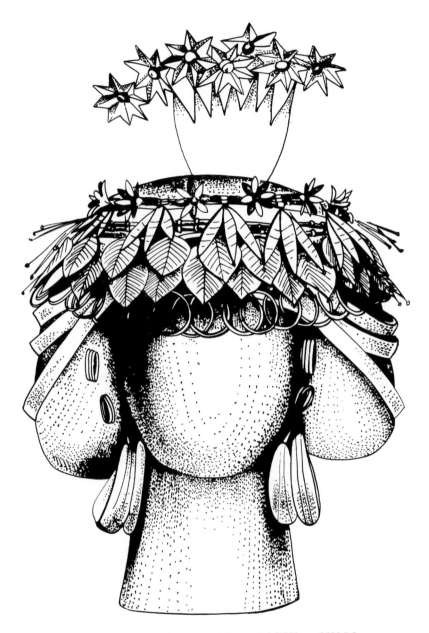

**Fig. 24** Ceremonial headdress of Queen Paubi. Ur, tomb PG 800, ca. 2600 BC.

revealed a total of 17 large tombs consisting of a burial tomb built in a large mass grave that was accessed by a descending ramp and possibly also by a level corridor. The tombs held deceased men and women with an extreme abundance of personal jewelry, weapons, toiletries, tableware, furnishings and other luxury items made of precious metals and a broad spectrum of gems and semi-precious stones [24]. Burials of other bodies were found both in the burial tombs themselves and in the spaces of the access ramps and corridors. Often accompanying the deceased here were personal jewelry, weapons, armor (military helmets), pottery and musical instruments (the legendary harps). This altogether exceptional phenomenon was interpreted in the sense of human sacrifices accompanying powerful men and women to the next world. At present, the hypothesis of human sacrifices can neither be confirmed nor refuted owing to the state of the skeletal remains. The community apparently considered the deceased buried here to be an earthly embodiment of the dying and reviving god Tammuz and perhaps even Inanna, deities embodying the male and female aspect of nature's fertile power. These tombs thus hold the ancient *lords* and *ladies*, whom their community richly rewarded for the role they played in public life when alive by sending with them to the next life an unprecedented wealth of funerary objects. The Ur community did everything in its power and employed all its skills, ingeniousness and taste in providing these objects.

## The wise Owl of Minerva flies at dusk: the crisis of the 27th century BC and what came of it - LUGAL, ENSI$_2$, EN

For reasons unknown, this entire system of public organization lost its credibility and disintegrated sometime in the 27th century BC. The cause of this collapse still is not completely clear. It may have been due to the failure of a society depleted by excessive costs linked to an unbelievable wasting of material powers, such as the production of wealth ultimately buried in tombs of the *lords* and *ladies* of Ur. Of course, the system may have lost its credibility due to factors that are untraceable today. A natural catastrophe of unprecedented proportions may have, for instance, severely damaged society at that time, undermining the public's faith in the ability of the governing elite to intervene in major events for the good of the governed. The archeological situation documented in the city of Kish some 60 km southeast of Baghdad can be taken as proof of this kind of calamity. Kish, the later royal seat of all of Mesopotamia, was settled in the early 3rd millenium BC at roughly the same time as archaic Ur. The layers from this period are covered with about two meters of alluvial sediment, completely devoid of evidence of habitation, but containing fish bones. If Kish, located in Akkad to the north of Sumer, was swept away by a catastrophe of these dimensions, what kind of horror was in store for Ur, located far to the south? Can we even begin to imagine the massive torrent of water that rolled southward over the virtually flat Mesopotamian plain at a deadly rate, wiping out everything that stood in its way? A summary of an archeological view of the city of Kish is given below.

**Kish** – a historical city and the seat of one of the oldest kingdoms in Sumerian Mesopotamia. Today a group of tells 14 km northeast of the city of Hilla (Iraq). Settlement started in the 5th millenium BC and took the form of a city at the start of the 3rd millenium BC. Sometime during the 27th century BC, however, it was devastated by a massive, apparently long-lasting flood. After that, two monumental works of architecture were created – the royal palace and a building of indeterminate purpose ("plano-convex building")– and in their vicinity is located the final resting place of important figures laid to rest in mass graves with carts, harness animals and a rich assortment of weapons, tools, ornaments, pottery and interior accessories. At some point in the 25th century BC, however, both monumental buildings deteriorated, a temple of the local deity was erected over the abandoned burial ground, and an adjacent settlement was added.

At any rate, the social events of the late 27th and early 26th century BC were already taking place on a completely different social blueprint. The office of the ruler with the title NAMESHDA disappeared off the face of the earth; this was only preserved as one of the glossary terms of ancient Sumerian literature as well as the name of one of the lower deities of the spiritual world. His place was occupied by LUGAL, which the Sumerian term *lugal*, meaning king or secular ruler, comes from. But this was not just any old king: It was the king of the city of Kish, whose title now meant the supreme ruler, who assumed the position of absolute power in the society at that time. The king of Kish was the master of all and ruler of the universe of ancient Mesopotamia. The subject population and, above all, its governing elite accepted and identified with this ideological construct. A whole complex of buildings was erected in connection with Kish's elevated status in the city and expressing the power and glory of the new lords. In addition to the royal palace, architecture of an indeterminate function, a so-called plano-convex building, was also built here, and the complex included a burial ground of the powerful and influential where the deceased were buried with weapons, tools, teams of harness animals, battle wagons and domestic necessities, though less magnificent in amount and splendor than that buried for the lords and ladies of Ur.

All of Sumer and Akkad soon recognized the power of the kings of Kish, and the sovereigns of the city took steps to build an administrative center that could be used to control the dominions further to the south. This administrative center was located at the site now named Fara and long ago called Shuruppak. Numerous archives of written texts found during archeological excavations have provided us with in-depth information on the center's managerial and coordination activities. Shuruppak was, above all, an organizational and administrative center; the kingdom's elite families that lived there primarily oversaw the performance of work duties by the people of most Sumerian cities who came to Shuruppak to meet their social obligations. Some of them were most likely supported by royal resources during their stay at the site. Giant silos in the form of cylindrical brick towers attest to this. It was calculated that if these silos were filled with grain, they could have sustained a work force of roughly 20,000 people for half a year.[62] In some cases, troops of conscripts were dispatched from

---

[62] For details on finds of grain silos in Fara see Giuseppe Visicato, Archéologie et documents écrits: Les "silos" et les textes sur l'orge de Fara, Revue d'Assyriologie 87/1, 1993, pp. 83–85.

Shuruppak to war (we do not know their enemy). Shuruppak was also an administrative and legal center where significant agreements were entered into, transactions were made and important official documents were archived in local institutions.

The rulers of Kish apparently subjugated most of the lands of Sumer and Akkad. The highest title of most rulers of Sumerian cities, PA.TE. SI, today read as $ensi_2$, bears witness to this. We know that this title was held by "regional administrators" of the Kish kingdom, governing the individual cities, and that PA.TE.SI.GAL, the "highest $ensi_2$", resided at the Shuruppak center. After the disintegration of the Kish kingdom and its previous member communities became independent – the history of the greater Uruk community visibly repeated here – the originally subordinated rulers retained the title as a symbol of their now independent position.

The title EN now became the sole reminder of ancient times, albeit in its form designating a ruler. This title returned to where it came from, and starting in the 27th century BC it was used by rulers of Uruk, the city from which Mesopotamia statehood arose, and which therefore occupied an exceptional position within Sumer's power structure.

If a Mesopotamian ruler of the $3^{rd}$ millenium BC had wanted to claim a supra-regional position of power, he would have had to do so through the royal title of Kish or through the *EN* title of Uruk. There were, admittedly, elaborate constructs drawing only partially on tradition: The lord of Uruk and Ur at that time, Enshakushanna (2432–2403 BC), took the title of *en* in the form of ki-en-gi, in which we sense the renowned and long defunct league of cities, created as a successor monarchy of the greater Uruk community sometime around 3000 BC. This form of ki-en-gi probably represents Shumer in its Semitic linguistic form, supported by the title of ancient Babylonian kings (*shar māt shumerim u Akkadim*), the name of the land that we use for the oldest Mesopotamian organized territorial unit.

Only beginning in the 27th century BC does there occur in ancient Mesopotamia the full separation of state authority from sacral elements, and only from this period can we speak of Mesopotamian kingdoms. This, incidentally, is the starting point for the oldest chronological guide to Sumer, *The Sumerian King List*.

*The Sumerian King List* contains a list of the rulers beginning with the mythical periods and continuing all the way to the king of the First Dynasty of Isin in the 19th century BC. The author (or authors?) of the King List had a quite clear idea of the mythical beginnings of Mesopotamia. First the "kingdom descended from the heavens to earth" in five primordial settlements: the cities of Eridu, Badtibira, Larak, Sippar and Shurrupak. Then everything living was wiped clean by a flood and only at this moment do three cities – Kish, Uruk and Ur – begin to alternate ruling over Sumer. Their hegemony is only "revived" by interference of a foreign dynasty, such as that of the lords of Avan (in Elam) or Hamazi (in the northeast?). The ancient rulers of Mesopotamian cities are attributed supernatural legitimacy here in that they are allotted unbelievably long reigns, exceeding any conceivable length of an individual's lifespan. An interpretation of no more than two state-forming traditions of Sumer (Kish to the north and Ur to the south) was inserted into this document – most likely regarding the sovereignty of the rulers of the three Ur dynasties. The Sumerian King List resulted in numerous descendents, both in Sumer itself (apparently a fictional list of rulers of Lagash from the period of ancient Babylonia), and in areas speaking Semitic languages – especially in Babylonia and Assyria.

Since then, Mesopotamia was ruled by a single lugal, who was assisted by representatives bearing the title *ensi$_2$*. The ruling title *en* is restricted to the historical city of Uruk and to the social bodies directly linked to the hegemony of the ancient greater Uruk community (league of cities=ki-en-gi=Sumer).

## "THE END OF THE BEGINNING":
## THE SUMERIAN STATE AT THE CLOSE OF THE EARLY
## DYNASTIC PERIOD (CA. 2500–2334 BC)[63]

We are on surer ground here, since this period left behind relatively numerous and detailed written documents providing us with an idea of how the previously established state bodies of the Sumerian city-states appeared and worked.

### The king and his court

We will first exam their governing bodies, the royal office in particular. A sufficient economic base was of the utmost necessity for the king to perform his role. The Sumerian king of the early dynastic period usually came from a rich family and, therefore, had access to the fortune amassed by his predecessors and ancestors.

As a member of the community, he also had a right to shares of the revenues from property that he owned with other citizens. Such cases are evident in written sources, especially at the moment when land administered by a temple keeping a written protocol entered the game. The king then held the land originally belonging to the temple and under its direct administration ("$ni_3$-en-na" in the Sumerian language). He could even make use of the temple's "extra" land that was rented to tenants (even those not associated with the temple) for a share of the harvest ("$kur_6$" in the Sumerian language). However, all other free citizens, and not just the king, had (at least theoretically) rights to such tenure.

[63] Conclusions of my previously published work are summarized here: Petr Charvát, Social configurations in Early Dynastic Babylonia (c. 2500–2334 B.C.), in: Gwendolyn Leick (ed.), The Babylonian World, New York and London, Routledge – Taylor and Francis Group 2007, pp. 251–264.

The third category of the king's income consisted of contributions received by the king by virtue of holding the highest office in the land. This also consisted of revenues from land belonging to the royal office. The question if this consisted of an individual tenure by a specific king or if these lands were an inheritable and inalienable appurtenance of the royal position, passed down in the ruling family from father to son as part of the transferred, remains unanswered.

The king's powers also obviously included the rights and privileges of his office, from which he could also derive profit. For instance, the king could request that his subjects perform extensive corvée.

A fourth, apparently not overly predictable income category consisted of gifts, voluntary contributions and "compliments" given to the king by his subjects on various occasions. The king would, for instance, receive such "gifts of goodwill" when public offices would be newly filled. The first family of the state received gifts upon other occasions as well: when Barnamtarra, the wife of Lagash ruler Luga-landa (2358–2352 BC), gave birth to a little girl, the subjects' gifts to the royal family included livestock and beer.

The fifth and final source of Sumerian royal income was the kings' own "entrepreneurial" activities. These were mainly large public projects that kings commonly supported and organized, and in whose revenues the other citizens then shared. We know that the kings, for example, established irrigation canals, though the irrigated land then did not belong to them but to the city deities. This essentially meant that it was transferred into the ownership of the state-wide community. Sumer's rulers would also lease land to be farmed, and certainly reaped the spoils of war campaigns that they themselves often led. We know of "letters of complaints" by Sumerian temples that during wars were pillaged of their cult inventory made from valuable materials. After such a campaign, the victorious commander was supposed to credit the deities that had bestowed victory upon him. We know that some Sumerian kings, such as the ruler or Uruk, Enshakushanna (2432–2403 BC), following his victory over the city of Kish, dedicated a share of their spoils to the supreme Sumerian God Enlil in the city of Nippur. This generally consisted of precious metals and slaves.

Sumerian kings used these considerable incomes to cover the costs of the royal office. Among the higher costs were the "managerial services" required for the administration of royal assets.

The kings were obviously also expected to care for those citizens unable to care for themselves: mainly widows, orphans and "homes without heirs," i.e. those individuals of advanced years with no offspring to care for them. Yet it is not our intention to create the impression that Sumerian kings were self-sacrificing and altruistic caretakers of the weak and helpless: in the early Lagash dynasty period, kings had a propensity to place orphans of both sexes into the workforce of the royal manufacturers.

In general, ancient Sumerians logically assumed that their king would oversee the rule of law and public order. Here, for the first time in history, we come across a remarkable socially motivated measure aimed at protecting at least the poorest classes from the economy's unfavorable impacts. Already in this period the Sumerians king announced that in some cases the obligation to pay cases would be waived, which meant that indebted slaves would receive their freedom. It is here that we witness the very first use by public officials of the word "freedom" (in Sumerian *amargi*, most likely meaning "return to one's mother"). This measure was to remove at least the heaviest burden of debts that the poorest farmers in particular were simply unable to pay in the event of repeated poor harvests. As far as we know, Enmetena, the ruler of Lagash (2404–2375 BC), was the first to announce a waiving of debts. A similar measure announced by the Athenian statesman Solon (ca. 640–560 BC) and called *seisachtheia* ("the shaking off of burdens"), can thus boast of a venerable tradition. Sumerian kings also appointed public dignitaries, including priests, to offices.

Sumerian rulers' authority also involved the judicial sphere, including judicial and arbitration proceedings. We know that the most powerful kings of the land ruled on disputes between entire communities and issued legally binding resolutions. The rulers of the land also oversaw the fair use of units of weights and measurement.

Sumerian kings also naturally represented their people abroad and acted as their diplomatic representatives in negotiating with foreign powers. This did not only concern war campaigns in which the kings often assumed the role of the commander-in-chief in leading their troops into battle. The very first international peace treaty that we know of also comes from Enmetena, the aforementioned ruler of Lagash.

A vast archive of economic and administrative writings from the city state of Shuruppak (presently known as Fara) from the $27^{th}$–$26^{th}$ century BC has provided us with a unique view of the administrative makeup of one of the oldest states of humankind. The entire "government office" ("$e_2$-gal" in Sumerian) consisted of four "ministries" in Shuruppak. The "ministry of transportation" was led by a dignitary with the title "gal-nim-gir" (the great speaker). The "ministry of foreign trade" was the responsibility of a dignitary with the title "gal-dam-gar" (the great trader). The "ministry of the cult" was controlled by a dignitary with the title "gal-mah" (the great dirge singer). Lastly, the entire center was supplied by the fourth member, the "ministry of supplying" ($e_2$-geme$_2$).

This relatively developed administrative structure was maintained by a separate body, the "center's supplying office" ($e_2$-uru).

Unfortunately we do not know who headed this administrative and organizational body. It was most likely the king of Kish, the ruler of the most important center of the northern part of Mesopotamia that would later develop into the Akkadian Empire, some hundred kilometers southeast of today's Baghdad.

Sumerian kings paid special attention to religious matters. Above all, they richly and systematically endowed the temples of the land. This could come in the form of constructing the buildings themselves, providing the liturgical and other religious paraphernalia for the temples, and often even providing for the everyday needs of the cult personnel. The "personal chaplains" of kings may very well have resided in the courts of the Sumerian rulers, right on hand to care for a king's spiritual needs. Royal descendents, daughters in particular, often served in sacerdotal positions, sometimes focusing on temple music. We even have reports of a "conservatory for music" in the city of Eshnunna during the period that followed (23rd century BC).

Rulers of Sumer's early dynastic period were sometimes involved in liturgical activities; we know, for instance, that they performed sacrifice rituals. They were also responsible for ensuring that there was veneration of the royal family's dead, which was an entirely separate religious and, particularly, liturgical area. The earliest form of the cult of the royal office was already basically developing at this time; this included worshipping the ancestors of the reigning king. Some preserved sculptures might even depict mythical figures that are half-human and half-animal "the founders' fathers" of noble families. An artistic tradition of work linked to the royal office also took hold to a certain extent; in some city states, for instance, this was expressed through a repetition of certain seal images (Lagash).

## The powerful and revered

The families of leading men and women of the early dynastic period primarily sought to preserve and augment the wealth that they were born into. Income was derived from agriculture and crafts, though earnings from entrepreneurial activities were also welcomed. The cities of Sumer's early dynastic period were linked by a network of trade lines along which merchants actively exchanged material goods. Sumerian merchants even dared to go to remote corners of their world: to the river plains and oases of present-day Syria, to areas beneath the lofty mountain tops of present-day Turkey and Iran, but also venturing out on the waves of the Persian Gulf. In the 26th century BC, export goods from the Near East and Sumer, in particular, apparently began appearing in the Aegean region as well, as indicated by archeological finds in Crete.[64] Throughout this region Sumerian entrepreneurs bought everything they knew would sell well at home and sold everything they could find customers for.

From the relative abundance of silver objects found in numerous graves of the city cemetery in Ur, we can even assume that a certain "monetization" of Sumerian economic life of the 3rd millenium was beginning to emerge.[65]

---

[64] For the most recent analysis of this see Cynthia S. Colburn, Exotica and the Early Minoan Elite: Eastern Imports in Prepalatial Crete, American Journal of Archaeology 1 12, 2008, pp. 203–224.

[65] The expression used in early dynastic texts for "interest" (in banking – that's right, the

It was apparently in this very period that wealth first staked a claim for a higher social position, respect and esteem among fellow citizens. This is evident in the attempt to tighten family bonds and to prevent the dissipation of accumulated wealth. Many (blood) relatives had to consent to the sale of family land with each having a right to a portion of the price. This would inevitably overly complicate such transactions and make them more expensive, so we can assume that this was viewed as a less desirable solution at that time by the people. Decision-making powers began to be concentrated in a relatively tight circle of society's leading figures and the importance of women's social position clearly dropped. This strengthening of family hierarchies apparently had a sole purpose – to maintain control over the "family silver" and to prevent its unwanted dissipation.

Numerous elite members of the early dynastic period of Sumer actively took part in public administration and the organization of social life. We have already described the "government center" in the city-state of Shuruppak, so we can imagine how many experts, administrators and organizers were required to maintain this organism's operation. An especially arduous task was the organization of public work, "corvée," which, upon the Shuruppak's instructions, the people obliged to perform the service would come to the center to undertake. There were hundreds of workers and thousands of beasts of burden working on hundreds of hectares of land. Two texts even state a total number of 160,000 drudges, though this may be merely a theoretical number figuring in a mathematical exercise.

Sumer's leading men and women were actively interested in public cult ceremonies. They supported and endowed the temples, and even performed – or had performed on their behalf – ceremonies solidifying their prestige and esteem. These may have been similar to "damning rituals" deployed in ancient Egypt to magically damage the land's enemies.

---

Sumerians also introduced this invention) also appears here. "Kud-ra us-a" = "that which follows after cutting off." Interest was thus paid in silver: Michael Hudson, How Interest Rates Were Set, 2500 B.C.–1000 A.D., Journal of the Economic and Social History of the Orient 43/2, 2000, pp. 132–161, on p. 148.

Unfortunately, more detailed information on how temples were run comes much later in the form of texts on life in the temple of the goddess Inanna in Nippur from the Ur III dynasty (2112–2004).[66]

To a certain extent, the temple represented at that time a self-subsistent and autonomous center. It had at its disposal its own arable land that it partly cultivated at its own cost, partly allotted to its own employees as a natural wage and partly leased for a share of the harvest. Palm groves (horticulturally cultivated land), livestock herds and, later, fisheries were treated in a similar manner. Experts performed their trade, particularly in textile and foodstuffs, in the temple's spaces. In later periods, the temple was also involved in the sale of goods on credit and provided small loans, as well as business credit on a larger scale. Proceeds from the temple's own assets covered about 60% of the consumption of the temple's collective. The remaining 40% was supplemented by payments which the temple had a socially acknowledged right to, e.g. a share of taxes collected for the state's benefit. The temple was led by a succession of family administrators from father to son and provided a livelihood for some 250–300 employees.

Unfortunately, a dearth of information prevents us from knowing more about life in the Sumerian cities. The question is whether it is too early to apply to this period the findings made in studying Babylonian cities of the 19th–18th century BC, when married couples lived with their juvenile children in block-type homes without courtyards. They generally had 3 rooms at their disposal with a total area of around 23 m$^2$ per family (5.3 m$^2$ per person). Larger homes built around courtyards were then occupied by extended families with adult, married offspring.[67]

The elite culture, the "civility" of the age, is well captured by the "Instructions of Shuruppak," a literary work composed sometime during this period based on the popular and internationally oft-represented

---

[66] See Richard Zettler, The Ur III Temple of Inanna at Nippur, The Operation and Organization of Urban Religious Institutions in Mesopotamia in the Late Third Millenium B. C. (Berliner Beiträge zum Vorderen Orient 1 1), Berlin, Dietrich Reimer Verlag 1992.

[67] Elizabeth C. Stone, Texts, Architecture and Ethnographic Analogy: Patterns of Residence in Old Babylonian Nippur, "Iraq" 43/1, 1981, p. 1–18, and the author's monograph Nippur Neighborhoods, Chicago, The Oriental Institute 1987.

genre of "a father's advice to his son." Here the incarnate Shuruppak instructs his son, who has just reached the age of a young man, how to properly act in society. Given its ancient age, the text is not completely comprehensible, though some advice is still applicable today and will most likely continue to be. A young man should make sure that "his house is not managed in discord" and that "he acts toward his older brother as he would toward his father, and toward his older sister as he would toward his mother."

The sage warns the young man of disobedience and defiance toward those more powerful, but also of defying his parents and casting out his wife. The most eloquent advice given by the father to his son is interpreted literally here, since it is intended for all generations: "Loving hearts build homes, hateful hearts destroy homes." Let us quote another piece of advice from the Instructions of Shuruppak that my learned friend and colleague Jiří Prosecký took a liking to: "Don't choose your wife on a holiday. She has a borrowed dress, a borrowed face and a borrowed heart."

The culture and spirituality of cuneiform Mesopotamia would hardly have survived for thousands of years if the families of the leading men and women of Sumer had not continued to cultivate it. Immediately following the formative phase of their creation, ca. 3000 BC, most prominent inventions of the age, the cuneiform script and cylinder seals, began to be used by not only the state administration of the newly created city states, but also by the land's eminent households. Literary culture also blossomed through the endeavors of the Sumerian elite: Literary texts appeared for the first time ever – another example, in addition to the aforementioned Instructions of Shuruppak, were the first Sumerian incantations. Dictionary-type literature, whose roots go back to the discovery of cuneiform scripts (ca. 3500–30200 BC), also experienced a boom in this period. Writers were not only innovating older lists of a wide-range of terms, but also creating completely new ones (lists of deities or lands). Older deities with Semitic names were also appearing among the gods and goddesses worshipped in Sumer.

We do not know much about scholastic education of the early dynastic period, and must therefore rely on information from the old Babylonian period (19th–18th century BC). Pupils of Nippur schools at that time were first learning to engrave (more like punching) syllabic symbols, one after another according to the principle of their mutual resemblance, into still moist clay tablets. They then began to learn to write syllables in which the three basic vowels u-a-i were combined with a given consonant (tu-ta-ti, mu-ma-mi, etc.). Then, once they had a grasp of these "ABCs," the pupils would proceed to copying lists of individual words and vocabulary lists as practice in translating from language to language (most frequently from Sumerian to Semitic-Akkadian). Only then did students of cuneiform schools begin to copy literary works and were considered sufficiently prepared to start copying very complicated works of Mesopotamian literature.

## Careful and resourceful

We know much less about the ordinary inhabitants of Sumerian cities, villages and secluded dwellings than of the elite who were closely linked to the creation of the written records of that age. It seems that most of the ordinary population resided in rural areas and made a living by farming. Farmers harvested wheat and barley, as they had done for thousands of years, the women cultivated legumes and hemp in gardens and orchardists grew date palms, pomegranates and nuts in orchards. By fermenting the juice extracted from the trunks of palm trees, experts produced a palm wine that was light and delectable with a taste resembling Riesling wine. The people were familiar with hops, but it was not cultivated and we do not know what Sumerians used it for. Beer was brewed from barley malt. Sumerians farmers already knew how to improve soil quality through fertilization, most likely using household waste of an organic origin. It seems that in this period there still was no need to engage in the extensive uprooting of forests to acquire arable land; this apparently began sometime after 2000 BC. The reapers appear to have cut the stalks close to the ground and used the straw as crude material or additives in opening materials improving the properties of clay products (ceramics, bricks from unfired clay or adobe). The farmers and their families threshed the harvested grain, coarsely cleaned it by throwing it against the wind and then sifted it – first coarsely, then finely. Only then did they deliver the prepared grain to the millers.

Besides crop farmers, livestock farmers also contributed to Sumer's subsistence. Cattle were now added to the traditional herds of sheep and goats, while mules and horses were largely used as draft animals. Shepherds raised sheep and goats for milk and fleece (wool, mohair); pigs were raised for meat. Finds of mule skeletons from an earlier period (23rd century) speak well of ancient livestock farmers: the animals were well fed and cared for, kept in stables and most likely used as transport animals, as well as pack animals used to being bridled. Ducks waddled around the courtyards of Sumerian farmsteads.

Sumerian villages offered a wide range of craftworks. Refuse from chipped-stone industry and slag from copper smelting have been found in villages. In addition to being made of available, albeit relatively precious metal, common household tools were also made of chipped rock the entire period. Products from a wide range of organic materials were also undoubtedly made. These materials included wood, leather, cloth, and even reed. Date palms offered many useful raw materials for building purposes and for manufacturing everyday consumer goods (leaves for matting, the midrib as construction material or for making rope, etc.).

Merchants also supplied consumers in Sumer's rural areas. Villagers indulged in dishes prepared from fish imported from river and sea fishermen. Merchants from distant lands imported rare delicacies such as grapes to the tables of noble families.

Sumerian villagers also had their own social organizations. They set up farmer groups, most likely subsistent and autonomously controlled bodies linked by blood relations (among other types of bonds). Communication with central authorities was conducted through a "contact officer," whose primary duty was to oversee that obligations to superior authorities were met.

Nomadic elements of the population are also apparent from the written sources of that period: mainly groups of hunters and fishermen living in wetland areas or present-day southeast Iraq. The administration of the city-states at that time assigned to them specialized tasks (e.g. military service) and attempted to force them to accept a settled way of life and agriculture-based livelihood. The mythical correlate of nomadic groups' absorption by the Mesopotamian majority society is a Sumerian narrative from the 19th–18th century BC on the engagements and marriage of the god Martu, the personification of the nomadic and hunter-gatherer way of life. Martu's request for the hand of the daughter of the city god Numushda is granted by the "civilized" father, even though Martu has no stable home, does not know how to prepare food on a fire, is constantly traveling through the desert and does not even find a permanent final resting place after death.[68]

The ordinary inhabitants of Sumer were seen as customers for the elite of that period. We have already seen that the kings themselves initiated the building of irrigation facilities that, upon completion, belonged to the city deity and thus represented to a certain extent the property of the entire community. It is clear that it was actually ordinary villagers whose work on such land yielded a considerable profit for the authorities, which is why Sumer's elite desired their settlement on arable land. "Service to the landlord pays off" – we see in the royal documents from Lagash under the reign of King Enentarzi (2364–2359 BC) a number of lacklands fed year-round who, under the Enentarzi's successor Lugalanda (2358–2352 BC), rose to the category of leaseholders. They were thus responsible for the land's maintenance, became independent and clearly climbed the social ladder.

The masses of the non-elite population could, however, also act as a political factor.

Although rulers of early dynastic Sumer emphasized that they were the ones chosen by the gods from thousands of others to rule the land, they did indirectly concede that non-elite Sumerians were at least theoretically entitled to an eminent social position. The sudden increase in written agendas by Lagash's temples starting in the period of the aforementioned ruler Enentarzi represents further proof of this. We know of a number of temple communities that were active in Lagash even

---

[68] Austen Henry Layard's description of nomads of the modern age from the 19th century has retained its value for ethnography, Elizabeth Carter, The Piedmont and the Pusht-i-Kuh in the Early Third Millenium BC, in: Colloques Internationaux du CNRS: Préhistoire de la Mésopotamia, 17-18-19 décembre 1984, Paris, Editions du CNRS 1986, pp. 73-83, on pp. 81-82.

before Enentarzi's reign and whose managers did not need to write a single cuneiform tablet as part of the day-to-day operations. We must therefore assume that non-economic reasons are concealed behind this sudden increase in written agendas, and perhaps even public pressure for the temple administrators to periodically release in writing the accounting details of certain temples.

As for the spiritual side of life, Sumerian villagers most likely embraced the ancient tradition of set rituals drawing predominantly from natural vegetation cycles. We can assume that fertility-initiation ceremonies played a leading role, as did those giving thanks to the harvest, those involving protective magic, "ceremonies of passage" (marking an individual's birth, attainment of adulthood, marriage and death), as well as the cult of the ancestors of individuals or of entire communalities.

## "He who shackles slaves..."

The lower rungs of the social ladder of early dynastic Sumer were occupied by slaves (in Sumerian $igi$-$nu$-$du_8$) and war captives serving as a workforce source. Mesopotamian slaves were originally only distinguished from the free by their hairstyle. Slaves evidently performed the hardest manual labor such as digging irrigation ditches or wells. The arduous work of grinding grain on prehistoric-type grinders consisting of a large flat bottom stone (slab) and a smaller rounded top stone (hand-held grinder) was performed by female slaves. The workplace where female slaves ground grain has been preserved in a royal palace in the Syrian city of Ebla (end of the 3rd millenium or beginning of 2nd millenium BC). This smallish room consisted of four benches by the walls with four grinders set into the ground next to the benches. Just imagine kneeling there the whole day in the gloom and heat, grinding grain with the same pendulous motion in the upper part of your body. In some cases originally free Sumerians fell into this unenviable position due to debtor slavery, in other cases they were already bought as slaves. Recorded prices for slaves ranged from 14 to 20 shekels (a unit of weight of approx. 8 g of silver, equivalent to 4,200–6,000 l of grain).

Slaves also worked as assistants in operations involving gardening and crafts and received annual food rations. They are distinguished in written records only by place of origin.

The position of war captives, commonly depicted in Sumerian art monuments as naked and shackled or even bound to a kind of neck beam, was probably quite similar to that of slaves. More detailed information on captives is lacking, but we know that most of them ended up as slaves.

# CONCLUSION

In general, it seems that the 3rd Early Dynastic Period of Sumer in many ways resembled our own times. The gods held lofty positions and the good old times "when everyone knew what was right and proper" were long gone. The highest political positions were open to all who heeded the call to enter the public arena and were indeed assumed by capable organizers and military leaders, though more often than not they went to those merely skilled in political maneuvering. The ordinary population, which increasingly experienced firsthand that "the Achaeans must pay for all follies of the kings," gradually intensified pressure for control and eventually even socially reformative measures. The Sumerian elite sought to preserve wealth and the privileges of their families and lineage, as well as the spiritual assets created by their ancient ancestors. They were familiar with both the turmoil of battle and the silence of scholarly contemplation. However, rising social conflict forced them in the interest of society to come out unwaveringly on the side of justice (whatever they may have imagined justice to be) and to employ the most sacred reference to ancestors – cuneiform script. Here a political polemic arises through writing; here terms such as "freedom" and "justice," as well as "guilt" and "sin" enter into human history.

# ANCIENT INDIA

The Indian subcontinent was created during the Tertiary Period when a tectonic shift thrust the continental block forming its bulk into the Euro-Asian land. This led to the orogenesis of the world's highest mountains – the Himalayas – from which flowed India's two great rivers, the Indus in a southwest direction and the Ganges toward the southeast, along the faults created on the contact lines of both geological units. Even today, tectonic pressure continues to push the Himalayan Mountains to greater heights, though erosion by water-courses and climate factors work to maintain their peaks at relatively stable altitudes [25].

The Indus River flows through historical northwest India and measures 3,200 kilometers in length. Most of its course is marked by a very moderate gradient of the riverbed acting as a strong sedimentation factor. Every year the Indus River deposits 150 million tons of alluvial sediment in the sea at a rate of roughly 1–2 meters of deposit per thousand years. The Indus flows southeast from the present-day city of Karachi, Pakistan to the Arabian Sea.

The ancient existence of a river that once followed the flow of the

---

[69] A guide to the history of India was submitted by Jaroslav Strnad, Jan Filipský, Jaroslav Holman and Stanislava Vavroušková, Dějiny Indie (The history of India), Prague, Lidové noviny publishing house, 2008. I've also drawn from the following publications: Charles K. Maisels, Early Civilizations of the Old World, London and New York, Routledge – Taylor and Francis Group 2001; Alexandra Ardeleanu-Jansen (ed.), Vergessene Städte am Indus – Frühe Kulturen in Pakistan vom 8.–2. Jahrtausend v. Chr., Mainz am Rhein, Philipp von Zabern 1987; Ute Franke-Vogt, Die Glyptik aus Mohenjo-Daro- Uniformität und Variabilität in der Induskultur: Untersuchungen zur Typologie, Ikonographie und räumlichen Verteilung, Mainz am Rhein, Philipp von Zabern 1991; Jonathan Kenoyer, The Indus Civilization, in Joan Aruz, Ronald Wallenfels (edd.), Art of the First Cities – The Third millenium B.C. from the Mediterranean to the Indus, New York – New Haven and London, The Metropolitan Museum of Art, Yale University Press 2003, pp. 377–413; Norman Yoffee, Myths of the Archaic State, Cambridge, Cambridge University Press 2005.

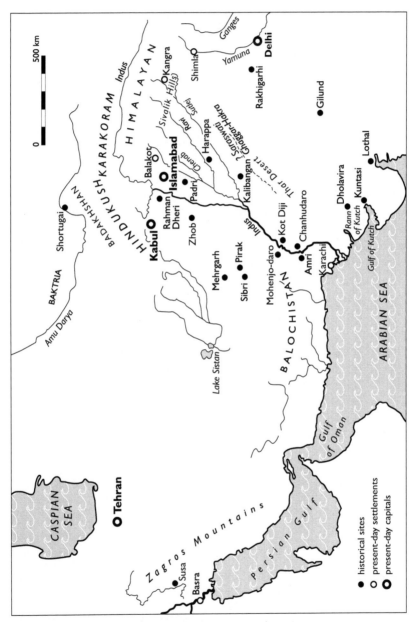

**Fig. 26** Main historical and archeological sites of the proto-Indian culture.

Indus, but which no longer exists, is noteworthy. Previously known as the Sarasvati (today the Ghaggar-Hakra Valley), it once flowed almost collaterally with the Indus for some 1,000 km, but is now completely dry. The cause of its current state seems to be the geographical situation of the Sarasvati's source.

This river flowed from the Sivalik Hills, where it was not supplied by water from melting snow to the same extent as the Indus was from the great Himalayan Mountains. Moreover, its main sources of water, the Sutlej and Yamuna rivers, drawing moisture from the melting Himalayan snow, later diverted their courses and fed into the Ganges instead of the Indus.

The land where proto-Indian culture began was therefore very similar to that where the earliest Mesopotamian civilization formed.

The orogenesis of the Himalayan Mountains also had an effect on the climate of northern India. The areas immediately inside the mountain massifs thus became frigid wastelands of high altitudes. Riverless areas in northwest India possess a very hot and dry climate with summer temperatures reaching 50 °C and an annual rainfall of less than 200 mm. Yet this situation changes in the region of northern India where north of Delhi near the Yamuna River the annual rainfall is 200–700 mm.

# PREHISTORIC BEGINNINGS

The territory later settled by the proto-Indian culture is situated in the central area of the Indus River, right in its fluvial plain. The Thar Desert forms its eastern border, while the western border consists of foothills in the Balochistan region on the northwest border of today's Pakistan.

Noticeable right from the start is the expanse of arable land, currently estimated at 650,000 km², that the bearers of proto-Indian culture most likely worked.[70]

The most complete and best assessed sequence of a prehistoric settlement in historic northwest India is the Mehrgarh site in the hills situated in the northwest end of the Kachi plain on the Bolan River, the northern (right-bank) tributary of the Indus River, under the Bolan Pass. The sequence here consists of seven settlement phases dating back to the Pre-Pottery Neolithic (I, late 8th, early 7th millenium BC) and continuing to the early 2nd millenium BC (VII).[71]

Findings show that the people here gradually replaced their hunting-gathering lifestyle with that of productive farming, agriculture and livestock breeding.

The people of Mehrgarh made their living in agriculture, namely by cultivating wheat and barley. The fact that we come across both wild grasses, as well as their cultivated offspring, may indicate that the people here made use of the lush growth of wild grasses following the spring floods and systematically worked to ensure high-quality seeds.

---

[70] Charles K. Maisels, Early Civilizations of the Old World, London and New York, Routledge – Taylor and Francis Group 2001, p. 186. A more modest estimate in Jonathan Kenoyer, The Indus Civilization, in: Joan Arur, Ronald Wallenfels (ed.), Art of the First Cities – The Third Millenium B.C. from the Mediterranean to the Indus, New York – New Haven and London, The Metropolitan Museum of Art, Yale University Press 2003, p. 377–413, on p. 378.

[71] For more details on Mehrgarh see Charles K. Maisels, Early Civilizations of the Old World, London and New York, Routledge – Taylor and Francis Group 2001, pp. 192–205.

With the help of domesticated dogs, they also raised sheep, goats and cattle; evidently zebus (Indian cattle) breeding had already acquired an importance in the Neolithic period – though later this domestic animal would become less significant. Surprisingly, the zebus seemed to get smaller through the ages. Hunted game included wild sheep and goats, gazelles, deer-like animals, boar, various antelope species and onager (wild predecessor of the ass), as well as African buffalo, a wild form of cattle and elephants. This rich assortment of game indicates that a broad range of landscapes were hunted – from mountainsides to the open steppe-forest, to shady and wet woodlands and pools. The presence of especially skittish and wary species, such as the onager, betrays the use of specific hunting techniques, most likely those that involved chasing the animals into pens or hazardous places (precipices, chasms, river valleys?) by organized groups of beaters.

The people of Mehrgarh made their hunting equipment from clay, stone, bone and, starting in phase II, also from copper. It is in phase III (5th–early 4th millenium) that we first come across proof of the mass production of pottery in "pottery districts," where the masters of the craft left behind layers of production waste up to 6 meters thick [26]. The process of making pottery on a fast potter's wheel and sometimes even fired in two-chamber kilns was most likely begun at the end of the site's development, in phases VI and VII. The presence of plates, dishes, bowls, cups, vase-like vessels, goblets, miniature vessels and lids and even storage containers attests to diverse forms of pottery for this period and indicates the use of pottery for cooking and storage, as well as for ceremonial purposes.

Sometime around 3000 BC the potters of Mehrgarh even mastered the technique of firing pottery in a reduction atmosphere, in which oxygen is reduced, and began to produce and supply popular grey pottery, often painted with elegant and colorful patterns.

The people of Mehrgarh mainly used local raw materials for the production of chipped-stone industry, particularly for sickle blades fitted sideways into handles to create a tooth-like edge, as well as for the production of asphalt cement. Some pieces of the chipped-stone industry even served as projectiles shot by bows, most likely for hunt-

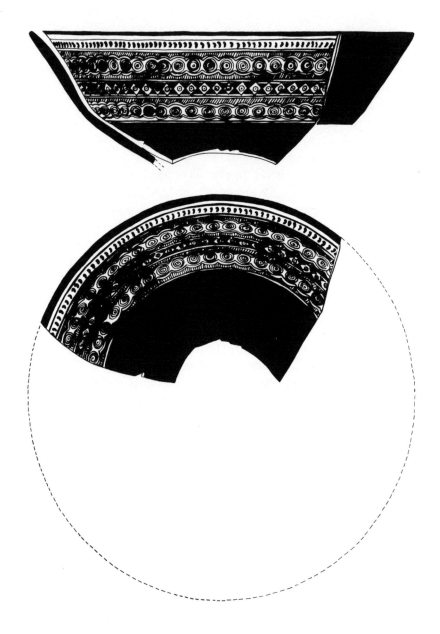

**Fig. 27** A piece of a painted bowl from Mehrgarh. Phase V, ca. 33rd century BC.

ing. Stone hatchets were honed here from coarser nodules of silex. The inhabitants wore necklaces, bracelets and belts made of stone, bone and shell beads. Raw materials used to make these accessories included lapis lazuli, carnelian, turquoise, chrysoprase, seashells, bone and copper. Silex drills used to make such beads dominated in phases I–III, though later they became less common and eventually disappeared from use. It is in the Neolithic period that stone vessels first make their appearance.

Bones were used to make everyday tools – spikes, bodkins, chisels, trowels and smoothers. Ivory was also worked with here (phase V).

In phase III (4000–3500 BC), copper was smelted here to make bodkins, hooks and blades. A hand drill and potter's wheel were used in workshops to make stone beads.

Baskets were woven from organic mesh and, in some cases, were impregnated with bitumen from local springs.

As for the site's contact with remote lands, the people of Mehrgarh had already figured out how to obtain seashells in the Pre-Pottery Neolithic. Semi-precious lapis lazuli appeared here in the same period (phase IA). This stone later became more widespread, particularly in phase III (4000–3500 BC). In contrast, the craftsmen of Mehrgarh did not become acquainted with "compartmented seals," most likely of Iranian origin, until phase VI (late 4th and early 3rd millenium BC).[72]

The inhabitants of prehistoric Mehrgarh lived in clay houses built from oblong adobe (unfired brick) with several (4–6) rooms under a roof of timber, thatch and clay. Fire pits and kitchens were often located in the corners of rooms. Public spaces used for domestic work and as occasional burial grounds were situated between the houses. Supplies were stored in special buildings that consisted of storage spaces arranged in parallel rows (there were usually 15 of them) with a central access corridor. These buildings were built together in a single enclosed "quarter" of the Mehrgarh village.

The seals, characterizing social mobility and probably the first indications of the boundaries of private property, first appeared in Mehrgarh in phases (IV?–V), i.e. even before the end of the 4th mil-

---

[72] Seals with contoured images protruding.

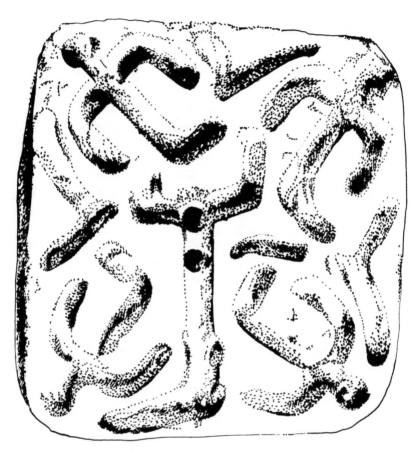

**Fig. 28** Seal. Mehrgarh, phase VII, ca. 26th century BC.

lenium BC, but became widespread only in phase VII, before the settlement was abandoned at the end of the 3rd millenium. One of the seals of this period depicts a remarkable scene with a central human figure squatting, raising his hands to the sky and surrounded by four crouching figures with their hands lowered to the ground [27]. Did the artist portray here a ceremony performed by a member of the elite of prehistoric Mehrgarh for the benefit of all the people of Mehrgarh, represented by symbols of the populated four cardinal points?[73]

Another question is whether it is possible to apply a social-historical interpretation to the various hairstyles and headdresses on figurines found in Mehrgarh. While representations of women in phases VI (late 4th and early 3rd millennium BC) and VII (early 3rd millennium) mainly feature finely curled hair and jewelry, men are presented, especially in figurines from phase VII, with headdresses emphasized in greater detail. Only additional research will tell us whether these circumstances can be interpreted in a binary sense of the primary female role of reproduction (hair as a symbol of the individual's inner-most essence and, in the case of women, emblematic of the ability to give new life) opposed to the primary male role of organizing the cult and social structures (symbolized by the headdress). The "third power," represented for the first time in phase VII by male figurines with shaved heads, could even stand for primary status, experts in the area of the spiritual, primal Brahman. This is, however, pure speculation.

Excavators also discovered here burial grounds where the people of Mehrgarh laid the deceased to rest. The dead were commonly buried with personal decorations, tools, weapons and pottery. In the 7th millennium BC, a red ochre dye was poured over the deceased. They were also often buried with personal decorations (necklaces, pendants, bracelets, belts and anklets), tools (stone chisels), pottery and even raw materials (silex or chunks of ochre dye). Up to five young goats were also buried at the feet of the deceased at that time. In one case, the deceased also received with the goat a sickle with the cutting edge made of a stone blade set in asphalt.

The mostly uniform material composition of the jewelry that accompanied the deceased on their final journey is noteworthy. Most of the beads in the various necklaces, belts or anklets come from a single type of stone (white or black soapstone/steatite, *Dentalium* shells, turquoise, limestone) with supplements varying in color (shells and steatite among the turquoise, turquoise and carnelian among the

---

[73] Alexandra Ardeleanu-Jansen (ed.), Vergessene Städte am Indus — Frühe Kulturen in Pakistan vom 8.–2. Jahrtausend v. Chr., Mainz am Rhein, Philipp von Zabern 1987, p. 252, No. A 70.

shells, turquoise among the limestone beads, lapis lazuli among the steatites). Exceptionally abundant and opulent necklaces were found in the graves of children (up to 520 beads).

Surprisingly, a uniform burial rite already appears in this period. The deceased were laid on an east-west axis with their heads to the east and their faces to the south.

A unique characteristic of the burial ceremony from this period consists of burying the deceased by a brick wall approximately 1.0–1.2 m long and walled up to a height of 3–8 rows of an adobe wall located generally to the north of the body. Then, after the body was laid into the burial chamber that was dug out partly to the side of a tomb shaft, the descendents apparently enclosed the burial chamber with a brick wall and filled the tomb shaft with dirt. This is how men, women and children were often buried, sometimes in a secondary position (the burial of an already disintegrating body). It seems that these "tombs" were used on a long-term basis; in at least some cases they were clearly reopened and the older bones were piled to the side to make room for the newly deceased.

A paleodemographic analysis of 71 graves from this site shows the normal representation of youth (35% of all buried, of which 68% died before the age of 5). The people were generally better off health-wise, and the average lifespan was 31 years. The estimate for the number of births per woman is slightly lower than with the Chalcolithic population, which may have been caused by the nomadic way of life of Mehrgarh's Neolithic population.

In phase III at the beginning of the Chalcolithic period (5th – early 4th millenium BC), the people of Mehrgarh established a vast burial ground that they used for a long time. The deceased here were still laid on an east-west axis, on their left sides, their heads to the east and with slightly bent legs, but without the ochre dye poured over them. Here we come across mass graves and burials of already decomposed human remains. The deceased were usually laid to rest with personal ornaments. In nearly all cases these consisted of necklaces made of soapstone beads and pendants of semi-precious stones. Despite the relatively meager personal effects buried here, three types of burials can be discerned: those entirely without funerary objects, with standard objects (necklaces) and with non-standard objects (pottery, bronze, semi-precious stones). Children were usually buried without objects, while the graves of adult women had the most objects. Adult men fell between children and women on this scale.

Paleodemographic analysis of the remains from this burial site shows that, of the 99 total buried bodies, 73 were adults (over 20 years of age), of which roughly half were men and half women, and 26 were youths (under 20 years of age). The estimated average lifespan for these individuals is 24 years. The low number of young people tells us that they were buried elsewhere. The estimate for the number of births per woman is slightly higher than with the Neolithic population here. All in all, this seems to have been an average prehistoric group of the population, void of traces of catastrophes, calamities and suffering or of other extraordinary influences and situations.

The Mehrgarh population of the Bronze Age (phase IV–VII, ca. 3500–2500 BC) left behind only a single burial ground, at which the remains of some 70 newborns and small children were laid to rest. They, too, lie in a crouched position in an east-west direction.

This uniform positioning of the deceased is noteworthy and signals to us the formulation of a uniform world view regarding the burial of the dead in observing the rules of the world of the living and dead.

The question arises to what extent a pottery vessel in the form of a shell, coming from the end of Mehrgarh's Neolithic stage, can be interpreted as a ceremonial object. Could this be interpreted as a liquid-pouring symbol referring to the (female aspect of) procreative power?

Clay figurines, especially those of woman, but also of horned cattle, begin to appear in Mehrgarh in the earliest phases of the settlement. They were usually highly stylized and often depicted a seated woman; the fact that these earliest figurines were colored with red ochre is worth noting. No female figurines have been found from phase III, though forms of the horned cattle do appear. The female figures do, however, begin to make an appearance in phase IV (ca. 3500 BC). They were usually made from a red material and consisted of several parts glued together; in some cases the depicted woman is holding a child. Traces of original colors are preserved on some of these: eyes and hair were

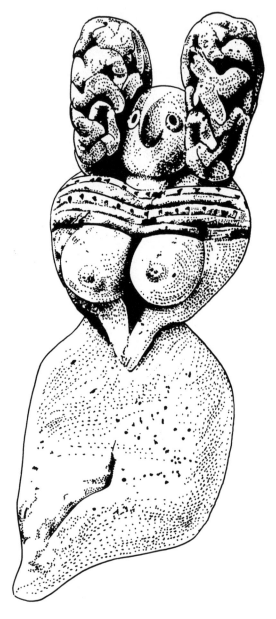

**Fig. 29** Female figurine. Mehrgarh phase VI, ca. 30th century BC.

at one time black or red (dyed using henna?), while ornaments such as headbands, necklaces, bracelets or pendants were yellow. The figures of the beautiful women of Mehrgarh were gradually perfected with women of voluptuous and even Rubenesque proportions depicted, frequently featuring elaborate hairstyles and opulent jewelry [28]. At the very end of phase VII development, male figurines also begin to appear in Mehrgarh, in some cases in pairs in living quarters. Similar small works of art frequently appear, often broken or burnt, in the settlement's refuse areas.

# THE PREPARATORY PERIOD

An essential period for the birth of the proto-Indian culture is undoubt-edly the first half of the 3$^{rd}$ millenium BC (the Early Harappan Period), when there occurred in the society of historical northwest India a number of transformations that can be seen in archeological finds.

We will first examine the changes revealed from traditional excava-tions. In Mehrgarh, the South Cemetery is one such site and features a number of empty tombs (cenotaphs) created during phase VII (ca. 2500 BC). If we look far to the north, in Afghanistan and southern Turkmenistan, we can find materials analogous to those found in the South Cemetery cenotaphs. We can therefore assume that a change in the site's cultural orientation occurred. The South Cemetery of Mehrgarh offered many remarkable finds – in addition to pottery, we find objects made from metal and stone, ornaments, cosmetic acces-sories (mirrors) and stamps. One of the tombs held a "scepter" made of grey limestone similar to those from Iran, northern Afghanistan and Turkmenistan.

There is no more evidence of settlement of Mehrgarh at this time, though there is proof at the nearby Sibri site. At Sibri, the site's resi-dential and production functions are combined with burial finds. Two cylinder seals were also found here: one bears the depiction of a zebu bull confronting a lion with a scorpion on the lower base. The second shows a lion attacking a zebu bull accompanied by a human figure holding a spike with the image of a fish and other animals at the end. These motifs also exhibit similarities with the iconography of sites lo-cated to the north of Mehrgarh. Nevertheless, a number of finds from there and from the South Cemetery of Mehrgarh show characteristics that are similar to monuments of proto-Indian culture, including symbols used in proto-Indian writing. Pottery, some tools and weap-ons also show resemblances (even emblematic battle-axes). This can therefore be seen as further growth and maturation of the Mehrgarh culture, accepting impulses from the north, but also drawing from its own resources.

Finds from excavations of a number of sites show that some components of the proto-Indian culture picture originate as far back as the 4th millenium BC. This includes excavation at the Kot Diji site, which is not far from Mohenjo-daro and which was probably already fortified in prehistoric times (pottery, clay toys, figurines of women and animals), and Amri in southwest Pakistan (pottery).

Surface surveying of the ancient Hakra River basin in Cholistan, the desert part of the original state of Bahawalpur in today's Pakistan, clearly show these changes. An increase in the area and number of function-specific sites is the main difference with regard to the earlier situation. The number of short-term encampments markedly drops from the earlier share of 52.5% to 7.5%. The number of excavated sites with exclusively residential functions (57.5%) slightly increases. Yet the strikingly high increase in sites linking residential and production functions – from a previous 2% to the current 35% – represents a very distinct factor. The production areas are situated in close proximity, though not directly within residential areas in 35% of all excavated sites.

It is also worth pointing out that the total number of excavated sites from this period stands at 40, compared to 174 from the proto-Indian period and 50 from the "dark age" (1900 to 1500 BC).

Social mobility in the sense of the stability of settlement structures and an increase in production specialization comes quite clearly into view here.

The differentiation in the size of excavated sites is also already clearly visible in this period. Around 60% of the sites are of an area less than 5 hectares. Mid-size sites, between 5 and 10 hectares, represent 25% of the excavated sites here. Only one settlement, Gamanvala, is of exceptional size with 27.3 ha.

Finds from the period preceding the proto-Indian culture, most likely the first half of the $3^{rd}$ millenium BC, provide evidence of sites obviously built in taking cult or ritual aspects into consideration. Of the 40 total settlements that can be included in the culture named after the Amri site near Mohenjo-daro, 13 consist of the upper and lower city. The upper city is usually represented by a cone-shaped mound, sometimes even artificially raised, rising to a height of ca. 25 m. Appearing on its slopes are the remnants of 2–4 rows of terraced walls and the remnants of stairways or access ramps adjoining the south side to the steep side of the mound. The upper city has numerous remnants of residential structures located at the foot of these artificial mounds. The architecture is believed to possess cult aspects.

# THE PROTO-INDIAN CULTURE
## (2500–1900 BC)


## Economy

Irrigation ditches were not a part of the proto-Indian agriculture culture. They were not necessary since during the flooding (from June to September) the river inundated the entire fluvial plain and brought fertile soil to the arable land as in Egypt. The wheat and barley sowed after the floods could be harvested in March and April of the following year.

In overflowing its banks and flooding the uneven terrain in the fluvial plain, the river turned the depressions and low grounds by its banks into ponds. Farmers could then either drain these ponds in irrigating lower lying fields or, by using mechanical equipment such as a shadoof (counterpoise lift), could reclamate upper lying fields.

The use of plowing equipment is evident here in the traces of cross-plowing in a field found at the Kalibangan site from the first half of the 3rd millenium BC. We can also assume that harrows and hoes were used and that cereal was threshed by a team of steers trampling it. The grain was then cleaned by throwing it against the wind with shovels made of organic mesh (matting).

Cereals that farmers of the proto-Indian culture cultivated included wheat, barley, millet, rice and sesame. Horticulturists grew legumes, flax and cotton, sesame and even mustard, while orchardists tended to date palm and jujube tree groves and vineyards where the grapes were ripening.

In later periods following 2000 BC, they sowed crops such as sesame and cotton to be harvested in autumn. Sometime during this period the agricultural of proto-Indian culture developed to include new crops introduced from Africa. These included sorghum, various types of millet and some other kinds of legumes and vegetables.[74]

---

[74] See Charles K. Maisels, Early Civilizations of the Old World, London and New York, Routledge – Taylor and Francis Group 2001, pp. 206–214.

Trained dogs helped people raise animals such as cattle, buffalo, pigs, sheep and goats.

It is perhaps unnecessary to emphasize that the proto-Indian people supplemented their diet with wholly traditional subsistence strategies such as hunting (deer, wild pigs, elephants, tigers, lions, bison, wolves, jackal and rhinos) and fishing.

Proto-Indian culture craftsmen excelled in a wide range of fields that entailed the processing of natural materials. They used the potter's wheel to create elegant pottery that was often painted and engraved and featured symbols that sometimes show similarities to the script of proto-Indian culture. They were able to make stone products (bracelets, sometimes even with writing) fired at temperatures around 1,000 °C. A pair of fitted crucibles, which they would place in the furnace to be exposed to the most intensive heat and which would undergo firing in a reduction (oxygen-less) atmosphere, was used for this. Surprisingly, this type of product seems to have been carefully controlled, since even closed pairs of these kinds of crucibles secured on the contact surface's clay daub by seal impressions were also preserved. Numerous smaller clay objects were also made. Among these were figurines of people or horned cattle sometimes accompanied by clay carts and which, as toys, long ago captivated early excavators of proto-Indian sites.

Stone was used to make common tools for everyday needs. Chipped minerals (silex) was used to make blades and similar tools, resilient and hard rocks (granite, limestone) were then used for grinders in preparing vegetable aliment or for drilled spherical objects, the purpose of which we still do not know. They also produced stone beads made from semi-precious stones (carnelian, agate and turquoise). When drilling especially long beads from semi-precious stones, they used special drills from a particular kind of rock that became extremely hard after it was heated. Even so, it was an extremely arduous process; a master craftsman could spend a whole week drilling a long bead. Stone-cutting saws, chisels, hole punches and drills were used to make seals.[75]

---

[75] Ute Franke-Vogt, Die Glyptik aus Mohenjo-Daro – Uniformität und Variabilität in der Induskultur: Untersuchungen zur Typologie, Ikonographie und räumlichen Verteilung, Mainz am Rhein, Philipp von Zabern 1991, p. 43.

The craftsmen here worked with bone, ivory and sea and river shells, which they often used to make tools, ornaments (bracelets), furniture marquetry, game pieces and commodities such as spoons and ladles.

They knew how to make numerous bronze tools, ornaments and cosmetic accessories (mirrors) and vessels that they supplied to consumers throughout the area of the proto-Indian culture. They also made vessels and other useful objects from metal.

Given that copper does not exist in the Indus valley, they imported it in smelted ingots, probably from somewhere on the Arabian Peninsula, perhaps from present-day Oman. They were adept at working with both gold and silver.

Materials of an organic nature were very commonly used, but very little has been preserved of them, leaving us without any information to convey. A shred of cotton material comes from Mohenjo-daro.[76] The existence of miniature vessels serving as flacons tell us that various cosmetic agents – oil, aromatic ointments, makeup, perfumes and the like – were probably used. Unfortunately, more specific details evade us. Knowledge of the use of bitumen was preserved from prior ages.

Craftsmen of that period were also skilled in working with faience, the first glass-like material in the world. This was made from crushed silica sand, to which a material containing magnesium, iron oxide, copper and aluminum was added. Water and a binding agent were then added to the mixture and everything was thoroughly kneaded. Small artistic works were then created usually by pushing the soft mixture into a mold, letting it dry and, lastly, firing it at a high temperature. This process was used to create miniature vessels, boxes, marquetry, beads, amulets, bracelets, buttons, chess figures, seals and figurines. Unfired faience is called fritted glass.

One remarkable finding is that the production of stone tools in particular shows traces of a mutual connection between the various production centers, enabling one to share their specialized production of components with another.

---

[76] Jan Filipský, Zrození indické civilizace (Birth of the Indian Civilization), in: Jaroslav Strnad, Jan Filipský, Jaroslav Holman and Stanislava Vavroušková, Dějiny Indie (The History of India), Prague, Lidové noviny publishing house, 2008, pp. 23–123, on page 31.

Enterprising Indian dealers and suppliers used steer-pulled carts as well as river and sea vessels for business purposes. Domesticated camels were also used as carriers and guides.[77]

Supplies of valuable goods from surrounding regions were mutually centralized in Harappa and Mohenjo-daro: lapis lazuli from Badakhshan, quality wood from the forests of the Himalayan temperate and subtropical zone, copper and steatite from Zhob Valley and gold mined on the upper part of the Chenab River, and perhaps even copper from deposits in the vicinity of Simla and Kangra. Copper ingots might have even been imported from the Arabian Peninsula, possibly from present-day Oman.

A chlorite vessel imported from regions near the Persian Gulf was found in Mohenjo-daro, and we also know of two compartmented seals found here, most likely from central Asia.

Various goods are assumed to have been exported from the proto-Indian culture. Contact with the Sumerian and Akkadian civilization through Persian Gulf transfer points is also considered highly probable. Carnelian beads from India appeared in the 26th century BC in the Sumerian city of Ur.[78] A stamp seal from the proto-Indian culture, impressed on a vessel closure, probably comes from the Sumerian city of Umma. This supports the notion that the trade of some centers of proto-Indian culture extended all the way to Mesopotamia. A proto-Indian seal was found in the Iranian city of Susa.[79] It seems, however, that the introduction of cultivated sesame and raised African buffalo was a more essential contribution of proto-Indian civilization to the crafts and skills of Sumer and Akkad.

We know from cuneiform records that trade relations existed be-

---

[77] Ute Franke-Vogt, Die Glyptik aus Mohenjo-Daro – Uniformität und Variabilität in der Induskultur: Untersuchungen zur Typologie, Ikonographie und räumlichen Verteilung, Mainz am Rhein, Philipp von Zabern 1991, p. 75.

[78] Charles K. Maisels, Early Civilizations of the Old World, London and New York, Routledge – Taylor and Francis Group 2001, p. 237, and also Alexandra Ardeleanu-Jansen (ed.), Vergessene Städte am Indus – Frühe Kulturen in Pakistan vom 8.–2. Jahrtausend v. Chr., Mainz am Rhein, Philipp von Zabern 1987, p. 45.

[79] Jonathan Kenoyer, The Indus Civilization, in: Joan Aruz, Ronald Wallenfels (edd.), Art of the First Cities – The Third millenium B.C. from the Mediterranean to the Indus, New York – New Haven and London, The Metropolitan Museum of Art, Yale University Press 2003, pp. 377–413, on page 411.

tween areas of the proto-Indian culture and Sumerian Mesopotamia. The Sumerians imported copper, ivory, gems, quality wood, rare animals and various decorative fabrics from historical northwest India. A cylinder seal bearing the name of Mr. Shu-ilishu, an interpreter of Meluhha (probably a language of the proto-Indian culture), dates back to the Akkadian Empire (ca. 2334–220 BC).[80] We even know that around 2000 BC people of Meluhha, as the area of proto-Indian culture is referred to in cuneiform sources, settled in Sumer.

A lack of evidence has left us somewhat in the dark concerning relations between the proto-Indian culture and other neighboring regions and areas. It seems that vigorous contact occurred prior to 2500 BC. The sphere of proto-Indian culture then became more closed and it was not until after 2000 BC that active contact was once again established with surrounding lands. Three proto-Indian seals come from the central Asian site of Altyndepe (phase IV–V).

Relatively vigorous relations were established within the very sphere of proto-Indian culture as demonstrated by, for instance, the widespread prevalence of seashells, often gathered at shores and transported to interior lands to be processed in specialized workshops.

## City life

One conspicuous finding is that cities of the proto-Indian culture played a role that was markedly different from that of Mesopotamian cities. This is indicated by the percentage of the population living in cities (in settlements with an area exceeding 40 ha) and in the country. In Sumer, this ratio was 78:22%, while in the proto-Indian culture it was 44:56%. A comparison of 50 sites of the proto-Indian period with 56 Sumerian sites of the early dynastic period (ca. 3000–2330 BC) tellingly shows that, though there are 11 Sumerian sites whose area

[80] Francoise Demange, 303 – Cylinder seal of Shu-ilishu, interpreter for Meluhha, in: Jonathan Kenoyer, The Indus Civilization, in: Joan Aruz, Ronald Wallenfels (edd.), Art of the First Cities – The Third millenium B.C. from the Mediterranean to the Indus, New York – New Haven and London, The Metropolitan Museum of Art, Yale University Press 2003, p. 377–413, on page 413.

3222222222322223222222222322222322

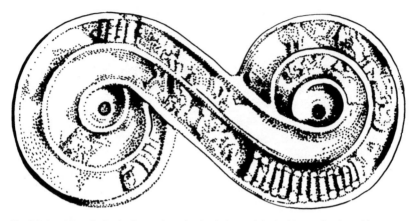

**Fig. 30** A golden clip in the form of a pair of spirals garnished with steatite, from Harappa, 2500 to 1900 BC.

exceeds 40 ha, there are only three such proto-Indian culture sites. While the proto-Indian culture did not have any large sites exceeding 200 ha, the Sumerian city of Uruk reached an area of 450 ha already at the beginning of the early dynastic period.

We are familiar with one of the oldest city centers of the future proto-Indian culture from excavations of the Rehman Dheri site in the Indus basin to the north of Mohenjo-daro. This site possesses a rectangular layout with an area of 21 ha and apparently dates back to the late 4th and early 3rd millenium BC. The city was probably home to 3,000–5,000 inhabitants, who created for their own needs ceramic goods marked with symbols that in many ways anticipated the writing of proto-Indian culture. They also used all kinds of bronze tools and were engaged in the production of stone beads from carnelian, agate and turquoise. Compartmented seals and abundant finds of lapis lazuli provide a vivid picture of the site's long-distance contacts.

It seems that seals with symbols of proto-Indian script had already appeared here.[81]

---

81 Alexandra Ardeleanu-Jansen (ed.), Vergessene Städte am Indus – Frühe Kulturen in Pakistan vom 8.–2. Jahrtausend v. Chr., Mainz am Rhein, Philipp von Zabern 1987, p. 118.

Finds from the Kot Diji and Kalibangan sites show that some city centers already had walls around them during this developmental phase.

Excavation of the city of Mohenjo-daro and the fortified site of Harappa has provided us with the main source of information on the urban milieu of the proto-Indian culture [29]. Large agglomerations on the now dried-up Sarasvati River – Ganverivala in Cholistan, Pakistan (81.5 ha) and in Rakhigarhi in Haryana, India – still remained unexamined, although excavations were recently commenced in Rakhigarhi.

The position of Mohenjo-daro and Harappa outside the main area of agriculture settlement shows some indications that, instead of perceiving both agglomerations as urban centers, they can rather be understood as "gates" situated in an area easily accessible to the bearers of the proto-Indian culture and their surrounding neighbors. The urban settlement of Shortugai in present-day northeast Afghanistan, some 1,000 km to the north of the heart of proto-Indian culture, represents a similar outpost of proto-Indian urbanism.

## Mohenjo-daro

Mohenjo-daro – literally "Mound of the Mohans" in Sindhi (the traditional interpretation as "Mound of the Dead" is most likely folk etymology) – is the most renowned city of proto-Indian culture on the Indus River, in the Sindh province of present-day southern Pakistan. It was built sometime between 2500 and 1900 BC in the flood zone of the Indus on massive brick platforms approximately five meters high to avoid the threat of the river's regular flooding. An acropolis (a citadel) surrounded by a wall originally rose above the city. This was built on giant brick platforms, 200 × 400 m in size and at least seven meters high.

The city itself spread out over an area of roughly 90 ha and it is estimated that 35,000–40,000 inhabitants resided there. Adobe residential structures were built into the network of perpendicularly crossing roads up to 10 m wide that were aligned with the cardinal points and probably measured and built according to a planned layout. These were generally 7 × 15 × 31 m in size and their exposed parts were made of fired brick. The residential buildings of Mohenjo-daro appeared remarkably similar to those outside the city. They were generally situated on a north-south axis, often had courtyards and very few windows. Their walls were massive and the dwellings were often equipped with baths. The houses, built around a courtyard, frequently featured an above-ground floor. Water from an adjacent well, of which the city had 700 at its disposal, was used in the baths of these houses. Their roofs were equipped with rain gutters made from burnt clay. A carefully built sewage system led waste water from the dwellings, even from their upper floors, into drains under the roads. Since food grinders were found in the courtyards; we can assume that cooking was done outdoors using vessels of burnt clay and metal. The interiors of homes featured opulent furniture adorned with shell-work, while metal dining wear was also used here. Miniature containers, perhaps small flacons for cosmetics, attest to the upkeep of personal appearances. Dice and game pieces show one of the ways leisure time was spent. Caches with valuables, sometimes stored in copper or silver vessels, were found under the floors of some homes. They contained an abundance of valuable jewelry of gold, bronze, copper, carnelian, agate, jasper, chalcedony or steatite. Elsewhere, however, perhaps under a home's threshold, multiple metal tools were discovered, including four pieces of writing on the blades of three axes and one chisel.[82]

The "Great Bath" found here with large dimensions ($7 \times 12 \times 2.4$ m) and treated with bitumen may have served as a kind of public cleansing ritual [30]. This structure was not part of the original urbanistic concept and was added to the urban development during one of its later phases. The people would enter the bath from the north and the south using two stairways of 10 steps. The bath itself was enclosed by a wall of burnt brick 1.35 m thick with another 3-cm-thick isolation layer of bitumen on the outside of the wall. A pillared courtyard, entered from the south through a vestibule, extended around the bath. "Bathing cabin" wings were situated adjacent to the north and east walls. It is

---

[82] Ute Franke-Vogt, Die Glyptik aus Mohenjo-Daro – Uniformität und Variabilität in der Induskultur: Untersuchungen zur Typologie, Ikonographie und räumlichen Verteilung, Mainz am Rhein, Philipp von Zabern 1991, p. 55.

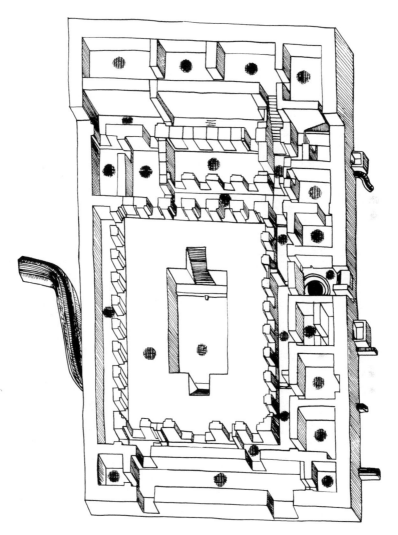

**Fig. 31** The "Great Bath" in Mohenjo-daro (ca. 2200–1900 BC), ground plan.

not clear how the bath was filled with water; perhaps the well in one of the rooms of the eastern wing of "cabins" served this purpose. A drain in the southwest corner of the bath served to drain the bath, emptying into a brick conduit drain approximately 1.8 m high.

A large enclosed structure, originally thought to be a granary or even public baths (50 × 27 m) and older than the "Great Bath," was found to the west within the city's built-up area. Its foundation, built on a massive terrace of bricks up to 6 m high, featured a total of 27 rectangular blocks of burnt brick arranged into three east-west and nine north-south rows. The passages between them were 0.8 m wide and 1.4 m deep. It appears that this configuration of a 27-brick platform was constructed some time after the existence of the foundation terrace and that the two construction phases were not carried out at once. These platforms date back to the existence of the "Great Bath," whose conduit drain had to be installed through the northwest corner of the already existing "granary." A sure interpretation of this structure still eludes its researchers. A massive building, 74 × 34 m in size with its outer walls over 1.5 m thick, was found in the northern part of the city.

To the south, a structure originally interpreted as a palace was revealed by excavators. This was another vast building (67 × 35 m) built from quality brickwork (walling 1–2 m thick), situated around two courtyards and featuring many rooms. There is also evidence of pyrotechnic worksites here. Three wells and at least one bread oven were found here. The building had three entrances leading into it from the city streets.

Modern research has, however, expressed doubts of whether this district would have had a palace. Our attention is immediately drawn to one of the "suburban" buildings, building I in the HR-A district. The building in this case most likely did not serve standard residential purposes and is now interpreted as a temple. Coming from the south, the visitor would first enter the front courtyard and come upon a rotund structure. Facing north, he would then have before him a part of the building that was raised by roughly 2.4 m and that was entered by a double staircase. Fragments of human sculptures, limestone vessels and other objects, including a set of seals featuring a "unicorn" were found here.

The city district included a quarter where craftsmen often worked with fire (e.g. potters, but also manufacturers of earthenware and faience shell cutters, stonecutters and coppersmiths) and with raw materials to be chipped into tools, with steatite or with semi-precious stones (chalcedony, jasper and serpentine) that they would make into ornaments. There were, however, no workshops here that created every-day consumer goods, nor were there smelting works for the production of copper and bronze. It is not clear who made the millions of bricks needed to build the city or where these bricks were created. Sets of weights served trading purposes, clearly indicating a universally ac-cepted system of weights and measurements.[83]

Merchants supplied the city with foreign goods such as copper, which the local land lacked, importing it in disk-shaped ingots. Evi-dence of the high level of professional craftsmanship of local producers has been found; these masters were able to make earthenware and ceramic ornaments at temperatures around 1,000 °C.

The burial of the city's deceased remains a complete mystery to us today. The remains of a total of 38 people were found in various positions here, but in none of these cases was there evidence of ritual burials. The 13 skeletons found in room 74 of building II in the HR district included men, women and one child. Six other skeletons were found in one of the streets of the HR district, which acquired the rather morbid name of Dead Man's Lane. The remains of four adults and five children were buried in a ditch in the DK district. Lastly, four skeletons were found lying on a stairway leading to one of the wells in the DK-G district. Yet that is all we know of the dead of this ancient city in present-day Sindh.

The remains of artistic monuments, such as stone, metal, terracotta, faience and shell-work sculptures, were also found in abundance here. They more depict acknowledged leaders or ancestral figures than act-ing rulers; the famous "priest king" represents a sculpture type that we are familiar with from at least another six specimens [31]. We can-not rule out that this is a portrayal of an individual with the ability to activate nature's fertile power; something in this spirit is implied by the depiction of a whole group of men similarly dressed and sitting in a similar position, accompanied by a picture of field plowing on a

[83] See Jonathan Kenoyer, The Indus Civilization, in: Joan Aruz, Ronald Wallenfels (edd.), Art of the First Cities – The Third millenium B.C. from the Mediterranean to the Indus, New York – New Haven and London, The Metropolitan Museum of Art, Yale University Press 2003, pp. 377–413, on p. 402.

silver goblet allegedly from Afghanistan. This artifact was obtained at an antique shop in Kabul. Trilobate motifs adorning both human and animal sculptures may evoke an astral theme, and consequently a fertility one involving the cyclical dates of farming. Other works consist

**Fig. 32** Reconstruction drawing of the "priest king" sculpture from Mohenjo-daro (2500–1900 BC).

of bronze-cast forms of female sacrifices or dancers. Female sculptures were normally made exclusively from clay, perhaps considering the earth to be a goddess. Figurines of animals, cattle in particular, were also found, as were small pendants depicting human faces, sometimes with horns or animal ears.

Famous seals made from fired steatite feature a certain quadruped usually accompanied by a group of symbols, the so-called proto-Indian script (most frequently in groups of 5), that we still do not know how to read. One of the newly formulated hypotheses postulates that this is not true writing depicting spoken sounds, but a system of symbols using emblems to express something like a "public announcement" (see below). In addition to the mysterious "quadruped," the seals also feature cattle, a zebu, an African buffalo, an elephant, a tiger, a crocodile and a rhinoceros. One of the temples here (building I, HR-A district, see above) provided a vast collection of these kinds of seals, all with pictures of the "rhinoceros;" a certain picture can therefore be linked to a group of people of a specific residence (profession, social standing or blood relations?).

Some seals depict even more complex scenes, documenting at least three religious cult levels (people subordinate to mythical creatures and these creatures subordinate to "gods" in human form).

A Buddhist monastery with a stupa (a mound-like reliquary) was built in the central part of the city in the 2nd century BC.

## Harappa

This fortified site of proto-Indian culture (ca. 2500–1900 BC) in the Punjab region at the confluence of the Indus and Ravi rivers features a "castle" in an elevated position on a giant, brick-built terrace surrounded by a massive wall, inside of which are structures of monumental architecture, with an area of 65 ha (ca. 1.5 km$^2$). Extensive residential quarters situated under the Harappan acropolis probably provided shelter for some 35,000–40,000 inhabitants. A brick-built building, probably used for storage purposes, was found north of the "citadel" in the river plain.

Next to the residential buildings were extensive cemeteries where the deceased were laid to rest in ditches; the dead were in a supine position with their heads first pointing east, though later north. Other necropolises contained the remains of the dead that were exposed to the climate's effects and were therefore void of organic tissue. For their final journey they received vessels, ornaments (earrings, necklaces, bracelets, rings, belts and anklets) and sometimes even bronze mirrors.

Cemetery R37, lying further to the south from the fortification than cemetery H, dates back to the period of proto-Indian culture. The recurrent superposition of graves, in which the more recent graves disrupt the earlier ones, attests to the long tradition of this burial site and the permanency of choice of a final resting place. Burial pits found here show a north-south axis orientation and were very large, though shallow (3–4.57 m long, 0.76–3 m wide, 0.61–0.92 m deep). The dead were usually laid in them on their backs with their heads pointing north. In one case, a deceased woman was wrapped in a reed blanket and laid to rest in a wooden coffin 2.13 m long and 0.76 m wide. There is also evidence of the brick lining of burial pits. The deceased usually received pottery, plates, footed bowls, vase-like vessels and pitchers, i.e. tableware pottery. A child's grave is noteworthy in that it contained miniature vessels of the same kind placed in adult graves. In another case, a copper mirror, sticks made from antimony and spoons and vessels made from shells were found. Ornaments that accompanied the deceased on their final journey included earrings, necklaces with beads made of steatite or semi-precious stones, shell bracelets, rings, belts of semi-precious stones (with two women and one man) and anklets of faience beads with golden clasps. There were even animal bones and tools made from silex.

At the H cemetery directly south of the fortification and dating back to the post-proto-Indian period, the deceased were buried in two layers, one on top of the other (layer I and II). The lower layer II revealed burials in a supine position on an east-west axis with an average depth of 1.8 m. For their final journey the deceased received gifts of pottery baked red and with ornamental and figural paintings made in black.

Remains of bodies were found buried in urns on the upper layer I. The deceased were not cremated though, instead their bodies were

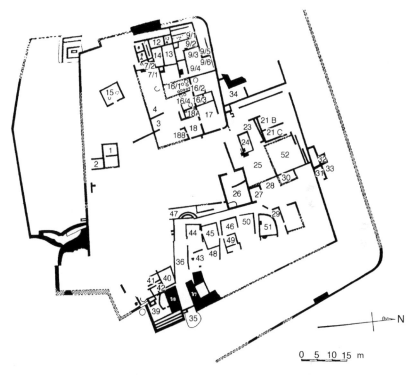

**Fig. 33** Ground plan of the proto-Indian city of Kuntasi.

exposed to the elements and the bare bones were placed in containers covered by lids or by smaller containers. This always entailed a selection of certain bones and never the whole skeleton. These urns also featured rich ornamental and figural decoration painted in black.

An abundance of household contents was also found at the site. Craftsmen here made elegant red pottery with black painted geometrical patterns and plant (and animal) figural motifs; we even have proof of ceramic sculptures (human and animal figurines). They also worked with stone (semi-precious stones), metal, organic materials (wood, reed mesh) and artificial materials (faience). The people of Harappa were also engaged in trade, as sets of weights and objects imported from the Indian Ocean over 700 km away (seashells) attest to. A Harappan bracelet made of seashells was found in the ancient city of Susa in present-day Iran.[84]

Finds of small ceramic flacons for valuable substances (perfumes?) speak of the importance that was attached to personal appearances. Some from Harappa even prided themselves on their impressive jewelry. Many such accessories were found together here: an eight-shaped brooch made of silver and gold, beset with beads of various shades of blue steatite, another similar brooch, gold bracelets and numerous necklaces with beads of jasper and agate. Other finds from this site include a seal with various symbols and proto-Indian writing that we cannot read, but which we assume expresses a message in one of the proto-Dravidian languages of India (perhaps already using some Indo-European elements). The seal's impressions were also found here on some goblets with tapered bottoms and on terracotta cylinders of indeterminate purpose, of which some were even found piled together as a small depot (28 pieces).

Harappa is estimated to have had 6,600 km² of arable land.

## Towns and cities

An examination of the smaller urban sites of proto-Indian culture can reveal interesting information. Such sites include the river port of Kuntasi near the Gulf of Kutch in the present-day state of Gujarat in northwestern India, approximately 5 km from the shores of the Arabian Sea [32]. This square-shaped city with an area of 2 ha has a central quarter of about one hectare surrounded by a double fortification wall. It was built of quarry limestone with clay mortar or from adobe with standard proto-Indian dimensions (38 × 19 × 9.5 cm) on stone foundations. The buildings are situated in the northern half of the site, while its southern part served more as a town square or public communication area. Granaries and storage spaces tell us that shipments (food) from

---

[84] See Jonathan Kenoyer, The Indus Civilization, in: Joan Aruz, Ronald Wallenfels (ed.), Art of the First Cities – The Third Millenium B.C. from the Mediterranean to the Indus, New York – New Haven and London, The Metropolitan Museum of Art, Yale University Press 2003, pp. 377–413, on p. 398.

near and far were centralized here. Evidence of pyrotechnic worksites (kilns and furnaces) confirms that the people of ancient Kuntasi often used fires, most likely for purposes that included the production of both greige and impressively painted pottery. Steatite beads, of which over a thousand were found here, were produced in large quantities. A pier about 12.5 × 3.2 m in size built on the riverbanks here and used for loading goods points to the importance of trade for the city. One of the structures on the central square is interpreted as a ritual podium on which ceremonies were performed.

Some sites of proto-Indian culture show a clear economic specialization, such as trading. The Padri site in the present-day region of Saurashtra, India, which evidently adopted the habitus of proto-Indian culture in connection with supplying local salt to consumers from the proto-Indian culture, can be described as such. The salt was exported from here in massive ceramic containers baked red. One of these containers bore a picture of the Harappan "horned deity." Beads of carnelian and of other colorful semi-precious stones were made at the Chanhudaro site; in Balakot, northwest of Karachi, seashells were worked with and used for decorations and for furniture marquetry.

Excavation of the Proto-Indian phase of Kalibangan turned up extraordinary results in a different direction. Here the acropolis, fortified and elevated above the lower city, enclosed in its walls a dual settlement composed of residential buildings in the northern part, while the southern part, separated by a northern wall extending quite hazardously along the stairway ramp adjacent to the bulk of the fortification, contains at least five terrace-like structures made of adobe. One of these terraces holds seven "fire altars" with a north-south alignment. These were clay-lined ditches, 75 × 55 cm in size, containing ash, cinder, crude terracotta and the remnants of upright clay blocks in the form of steles. Similar steles, 30–40 cm high, were also found in residential buildings in the lower city, usually. Their diameters were 10–15 cm and they stood in the middle of fireplaces. The same terrace contained a well and several fragments of bathing room tiles made from burnt brick and equipped with small drainage conduits. Another of these terraces, also equipped with a well and a "fire altar," contained a square pit, 1.0 × 1.25

in size, lined with burnt bricks. Cattle bones and antlers, most likely the remnants of sacrifices, were found in this pit.

In this case, it seems that the city's acropolis was used exclusively for cult ceremonies involving in some form veneration expressed to (among other things) the elements (fire, water, the earth represented by wild and domesticated animals and, given the altitude of the site, the air as well).

The lower city of Kalibangan, also enclosed by walls, included a comfortable residential development, whose homes were also equipped with the aforementioned "fire altars."

Some 80 m east of the lower city looms the KLB-3 site, a mound with four or five "fire altars" that was probably used for ritual purposes. It seems, however, to date to a different period than the acropolis settlement. An unexcavated settlement, perhaps a crafting worksite, is located to the south of the acropolis.

In the case of Kalibangan, it is actually very tempting to regard those living in the acropolis with their cult obligations as the oldest discovered form of the traditional Indian cast of Brahmins, while considering the people of the lower city as representatives of embryonic forms of the Kshatriya (ruling and military) and Vaishya (suppliers) castes. We hope that future research will tell us how it really was.

The latest research of the site of the proto-Indian city of Dholavira has yielded very interesting findings. Set into the city walls above a gateway leading into the inner fortification of the city district (citadel) was a three-meter-wide inscription with at least four characters of proto-Indian writing.[85] We have no idea how to interpret this.

## Rural life

The aforementioned surface surveying by Dr. Mohammad Rafique Mughal in the basin of the ancient Hakra River in Cholistan, a desert

---

[85] See Steve Farmer, Richard Sproat and Michael Witzel, The Collapse of the Indus-Script Thesis: The Myth of a Literate Harappan Civilization, Electronic Journal of Vedic Studies 11-2, 2004, pp. 19–57, on p. 22 and pp. 35–36 (cited on 24 June 2008 from http://www .safarmer.com/fsw2.pdf).

area of the original state of Bahawalpur in present-day Pakistan, has provided a remarkable comparison with the conditions that prevailed before the birth of the proto-Indian civilization. In contrast to the previous 40 sites, the number of sites here during the proto-Indian period rises to 174, although during the "dark ages" (1900–1500 BC) this number once again drops to 50. Dr. Rafique Mughal claims that a shift in the settlements occurred from the northeast to the southwest during the proto-Indian period and also that there was an increase in the number of sites with an exclusively residential function (47.7%). Yet the number of sites serving manufacturing purposes also rose (45.4%), and they are distinctly separated from the residential sites. Purely manufacturing settlements contain evidence of the work of potters, brick makers, producers of small terracotta objects, producers of faience and coppersmiths.

We also see here a developmental trend within the proto-Indian period. During the late Harappan period (2100–1900 BC) there appears here a single regional center, the Kudwala site with an area of 38 ha. Once again the number of short-term camp sites rises (to 26% of all) and the number of exclusively manufacturing sites, which moved back to village settlements, drops (to 18% of all).

Everything here seems to clearly indicate the end of strict production specialization and a return to simpler and traditional subsistence strategies.

## A state organism?

Multiple finds from Quetta, Pakistan nicely demonstrate the nature of the social differentiation and the culture of the Indian elite at that time. Products of gold, copper, alabaster, semi-precious stones and ivory were found here. Other found objects included gold jewels as necklace beads, gold pendants in the form of figurines of horned cattle, splendid ornaments of chalcedony and carnelian set in gold and numerous cosmetics: alabaster vials, mirrors and small bronze makeup applicators. A goblet of wrought gold decorated with images of lions and snakes was also found here, as were discs, elongated sticks or "scepters" made of stone and similar to those found in the South Cemetery in Mehrgarh. Other emblems of this type, featuring the form of an animal hoof at the end, were found here. Of particular interest were "miniature columns" with a concave surface, sticks and game pieces made of ivory. Trilobate ornaments of ivory, originally colored red, were also found. We are familiar with these as sculptural motifs of proto-Indian culture, possibly originally sewn to cloth or used as furniture marquetry. Copper axes and chisels were also discovered here. There was also a copper censer and one pile contained the lower part of a human sculpture clad in a robe with fringes ("kaunakes"). Unfortunately, we are only familiar with these from Afghani antique shops. This points directly to contact with areas in present-day Iran, where similar artworks appeared around 2000 BC. This elite, adorning themselves with choice jewels, dining on splendid tableware, playing board games and even tending to the veneration of the deities of the day, apparently maintained remote contact with areas in present-day Iran, Turkmenistan and Afghanistan and exchanged know-how and experiences with partners, colleagues and friends there.

One of the most recent studies draws attention to the fact that, even though objects made from valuable materials did not play a significant role in public ceremonies and rituals, they did represent a tangible form of value that was guarded in personal property as a valuable asset.

One noteworthy fact is that terracotta figurines of women of the proto-Indian period are now shown with headdresses. This was missing in prehistoric works where women's hairstyles were depicted. Can we infer from this that women of the proto-Indian culture were now holding public offices? Moreover, the figurine of a "naked ascetic" could kindle ideas of cult specialists – the first Brahmins. Yet this is all pure speculation. As far as depictions of hairstyle are concerned, art monuments of the proto-Indian culture do not provide clear testimony to their possible emblematic roles, not even with regard to distinguishing sexes.

An effective exchange, perhaps even non-distributive mechanisms, clearly thrived in the proto-Indian culture, as attested to by an elaborate and evidently uniform system of weights and measures substantiated by discoveries of weights.

Modern research has recently presented remarkable findings in this area. Not long ago an American archeological expedition found a massive adobe building measuring at least 20 m in length at the Gilund site in the southern region of Rajasthan, India. This location is at the eastern edge of the area settled by proto-Indian culture. The building, positioned on a north-south axis, has five parallel walls with two walls running crosswise, giving the impression of a storage complex. Excavators found a container with about a hundred clay seal impressions in the northwest corner of the structure [33]. In most of the cases these seals featured geometric motifs and were apparently taken from moveable containers, most likely pottery vessels.[86] This can be taken as convincing evidence that supplies of goods with supplier seals affixed to them were concentrated at a central collectorship. There the seals on the containers were unsealed, the goods were stored and the seals were apparently archived for accounting-reporting reasons.

The existence of city quarters surrounded by walls created in various periods and growing at various rates, though separated by empty spaces that were intentionally not occupied, is interpreted by Norman Yoffee as proof of competing social groups.

One proto-Indian seal depicting a number of standard or emblem bearers offers very interesting information [34]. It seems that these are symbols of individual communities or regions, indicating some of the more advanced forms of territorial organization. In another case, the picture of a standard fills the entire field of the seal, which, accompanied by writing, evokes the idea of a regional unit (symbolized by the standard) associating multiple communities (represented by the writing)

Walter A. Fairservis has presented a stimulating interpretation of the social impact of proto-Indian seals.[87]

---

[86] Cache of seal impressions discovered in Western India offers surprising new evidence for cultural complexity in little-known Ahar-Banas culture, circa 3000–1500 B.C., in: http://www.museum.upenn.edu/new/research/possehl/ahar-banas.shtml, cited on 4 Feb 2004. See also Gregory Possehl and Vasant Hinde, Excavations at Gilund 2001–2003: The seal impressions and other finds, in press in South Asian Archeology 2003. My gratitude to Professor Gregory Possehl for providing access to the manuscript.

[87] Walter A. Fairservis, Jr: G. L. Possehl's and M. H. Raval's "Harappan Civilization and Rojdi," Journal of the American Oriental Society III/I, 1991, pp. 108–114, and pp. 111–112.

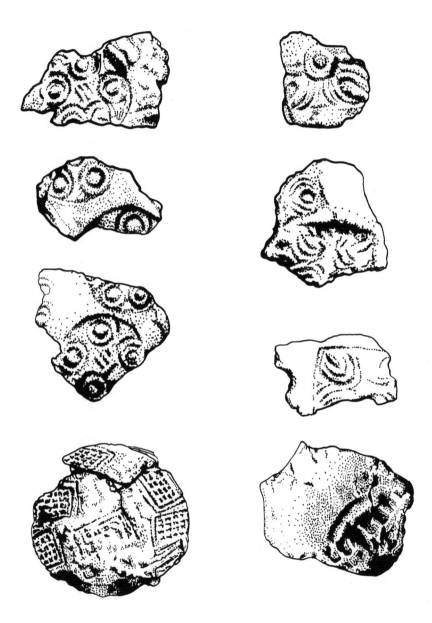

**Fig. 34** Seals from the proto-Indian site of Gilund.

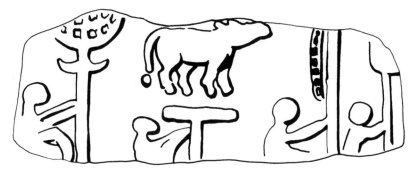

**Fig. 35** Proto-Indian seal from Mohenjo-daro. Standard-bearers (?).

The fact that the images on the seals are oftentimes standardized and repeated many times, whereas the writing exhibits a markedly individual and distinguished nature, is interpreted as references to sodalities (animal symbols) connected to the identification of an individual (writing). In his view, the antithesis of domesticated and wild animals, featured as motifs on seals, indicates the existence of binary kinship structures (moiety), while mythical creatures consisting of various parts of animal and human bodies characterize sibship or alliance. Hopefully, future research will either confirm or refute this bold assertion.

Archeological excavation of the proto-Indian culture has not revealed much in the way of militaria and defensive or offensive equipment. Spear or lance heads have been found, though certainly not in large numbers. In some cases, the exact nature of the enclosure around urban settlements (such as at Kot Diji) is not clear. Is this a symbolic delineation of a space for domestic peace, or is it a defensive wall?[88] Pictures depicting scenes of battle and conflict, which could carry heroic connotations, are also worth pointing out. One such scene shows a lancer vanquishing a water buffalo.

Another thing we do not find here is clear proof of the presence and involvement of a socially distinguished elite. The damaged "priest-king" sculpture from Mohenjo-daro (see fig. 31), made of burnt steatite

---

[88] There is an eloquent German expression for such a delineation of space: *Umfriedung.*

and depicting an adult male in a flowing robe originally beset with red ornaments in the form of a trilobate arrangement, is often cited in this sense.

Remnants of dark colored materials were apparently still visible between the trilobates when the sculpture was found.[89] It is worth noting that these trilobates appear only very rarely in the proto-Indian culture, that instead it seems that this decorative element entered historical northwestern India from somewhere in the west, most likely from Iran. At least in one case these trilobates also decorate a picture of a standing bull. One of the most recent compendiums characterizes proto-Indian communality as an "example of archaic social-cultural complexity, but without a state."[90]

Anthropologists contributed to the substantial findings: based on the skeletal remains found, the state of health of the bearers of proto-Indian culture was, on the whole, well-balanced; they evidently did not live in destitution. This fact also bears witness in a sense to the culture's relative homogeneity and a certain egalitarianism. Increased deficiency in enamel formation (*linear enamel hypoplasia*) in girls of the proto-Indian culture represents the only exception. This seems to indicate more intensive stress that girls were exposed to in childhood, perhaps due to the greater respect commanded by males in this culture.[91]

## The spiritual culture

We should at least take a cursory glance at the aforementioned burial customs of the proto-Indian culture. The prevailing orientation of the deceased in burial pits was on a north-south axis, lying in a supine position with their heads (if it was preserved) pointing north. The graves

---

[89] See Jonathan Kenoyer, The Indus Civilization, in: Joan Aruz, Ronald Wallenfels (ed.), Art of the First Cities – The Third Millenium B.C. from the Mediterranean to the Indus, New York – New Haven and London, The Metropolitan Museum of Art, Yale University Press 2003, pp. 377–413, on p. 385.

[90] Norman Yoffee, Myths of the Archaic State, Cambridge, Cambridge University Press 2005, p. 228.

[91] Charles K. Maisels, Early Civilizations of the Old World, London and New York, Routledge – Taylor and Francis Group 2001, p. 250.

were sometimes found to be lined with bricks. Some graves contained urns holding select bones; empty graves (cenotaphs) were also found. Highly noteworthy are the double graves, in which a deceased man and woman lie together. Could the widow have been sacrificed? For their final journey the deceased were provided with gifts of ornaments, cosmetics (even mirrors), tools and pottery. One grave contained goat bones that were probably added as a sacrificial offering.

Findings related to cult and ritual matters are extremely rare in the proto-Indian culture.

It is difficult to decide whether a small terracotta head from Mohenjo-daro depicting a human head with two faces looking in opposite directions represents a being from the spiritual world or not. This brings to mind a similar case from the iconography of seals, in which two depictions of a "proto-Shiva" portray a creature with three faces. The preserved masks of proto-Indian culture feature in some cases openings or eyelets so that they could be fastened to something. They, therefore, may have served as idols, as worshipped objects. Some pictures of buildings show two poles with emblems or flags built into the ends of these buildings. Could these be sacred symbols?

In some cases proto-Indian seals depict standards, "totems" or idols in the form of poles with, for instance, bovine skulls and leaves from a pipal tree. The figure appearing on proto-Indian seals as "yoke bearers" could refer to a *kavadi* sacrifice (relating to the sacrificial vessels carried to the place of sacrifice on a beam across the shoulder, literally a "yoke") made to the Dravidian deity Murugan.[92] Traces of scorching or smoke under the surface of some sculptures suggest the custom of lighting incense or aromatic substance, or merely having a flame burning – again for reasons that continue to elude us. The copper vessel found among other things in Quetta and interpreted as a censer comes to mind here. We find a cup-shaped object on a stick, which frequently appears on seals of proto-Indian culture, attached to a golden headdress from Mohenjo-daro. Could this be a kind of tiara worn by a high priest?

---

[92] Ute Franke-Vogt, Die Glyptik aus Mohenjo-Daro – Uniformität und Variabilität in der Induskultur: Untersuchungen zur Typologie, Ikonographie und räumlichen Verteilung, Mainz am Rhein, Philipp von Zabern 1991, p. 93, Taf. XXXV, 256.

Worth noting is the form of personal ornaments, much more varied than in prehistoric cultures. Although the bearers of proto-Indian
culture did wear, for instance, necklaces or belts made of one kind of
stone (e.g. carnelian), they often combined in them several materials
(agate/chalcedony/jasper; agate/jasper/carnelian, agate/jasper/gold,
gold/onyx/turquoise and others). Did they do so for purely aesthetic
reasons or was there a deeper meaning concealed?

Some 3,000–3,500 seals with proto-Indian writing have been found
in all types of proto-Indian sites. They are found in normal settlement
contexts, separately and in multiple numbers. The author of the last
synthetic work presented a total of 2,371 finds.[93]

These consisted of smallish rectangular tablets made from steatite,
recoated with a layer of powdered steatite mixed in water and baked
at a low temperature to better resist routine wear. At other times, seals
were made from other types of stone, clay, frit (unfired faience) and
very rarely from silver, marble, limestone or burnt clay. Semi-precious
stones that were otherwise known and worked with were not used in
making these seals. The seal image was engraved in negative on the
impression area. The back side of this seal usually had eyelets drilled
through it for hanging or wearing. Other longer rectangular-shaped
seals that had convex backs with holes drilled through them were also
found; these generally only featured script symbols.

Similar seals were found in the Persian Gulf region and even in
southern Mesopotamia. Proto-Indian writing was discovered at a Ras
al-Jinz (or Ras al-Junayz) site located in present-day Oman, at the
easternmost point of the Arabian Peninsula.[94]

---

93  Ute Franke-Vogt, Die Glyptik aus Mohenjo-Daro — Uniformität und Variabilität in der
    Induskultur: Untersuchungen zur Typologie, Ikonographie und räumlichen Verteilung,
    Mainz am Rhein, Philipp von Zabern 1991, pp. 78–79, motifs 32 and 34, Taf. XXXII,
    221 and 222.

94  Alexandra Ardeleanu-Jansen (ed.), Vergessene Städte am Indus - Frühe Kulturen in
    Pakistan vom 8.-2. Jahrtausend v. Chr., Mainz am Rhein, Philipp von Zabern 1987,
    p. 131–133, also Serge Cleuziou, Giorgio Gudi, Charles Robin, Maurizio Tosi, Cachets
    inscrits de la fin du IIIe millénaire avant notre ère a Ra's al-Junayz, sultanat d'Oman,
    Académie des Inscriptions et de Belles-Letters, Comptes-rendus des séances de l'année
    1994, avril–juin, Paris, de Boccard 1994, pp. 453–468, on p. 457 Fig. 4 (ostracon with
    proto-Indian writing).

**Table of the frequency of various motifs of proto-Indian seals[95]**

| Motif group | Group | % |
|---|---|---|
| Animal looking right | A | 75.9 |
| Writing | S | 16.2 |
| Mythical creature | B | 1.6 |
| Variety of animals | E | 0.1 |
| People | C | 0.3 |
| Scenes | K | 0.8 |
| Plants | O | 0.1 |
| Geometric motifs | Q | 4.1 |

**Recurrent motifs on proto-Indian seals[96]**

| Motif | Motif number | % |
|---|---|---|
| "Unicorn" | 01 | 58.3 |
| Writing | | 16.2 |
| Individual cattle | 03 | 4.7 |
| Zebu | 04 | 3.1 |
| Swastika | 86.87 | 3.0 |
| Elephant | 12 | 2.5 |
| Rhinoceros | 11 | 1.1 |

The most common iconography of proto-Indian seals combines writing of most frequently 5 (and sometimes up to 7) symbols with a picture of an animal. Seventy-five percent of all seals found in Mohenjo-daro are of this type. The "unicorn," perhaps an aurochs, clearly reigned among the depicted animals. It often appears accompanied by a special cup-like object on a stick (a "feeder"?), whose meaning we have yet to explain. In addition to the "unicorn," the common form of a horned cattle, a zebu, African buffalo, goat, elephant, rhinoceros, tiger, croco-

[95] Ute Franke-Vogt, Die Glyptik aus Mohenjo-Daro – Uniformität und Variabilität in der Induskultur: Untersuchungen zur Typologie, Ikonographie und räumlichen Verteilung, Mainz am Rhein, Philipp von Zabern 1991, p. 46.
[96] Ibid.

dile and various types of antelope is also used. Other animals, such as a hare or camel, also appear on copper tablets. We also find fabricated creatures: quadrupeds with human faces, cattle with several heads, a horned tiger and mountain goats with elephant trunks.

The mythical creature of a human form sitting on a lotus throne (Padmasana) on a rectangular pedestal with its hands on its knees appears here several times. A "horned crown" with Sacred Fig *(Ficus religiosa)* leaves is often atop its head, and it sometimes view the world with three faces while surrounded by animals. Although this creature had repeatedly been interpreted as Proto-Shiva or Pashupati (the god Shiva as lord of all animals), modern research has cast doubt on this

**Fig. 36** Proto-Indian seal from Mohenjo-daro. "Proto-Shiva" (?).

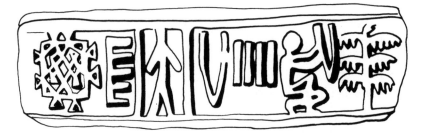

**Fig. 37** Proto-Indian clay seal from Mohenjo-daro. This could be a depiction of a sacrifice. The ceremony initiator, presenting the sacrificial offerings (a vessel?) to the idol in the form of the tree at far right. An object that could be interpreted as a sacrificial vessel (?) with the numeral 4 (?) is to the left of him. A man with staffs (?) in the left half of the picture could be the dignitary on whose initiative the ceremony was performed. The ladder-like symbol to his left could indicate his sphere of activity (region or specialization). The symbol completely to the right could indicate the kind of ceremony being performed. Or did it mean something else?

**Fig. 38** Proto-Indian seal from Mohenjo-daro. Worship of an idol in human form (?).

interpretation [35]. Some researchers interpreted the form of a horned human being dressed in a spotted robe (?) and holding a bow as the goddess Durga (or Proto-Durga), Shiva's wife, who is riding a tiger.

One of the proto-Indian seals features a sacrifice offering to a tree, which is either venerated for what it is or as a symbol representing another venerated being [36]. Elsewhere a human figure presents an object of veneration [37]. The motif of the soles of people's feet, already appearing here, also certainly warrants a closer look. This motif was to achieve considerable renown in India and even continues to be depicted in our present day.

**Fig. 39** Proto-Indian seal from Mohenjo-daro. A procession worshipping the human figure in a tree.

The human figure with a bun hairdo in a babul tree *(Acacia arabica)*, before whom a tiger stands on the ground and turns its head to the human, presents another solid link.

A naked figure with outstretched arms, braided hair and a horned crown standing on a garland of pipal leaves can also be found here. Animals, people and mythical creatures join the "person in the tree." Sometimes worshippers surround the entire scene, or walk to him, creating a procession [38].

Dextrorotatory and sinistrorotatory swastikas (fylfot) appear on frit seals.

**Fig. 40** Proto-Indian seal from Mohenjo-daro. The "Tamer" from Mesopotamian inspiration (?).

In some cases, proto-Indian seals betray foreign patterns and inspi-rations. The scene with a human figure holding with each hand a tiger by the neck as they stand on their hind legs is most likely related to Mesopotamian depictions of the "lord of all animals," often interpreted as Gilgamesh [39]. A half-man, half-bull creature is cited on copper tables from the same area.

Specific iconography appears on "amulets," dice, cylinders, prisms or cubes made from burnt clay or frit. We once again see many people or animals with legs apart, "giving birth to" scorpions or turtles. Working scenes appear on them rarely (two women with a basket in the garden?).

In the later period of the culture, seal impressions decorate a num-ber of cups from Mohenjo-daro.

A special kind of writing can be found on copper tablets, whose re-verse sides often bear a figural picture. In addition to the animals that we are familiar with from seals, we also come across hares, dogs, deer or mythical creatures in the form of animals. Writing can also be found on copper blades, ivory staffs, earthenware pottery and bracelets, tools and sometimes even on necklace beads.

The proto-Indian system of writing is composed of roughly 450 symbols.[97] This system most likely consisted of individual symbols representing either whole words or individual syllables. The fact that proto-Indian writing samples, possessing a completely different sequence of symbols, are known from different regions seems to al-low for the assumption that the symbols more represent syllables by which different local names were transcribed. Contemporary research has expressed the view that proto-Indian script is derived from some languages of the Dravidian language family. These languages were spoken by the pre-Indo-European population of (south) India.[98] We

---

[97]  An informative overview of the attempts to read this script was provided by Jan Filipský, Zrození indické civilizace (Birth of the Indian Civilization), in: Jaroslav Strnad, Jan Filipský, Jaroslav Holman and Stanislava Vavroušková, Dějiny Indie (The History of India), Prague, Lidové noviny publishing house, 2008, pp. 23–123, on pp. 32–36.

[98]  Walter A. Fairservis, Jr., G. L .Possehl's and M. H. Raval's 'Harappan Civilization and Rojdi', "Journal of the American Oriental Society" 1 1 1/1, 1991, pp. 108–114, on p. 111, and Asko Parpola, Special lecture: Study of the Indus Script, paper read at the 50th ICES, Tokyo Session, 19th May 2005 (cited on 24 June 2008 from http://www.harappa.com/script/induscript.pdf).

have already pointed out possible evidence in proto-Indian script of a *kavadi* sacrifice (this relates to the sacrificial vessels carried to the place of sacrifice on a beam across the shoulder, literally a "yoke") made to the Dravidian deity Murugan.[99]

There does not seem to be a fixed relationship between pictures and writing, at least not on the seals. The same inscriptions can accompany different pictures, even on different mediums or from different locations. Simple inscriptions usually repeat more often than that considered complicated.

Evidence of writing in both directions – from right to left and from left to right – has apparently been found.

One noteworthy fact is that, with the exception of blades bearing script, no other objects found in troves had writing on them.

An attempt has recently been made to draw sweeping conclusions from the fact that nearly half of all symbols of proto-Indian script appear only once.[100]

This could cast doubts on the nature of the proto-Indian graphic system as script, since, if it were really writing, the same symbols representing the same syllables would necessarily have to repeat more often. Researchers have therefore questioned whether this is instead a system of symbols of an optical nature, i.e. emblems that referred to concepts of a different or more complex nature. By combining several such emblems, a "statement" of, for instance, a social message could be made in which the individual symbols, perhaps representing social units, could express the willingness of these social bodies to join forces and "act in unison."

For the most part, traditionally oriented research has reacted by pointing out the inconsistencies and ambiguities in the interpretation by proponents of the new theory, as well as the statistical tests that the hypothesis on the purely symbolic nature of proto-Indian script

---

[99] Ute Franke-Vogt, Die Glyptik aus Mohenjo-Daro – Uniformität und Variabilität in der Induskultur: Untersuchungen zur Typologie, Ikonographie und räumlichen Verteilung, Mainz am Rhein, Philipp von Zabern 1991, p. 93, Taf. XXXV, 256.

[100] See Steve Farmer, Richard Sproat and Michael Witzel, The Collapse of the Indus-Script Thesis: The Myth of a Literate Harappan Civilization, "Electronic Journal of Vedic Studies" 11–2, 2004, pp. 19–57 (cited on 24 June 2008 from http://www.safarmer.com/fsw2.pdf).

is based on.[101] Such research can, however, be problematic in that it persists in the assumption that the symbols of proto-Indian script possess phonetic values and that they capture the sounds of spoken language on the rebus and charades principle. The working hypothesis here is based on the assumption that the graphic forms of the symbols captured the pronunciation of words of closely related expressions that stood for originally intended essences. The *signifiant* was supposed to be pronounced the same or very similarly as the *signifié*, whereby the idea of the *signifié* was to have been evoked and the communication function of the script accomplished.

In fact, the universal validity of this principle is unsubstantiated. The principle of the sound interpretation of written symbols was asserted relatively late in the early phases of ancient graphic systems, even up to roughly a thousand years following the introduction of written communication. Early writing systems are usually composed of icons, indexes and symbols, whose meaning are specified only in ambiguous or contradictory cases by phonetic complements (sound references to how to read a symbol) and semantic complements (determinatives, symbols determining the next highest class of terms which that word belongs to, e.g. symbols such as "person," "city," "country"). Egyptian hieroglyphics acquired such a form between the years 3200 and 2700 BC, and early cuneiform can also be characterized in the same way, at least between the years 3500 and 3000 BC.

The bearers of cuneiform civilization even used two writing systems in the 27th century BC: the one in which the symbols were chosen based on their meanings and the other in which they were chosen according to the written values.[102] As we will later see in this book, a similar trend also appeared in early Chinese writing.

---

[101] Asko Parpola, Special lecture: Study of the Indus Script, paper read at the 50th ICES, Tokyo Session, 19th May 2005 (cited on 24 June 2008 from http://www.harappa.com/script/induscript.pdf).

[102] The so-called UD.GAL.NUN system: Jean-Jacques Glassner, Écrire a Sumer – L'invention du cunéiforme, p. l.: Editions du Seuil 2000, pp. 212–213, as well as Claus Wilcke, Literatur um 2000 vor Christus, in: J.W Meyer, W. Sommerfeld (ed.), 2000 v. Chr., Politische, wirtschaftliche und kulturelle Entwicklung im Zeichen einer Jahrtausendwende, Berlin, DOG in Kommission bei Saarbrücker Druckerei und Verlag 2004, pp. 205–218, on pp. 213–214.

I therefore personally consider hypotheses based on attempts to interpret the earliest writing exclusively as systems of audio-oral symbols to be unpromising, since many, if not all, were used in a multilingual milieu where the need for general comprehensibility play a fundamental role. I am more inclined to accept the attempts to view them as systems of either graphic or mixed symbols. In such systems, although the primary message, encoded in symbols designed for optical reading, can be specified in ambiguous cases by references to their sound, this plays a supplementary role and not a primary one.

The actual meaning of proto-Indian script will, therefore, probably continue to elude us for a long time.

# THE DEMISE OF PROTO-INDIAN CULTURE

Among the still unanswered questions hindering our knowledge of this unique and remarkable culture enriching humankind's oldest history is the difficulty in explaining its demise. We have already learned that the other river supplying the proto-Indian farmers, the ancient Sarasvati, apparently dried up at the end of the proto-Indian period, and thus deprived the people of historical northwest India of an abundant source of subsistence.

Another factor that may have substantially contributed to the collapse of the public structure of proto-Indian life is that of health – and hygiene in particular. Indeed, the fact that water resources for normal consumption were dangerously close to drainage facilities for sewage water has been attributed to the demise of numerous ancient urban civilizations. The public and private wells of proto-Indian cities were located in perilous proximity to sewage drains, sometimes even in adjacent soakage pits where house sewage would be discharged into. It also seems that in some proto-Indian cities, after the sewage drains were blocked by sludge, the water would begin to simply spill out into the streets.

Although Europe was certainly no stranger to this problem in the Middle Ages, in tropical India and in sub-continental areas an outbreak of an epidemic such as typhus or cholera – typical diseases caused by contaminated water resources – could turn catastrophic.

The results of surface surveying in the Cholistan Desert can assist us here as well. In contrast to the 174 proto-Indian sites, the number of sites of the "dark ages" (1900–1500 BC) dropped to 50 here. We find a considerable contraction in the size of settled areas: none of the sites exceed an area of 5 ha. Fourteen percent of the sites combined residential and production functions, while another 14% were exclusively of a residential nature. This probably indicates that a collapse of the culture did not occur, but that a restructuring and a "move to the country" took place.[103]

However, in no way did this lead to a substantial restriction and "barbarification" of the culture. Finds from the Pirak site in Kachi plain dating back to ca. 1500 BC offer convincing proof that none of the original proto-Indian techniques had completely vanished. Grown here, along with wheat and barley, were rice and sorghum, the latter an African crop related to millet; many of these were now cultivated as spring crops. Camels and horses were raised here as well.[104]

[103] Charles K. Maisels, Early Civilizations of the Old World, London and New York, Routledge – Taylor and Francis Group 2001, pp. 248–249.

[104] Alexandra Areleanu-Jansen (ed.), Vergessene Städte am Indus – Frühe Kulturen in Pakistan vom 8.–2. Jahrtausend v. Chr., Mainz am Rhein, Philipp von Zabern 1987, p. 136.

# ANCIENT CHINA

Northern China is characterized by mountainous land in the west, with flat alluvial plains spreading out in the east from the foothills to the Shandong Peninsula and northeast Manchuria. Right about in the middle of this area we find the Ordos Plateau, north of which, beyond China's borders, lies Mongolia and the Gobi Desert. Southern China is hidden in the shadows of the giant Himalayan Mountains, whose foothills extend all the way to Chinese territory. The precipitation that this massif attracts provides most of the waters to the main Chinese rivers. The Yangtze's basin, extremely mountainous in the western part, is distinguished by numerous natural lakes [40].

The Tropic of Cancer traverses Taiwan and China's coast to the north of Hong Kong.

China's axis consists of two large rivers flowing from west to east and emptying into the Sea of China: the Huang He (Yellow River) in the north and Yangtze River in the south. The Huang He is 4,840 km long and flows through the plains in the northern flatlands, emptying into the Yellow Sea to the north of the Shandong Peninsula. The Yangtze first meanders through the massifs of southwest China then travels 6,380 km before emptying into the East China Sea.

---

[105] This following books provided the information base for this chapter: Charles K. Maisels, *Early Civilizations of the Old World*, London and New York, Routledge – Taylor and Francis Group 2001; David N. Keightley (ed.), *The Origins of Chinese Civilization*, Berkeley – Los Angeles – London, University of California Press 1983; Jakub Maršálek, *Sociální analýza pohřebišť pozdního neolitu* (cca 3000–2000 BC) na území provincie Shandong (Social analysis of late Neolithic burial remains (ca. 3000–2000 BC) of the Shandong Province), doctoral distertation, Charles University in Prague, Humanities Faculty, Institution of the Far East (department: The History and Culture of Asian and African Countries, adviser: Prof. PhDr. Oldřich Král), June 2003; Yang Yang et Zhao Guayan, *Culture de la Chine – L'archéologie*, Beijing: Editions en Langues étrangères 2003, as well as Norman Yoffee, *Myths of the Archaic State*, Cambridge, Cambridge University Press 2005.

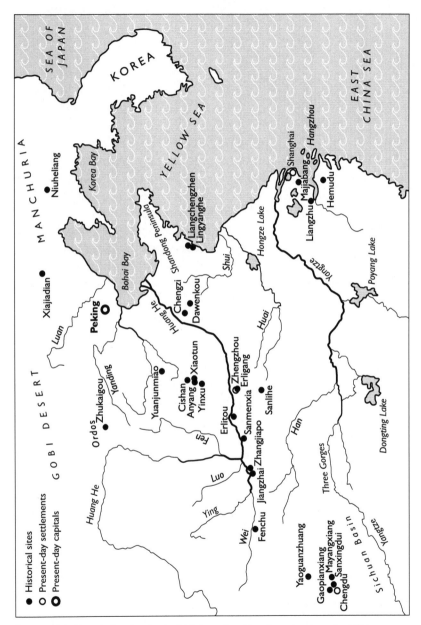

**Fig. 41** Main historical and archeological sites of prehistoric and early ancient China.

The geological foundation of northern China's plains consists of immense, wind-blown layers of loess. River and stream beds are often recessed in this loess, frequently bearing layers of fertile black soil. These beds are very susceptible to the erosion process, especially following ancient deforestation, to the effects of wind and to the summer monsoon rains.

There is an abundance of loess matter in the river water that often settles in the riverbeds, causing them to clog up and resulting in catastrophic floods and the unexpected redirection of river currents. In southern China, on the contrary, most of the soil comes from diluvium.

Northern China is characterized by an oceanic climate that mainly prevails in areas in close proximity to the Yellow Sea. The winters are mild here, while summers are not overly sweltering and rain falls frequently throughout the year. An inland climate prevails in the western part with a hot and damp summer (30–35 °C) and cold winter (around 0 °C). The rains here are not overly profuse, but it is enough for farmers to grow crops without artificial irrigation.

China features a uniquely remarkable biotope of vegetation from north to south, representing nearly all species of plants from a subarctic to a temperate and even subtropical zone. Its northern-most region consists of subarctic taiga, composed mainly of pine, hemlock, birch and poplar. Manchuria in northeast China represents a region of mixed and deciduous forests, while Mongolia to the northwest has steppe features, and we even find desert land toward the western border of China. The land's complexion south of the Huang He River is made up of deciduous trees, lakes, wetlands and low hill country. Steppe-forest land stretches out south of there. South China then surprises with damp subtropical evergreen forests. The zone of dense monsoon rainforests originally spread along the coast of the Sea of China and extended west to Myanmar (Burma), and even to northeast India. Yet China's geography also offers steppe, cold deserts and high mountain vegetation.

# PREHISTORIC BEGINNINGS:
## "MESOLITHIC-NEOLITHIC" – HUNTERS,
## GATHERERS AND FARMERS

Chinese archeologists discovered the first cultures of this type, dating back to the 6th millenium BC, at the lower part of the Yellow River (Huang He); the Cishan site in the Hebei province is the most renowned of these. In contrast to present-day climatic conditions, an examination of found animal bones tells us that a subtropical climate prevailed here in the 6$^{th}$ millenium BC. This undoubtedly facilitated the search for food by people that lived here at that time. They most likely moved in an environment of deciduous forests and swampy river valleys.

The people living here at that time were mainly hunters and gatherers (hares, moles, monkeys, badger, civet, leopards, sika deer, various other types of deer, muntjac, wild cattle, wild pigs, wild geese, carp, turtles and shellfish). The hunters here would frequently stalk deer in the shady forests.

We know that chestnuts, hazelnuts and hackberries were among the foods gathered. Farmers apparently focused on cultivating one kind of millet.

It appears that the people had tamed dogs and even domesticated pigs. They may have even begun the domestication of fowl – roosters, hens and chickens.

The clay here was used to make pottery baked at low temperatures and decorated with ornaments that were either impressed with a comb or string, or were painted. Handmade stone tools included sickle blades, grinders for plant food and long and thin diggers.

The remnants of settlement activities is represented here by a total of 80 pits of various shape, round and square, some of which are over 5-m deep. They were found to contain an abundant residue of cereals, consisting of one kind of millet. Apparently, this was already grown as a cultivated crop *(Setaria italica)* at this time.

Clay figurines of pigs also appeared in this period.

It was only after 5000 BC that Chinese history produced its first Neolithic culture complex, now called Yangshao (ca. 5000–3000 BC) with the bearers of this culture mainly occupying the area of the central part of the Yellow River.

Yangshao agriculture, namely the cultivation of the millet species *Setaria italica* and *Panicum miliaceum*, provided these people with basic subsistence.

Digging sticks, hoes and spades were used to cultivate the soil. The harvested cereal was kept in storage vessels made of pottery, and food was prepared using stone grinders.

Herdsmen raised dogs and pigs, and less frequently cattle, sheep and goats.

The Yangshao people also supplemented their diet with chestnuts, hazelnuts and hackberries. They carried on the older hunting traditions

**Fig. 42** Painted pottery of the Neolithic culture of Yangshao.

and dragged or carried home bandicoots, marmots, monkeys, badgers, raccoons, foxes, bears, wild pigs, ovibovines, deer, turtles, fish, clams and snails, leopards, wild horses, rhinoceroses and antelopes.

The culture produced handmade pottery that was painted before it dried and fired in temperatures around 1000 °C and higher. Finished products included bowls, dishes, pots and bottles. Geometric elements, animal figures and human faces were among the repertoire used as painted ornament [41].

Farmers here primarily used stone to create the working parts of hoes for cultivating fields.

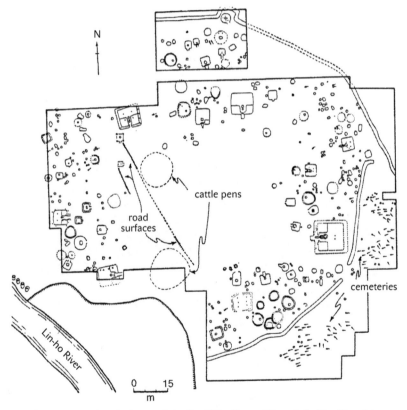

**Fig. 43** A map showing the layout of the Neolithic village of Jiangzhai of the Yangshao culture.

Primitive metal tools even appeared in later phases of Yangshao cultures.

The bearers of this culture complex usually chose loess terraces over riverbanks. As it seems that the bearers of the Yangshao culture complex practiced shifting cultivation, villages probably did not remain too long in one place. These villages were usually about 50,000–60,000 m² in size.

The Jiangzhai site in northeast China provides a nice example of a Chinese Neolithic village [42].

This site consists of approximately 100 dwellings accompanied by some 200 storage pits and enclosed by a moat and palisade. A common of about 4000 m² is situated in the middle of the village; cemeteries lie to the east and south beyond the village's barrier. Furnaces were concentrated in a special sector in the southwest. The square or round dwellings had sunken-featured foundations; their walls were made from an organic weave covered with clay, thatch was used for roofs and entrances faced the common. The village of Jiangzhai was composed of five residential groups, each with at least one larger building. This could be proof of five lineages, though the cemeteries had only three separate sectors. Chinese research estimates the size of the Neolithic villages to range from 5 to 100 houses with a size of 20–300 m². With five to six people per house, this would indicate the population of one village to be 200–3000 people, though 300–400 seems more likely.

An analysis of the burial grounds of Neolithic China has produced remarkable results. The Yuanjunmiao site in central China provided a total of 51 graves arranged in six rows oriented on a north-south axis. The entire cemetery was probably originally composed of an east and west half, and, based on the chronology of the material culture, it was deemed that the cemetery was gradually expanded from north to south and from east to west. Approximately two thirds of all graves were mass burials with 92% of the deceased buried in such graves. These graves usually contained a larger number of deceased – from two to twenty-five, though frequently more than four. The fact that the remains of the deceased show considerable manipulation and that, consequently, the cemetery represents an artificially constructed social work and not an objective source for interpreting the society's history is supported by the fact that these were mainly secondary burials, i.e. bodies that were already decayed were laid to rest here.

Researchers have presented the view that the cemetery's duality could mean that there was a binary social structure – the division into two moieties – and that graves with mass burials could indicate lineage. The cemetery did not provide evidence that could be interpreted in the sense of social stratification, but it did show differences in the prestige of individuals reflected in the number of funerary objects, especially pottery. Burial of women, often with as many or even more funer-ary objects than their male counterparts – with beads, hairpins and knives – offer extraordinary testimony. The separate burial of two girls, laid to rest in a grave with a specially prepared bottom made of red clay, was also documented. Grave M420 provided a final resting place of a mother and her two daughters and contains the largest quantity of funerary objects of the entire culture.

This could possibly be interpreted in the sense of the matrilineality of the Chinese Neolithic.

The deceased who did not reach adulthood were often buried outside the burial ground in, for instance, containers in graves under residential buildings.

In addition to the Yangshao culture complex, the Dawenkou cul-ture, also Neolithic, existed in the present-day coastal province of Shandong. The bearers of this culture subsisted on agriculture, namely by growing millet. The raising of livestock, mainly pigs, was supple-mented by hunting (deer, hares) and fishing.

Both slow- and fast-turning potter's wheels for clay work had already appeared here in isolated cases. Potters made legged bowls, three-legged pots, kettles on three saccate legs, cups and storage vessels. Experts divide the pottery of the late Dawenkou culture into black, grey, red and white. In the culture's later phase, cups on a *bei* leg, "wine glasses," were being used, apparently for ceremonial feasts.

Jade warrants attention as one of the lithic raw materials worked with by the craftsmen of the age. They made small elongated ornaments of a triangle-like cut, perhaps worn on the head, as well as earrings, rings, bracelets, pins, spikes, pendants and beads. Weapons were also made from this material (axes). Turquoise was used as a decorative material for making beads, for instance, but also for the marquetry of ivory objects. Other types of stone were used to make tools (discs, whorls) or ornaments (bracelets).

The industrious hands of craftsmen worked with another remarkable material, ivory, which they used to make unique cylindrical objects of a conical shape and of unknown function (tubes), knives, sickles and combs, or traded in its unprocessed state. Bones and antlers were also used to make various spikes and throngs or for special implements.

Objects made of organic matter were evidently at one time a quite common component of prehistoric Chinese cultures. Archeological finds in burial grounds include the remnants of drums made of alligator leather, most likely used for ritual purposes.

Dawenkou culture sites are usually located in the hilly and terraced areas beneath mountains in Shandong and along the coast. Smaller square and round sunken-featured dwellings have been found there.

Most of the information on the culture comes from their burial grounds. The deceased were buried in rectangular graves in a supine position on an east-west axis, usually with their heads pointing east, though sometimes to the north. In some cases, the graves are grouped in north-south oriented rows (Jianxin, Sanlihe).

The burial grounds are frequently found in the proximity of settlements and sometimes both locations converge and overlap. In such cases, it seems that the graves sunk into remains of residential buildings are more recent. This would indicate that the Dawenkou people buried their dead in areas of abandoned settlements.

The deceased were well equipped to enter the next world, taking with them pottery, stone tools, weapons (axes and adzes), implements (whorls) and ornaments made from bone, stone and ivory. An abundance of pig mandibles was also found.

The "inner coffins" first appeared in graves in the middle phase of the Dawenkou culture. These were actually burial tombs made of wooden logs with mutually overlapping ends and supporting a flat roof. The entire structure could also be doubled. These structures were probably already at this time linked to the burial of individuals with significant social status. History has shown that this attention paid to a final resting place is emblematic of an elevated social position.

The number of "wine glasses" (*bei*) found in a grave can be considered a barometer of social prestige; sometimes the deceased were buried with only one, elsewhere 35 of these luxurious vessels were found buried with an elite member of society. Another grave of an important figure contained 38 bottles (*ping*) (Dawenkou, grave M10). The occurrence of large storage vessels, whose contents were intended to accompany the deceased elite to the next world, is indicative of social position.

Upper-class male and female graves – though others as well – contained weapons and jade ornaments. Axes accompanied men more frequently than women on their final journey. Ivory objects were also found in graves; these were found in relative abundance at the Dawenkou site, thus clearly emphasizing their exceptional importance. Conical cylinders made of ivory often mark the graves of men.

Cooking, eating and storage vessels were accompanied by pig mandibles (sometimes even whole skulls) in graves of the Dawenkou culture. This is most likely evidence of funerary feasts or the "viaticum," provisions for the journey to the next world (up to 35 objects – Lingyanghe, grave 79M17). We find by the hands of the deceased unusual "hooked objects" made of handles cut from bone or horns with two deer canines with tips pointing up and away from the handles inserted in them. It is unknown what these were used for. Turtle shells, buried along with some of the deceased, sometimes contained bone needles, small spikes or pebbles and can therefore perhaps be considered musical instruments or ritual props.

The fact that the remains of subadults did not appear in some of the culture's burial grounds is noteworthy. These burial grounds do not therefore represent a completely objective source for interpreting the society's history, but show traces of a deliberate selection of the deceased buried here.

The bearers of the Dawenkou culture seem to be the ones who created a system of symbols that would later become the first Chinese script. We still do not know how to interpret the engraved symbols that appear on large storage vessels in particular. The bearers of this culture also devoted considerable attention to ceremonial communal feasts.

The prevalence of tableware sets found in graves attest to the codification of a dining etiquette and the classification of a socially important space for feasts. This consists of a pot for preparing food (*ding*), most likely a legged serving dish (*dou*), storage vessels *hu* and a "wine glass" (*bei*).

In the wealthy M10 grave from Dawenkou, a deceased woman is adorned with a necklace made from 19 turquoise beads, which is wholly unique within this culture. The question lingers whether this ornament made exclusively of a single kind of stone indicates the prestige value of turquoise or whether it points to something else. Could it refer to the connection between a deceased woman's being and a natural sphere, symbolically expressed and represented by turquoise? Were the color, appearance, "mythical coordinates" of the mineral or its rarity important here?

We thus begin to see the potential of further development toward the society's division into groups occupying different positions and orientations within society. Up to this point, the society seems to have been distinctly homogenous with the individual elite members vying for a superior position through ostentatious public displays in socially relevant spheres of activities. This should thus be interpreted more as a ranked society than a stratified one.

## The Neolithic Period in southern China

Let us now focus on the Neolithic Period of southern China. The Majiabang culture near the mouth of the Yangtze River, mainly to the south of Shanghai, played a significant role in the historical development here. The bearers of this culture grew rice and baked clay pottery at low temperatures. Another distinct southern culture complex, the Liangzhu culture, arose at the tail end of the Majiabang after 3000 BC. It is should be pointed out here that the cultures of this group cultivated, apparently with respect to their coastal position, relations with the Dawenkou culture in northern China.

Craftsmen of the Liangzhu culture produced a delicate black pottery as well as the first silk ever known in China.

The bearers of the Liangzhu culture markedly developed the production of ritual objects made of jade. It is here that we become
acquainted with the jade objects called *bi* and *cong*, disk-like and cylindrical in shape. History tells us that the *bi* discs were used to worship
the heavens, while the *cong*, often square-edged and profusely decorated, channeled the worshipper's veneration toward the earth. Another
surprise from this culture consists of the first *taotie* masks in the form
of a face that might be that of a person or animal. In one case, a *cong*
cylinder even bears the picture of a creature that beats two drums tied
around his waste and seems to be wearing a large *taotie* mask.

These people often buried the deceased under mounds accompanied
by jade ritual objects and burned sacrifices. In some cases the dead were
buried in square ceremonial terraces on the tops of hills.

Portentous and obviously emblematic weapons point to distinct
social differentiation in the Liangzhu. The handles of jade axes from
the culture's graves, sometimes made of ivory, bore varnished and/or
jade decorations and usually had a jade terminal. Artists were able to
carve in them impressive decorations that were visible when the axe
was carried in an upright position. The rulers of the ancient Chinese
states may have adopted the axe's emblematic function from there.

Another remarkable historical phenomenon of south China is the Hemudu site, which is also south of Shanghai and not far from the coast. This
site is about 40,000 m², of which 2,630 m² has been excavated. Four archeological layers have been discovered here, of which the two lower layers
belong to the Hemudu culture (the earlier dates to ca. 5000–4600 BC,
the more recent to 4300–3400 BC), while both of the upper layers
(ca. 3900–3700 and 3400 BC) belong to the Majiabang culture.

The Hemudu culture's subsistence was rice, which was found in
great quantities at the saturated site, including rice kernels, hulls,
straws and leaves. Farmers used hardwood digging sticks and hoes
with blades usually made from cattle shoulder bones. The people
supplemented their subsistence by hunting (elephants, rhinoceros and
monkeys, among other things) and by gathering edible wild plants.
The composition of the vegetation found at the site attests to a warmer
climate than today and the presence of dense forests.

The materials that the people of Hemudu made use of included clay for pottery (dishes, trays, pots and kettles), often lavishly artistically rendered and decorated with the imprints of cords and with engraved ornamental, plant and figural motifs. Jade objects were also found here, but bone was the most common raw material for making things of everyday use. Arrowheads, whistles, chisels, spikes and needles were all made from it. Ropes, strings and even thread were made from straw and other vegetable matter, as were woven boxes and containers.

The oldest layer of the Hemudu settlement provided proof of dwellings built on posts. One such structure was 23 × 7 m in size and featured a 1.3 m deep entrance hall. The wooden structures of the dwellings reveal quality carpentry, including mortise and tenon joints. Reed mats covered the floors here. Some of these larger structures seem to be "community houses" similar to those still used by people of the Indonesian islands.

In contrast to the fourth, deepest layer, the third Hemudu layer underwent definite changes in its inventory. Along with painted pottery, we also find here a wooden loom. Though butterfly-shaped ivory objects were found here, the material culture remained the same, except for a few minor exceptions (lower temperature for firing pottery, the appearance of a portable stove made of fired clay). The same can be said of the second layer.

A more substantial transformation can be seen in the first, highest layer.

In this period, expert potters fired the pottery at a temperature around 1000 °C and, in some cases, may have already been making it on potter's wheels. Decorative cord imprints again appear. The women here made whorls, flywheels set on the spindle and used in spinning thread from a tow.

Stone tools used in this period included axes, whose middle parts were drilled through, and rectangular adzes, carpenter's tools with the blade at a right angle to the handle. Objects made from jade included *huang*, square plates with holes in the middle, and semi-annular *jue*.

For the first time there appear only post holes for the insertion of standing structures instead of wooden buildings. Excavators also found 12 burials in supine position here.

Domesticated animals raised by the people included dogs and pigs and perhaps even water buffalo. Finds from Hemudu explicitly testify to the exploitation of a large number of uncultivated biotopes, i.e. the wilderness from the mountain forests to the riverine wetlands (the remains of carp, catfish and turtles) and influent streams (pelicans, herons, ducks). The same applies to pollen grains that prove the presence of different species of oak trees, wild cinnamon, plum trees and walnut trees, as well as aquatic plants and herbs found on land. The people here most likely also ate gourds, acorns and water chestnuts.

# THE CHALCOLITHIC PERIOD
## (WE ARE NO LONGER ALL EQUAL)

The Longshan culture, presently broken down into seven regional variations, gradually developed between 2600 and 1900 BC.

Animals reared during this epoch included pigs and horses.

It is predominantly in the use of clay that we see a difference from the Yangshao period's work with natural materials. Master potters of the Longshan culture, probably already professionals in their craft, often used potter's wheels and fired their clay at high temperatures to shades of grey or black. This pottery sometimes had distinctly thin walls and generally featured engravings, attachments or protrusions. Pottery made here included legged bowls, cups with handles, goblets, typical three-legged kettles, pots and pitchers, as well as storage vessels. This pottery can be classified as black, grey and white. We also find here cups on a *bei* leg, "wine glasses," apparently used for ceremonial feasts. Everyday household objects were made from clay (whorls used for spinning thread).

Jade and turquoise, perhaps of western origin, are among the noteworthy lithic raw materials used by Longshan craftsmen. Jade was used to make ornaments (beads, bracelets, pins with *Taotie* protective masks, burial M202, Xizhufeng), weapons, (axes) and ritual objects. A tablet depicting a human face with protruding fangs was found at an unknown Chinese site, most likely belonging to the Shandong strain of the Longshan culture. Turquoise was used to make ornaments (pendants), but was also placed in graves in its raw form (Xizhufeng graves M202, M203). Stone axes were no longer found among the everyday objects buried with the dead. Less rare types of stone were used to make stones (chisels), some kinds of household implements (e.g. whorls – aids for spinning thread) and weapons (arrowheads). A stone axe with a *Taotie* mask motif made on both sides comes from the Liangchengzhen site.

Bone or shell was used to make everyday tools and implements (e.g. knives, arrowheads, spearheads, whistles?)

In contrast to earlier periods, bronze castings were widely used in the Longshan culture and all kinds of bronze necessities were made. Parts of belts, mirrors and weapons were cast from bronze (later this would also include formidable axes and halberds), as were some types of tools (e.g. knives), parts of harnesses and even of musical instruments. Research has generally focused on ritual bronze vessels that experts divide into the following categories:

1. vessels for preparing and cooking the food offering, especially three-legged vessels and four-legged rectangular *ding* vessels;
2. vessels for storing the food offering *(gui yu)*;
3. vessels for warming up a wine-like fermented millet drink *(jia ajue)*, both three-legged with pointed legs, also used for libations. Another such vessel is the *he*, an oblate teapot standing on three or four cylindrical legs. This naturally was not a teapot *per se*, but was used for mixing wine with water.
4. vessels for storing wine: *zun* and *guang,* among all bronze artifacts these were most frequently made as sculptures, often in the form of animals;
5. vessels for tasting wine, *gu* or *zhi,* round or square in profile;
6. vessels for ritual washing, all broad and shallow with rounded bottoms and no handles.

It should be noted that the first objects made from gold and silver in China date back to this period.

Remnants of drums made of alligator leather found in the graves of this culture are, among other things, proof of their work with organic materials.

The finding that Chinese farmers and transporters were apparently not familiar with the wheel until the late Shang period is somewhat surprising. Evidence of the wheel's use does not appear until the later stages of the Shang Dynasty.[106]

---

[106] Jakub Maršálek, Sociální analýza pohřebišť pozdního neolitu (cca 3000–2000 př. n. l.) na území provincie Shandong (A social analysis of late Neolithic burial grounds in the Shandong province (ca. 3000–2000 BC), doctoral dissertation, Charles University in Prague, Humanities Faculty, Institute of the Far East (specialization: The History and

The primary difference between the Yangshao and Longshan cultures, with regard to civil engineering, is that the Longshan culture complex first used structures that were not sunken into the ground, but, instead, elevated on terraces made from packed clay. The culture's social centers – the early cities – which did not exceed 20 hectares in size, also became foci with a wide range of crafts. They were, however, already surrounded by walls of clay packed into frames, and larger surface buildings were also there.

Based on the size of the residential area, a four-level hierarchy of Longshan settlements can be distinguished: the 1$^{st}$ settlement with an area of 240 hectares, the 2$^{nd}$ with 70–230 hectares, the 3$^{rd}$ with 20–60 hectares and the 4$^{th}$ with 20 hectares. Already in the culture's final phase we find here extensive residential agglomerations surrounded by clusters of smaller sites.[107]

The fracturing of society into groups positioned differently on the social ladder is evident in burials.

The culture's burial areas generally appear to be less structurally aligned than burial grounds of the preceding period. The evenly arranged rows of graves prevalent in the Neolithic Age completely disappear. Here we encounter burials directly in residential areas – especially those of youths and children. Although the deceased were still predominantly buried in a supine position on an east-west axis and with their heads pointing east, a relatively large number of deviations were found (head pointing west, south-east orientation with head pointing north – Yaoguanzhuang). Intensive use was made of burial grounds and the superposition of graves (i.e. more recent burials disrupting older ones) was a common occurrence. The relationship between burial grounds and the settlements is more obscure than previously in the Neolithic period. Once again, however, we cannot rule out that the deceased were buried in abandoned settlements, and sometimes settlements were even built on ancient burial grounds.

Culture of Asia and Africa, supervisor: Prof. Oldřich Král, PhD.), June 2003, p. 82, note: 274.

[107] Norman Yoffee, Myths of the Archaic State, Cambridge, Cambridge University Press 2005, p. 50.

Funerary objects consisted mainly of pottery; weapons, tools and ornaments for the most part disappear.

In the case of high-profile burials, the bearers of the Longshan culture adopted from the Dawenkou culture of the Neolithic Period the custom of building "internal and external coffins" (actually timber lined burial tombs). The entire structure can even be repeated several (up to three) times with the tombs inserted into one another.

"Wine glasses" were found here too as funerary objects. Although this type was found in the graves of the deceased that had not been overly wealthy, more technically demanding variations were linked to large and opulent graves. The number of individual glasses found in each grave (up to six) did, however, markedly drop with one "wine glass" per deceased being the most frequent occurrence. Overall, the number of graves with these "wine glasses" also dropped and their imitations in cruder pottery disappeared. A change is apparent in the storage vessels found in graves as well: many of them completely disappear from the Longshan burial grounds and those that remain are of smaller types, including oval vessels with four horizontal handles, a cylindrical neck and cover *(lei)*.

The funerary objects also possess fewer jade components at this point and consist mainly of weapons (especially axes) and not of ornaments, as was previously the case.

One of the jades probably bears the depiction of a *Taotie* protective mask (Xizhufeng, grave M202). Perhaps the most important thing to note here is that axes, and especially golden or white axes, were a royal emblem during the Western Zhou period. The king would wield it in his left hand before a battle as he gave a speech to the assembled troops; then, after the battle, he would use it to decapitate the defeated enemy king.[108]

---

[108] Jakub Maršálek, Sociální analýza pohřebišť pozdního neolitu (cca 3000–2000 př. n. l.) na území provincie Shandong (A social analysis of late Neolithic burial grounds in the Shandong province (ca. 3000–2000 BC), doctoral dissertation, Charles University in Prague, Faculty of Arts, Institute of the Far East (specialization: The History and Culture of Asia and Africa, supervisor: Prof. Oldřich Král, PhD.), June 2003, p. 67, *(Shujing,* Book of Documents).

Along with other funerary objects, grave M202 in Xizhufeng) contained alligator scales, most likely the remnants of drums made of
stretched alligator leather for ritual purposes. They were found along
with a whetstone, a bone pipe and a "wine glass" in a 1 × 0.35 m wooden
box painted black and red and positioned between the inner and first
of the two external timber linings of the grave.

The lower jawbones of pigs, most likely attesting to funeral feasts or
supplies provided to the deceased for their journey to the next world in
the prior Neolithic Period, were apparently connected to the graves of
the elite in the Longshan milieu (up to 32 lower jawbones, Yinjiacheng,
grave M138). They appear there repeatedly in multiples of four.

The individual burials at the burial site in Chengzi containing a
total of 87 graves could be divided into four different groups according to the number and quality of funerary objects. The fact that the
entire burial site is divided into three sectors, of which each contains
burials of all four social levels, is of particular importance. This can
probably be interpreted as a common burial site of three lineages that
had already been internally stratified [43].

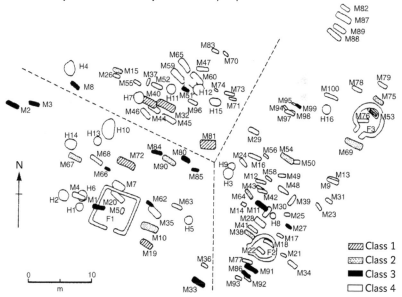

**Fig. 44** A map showing the layout of the Chengzi burial site of the Longshan culture.

Arrowheads found in the most opulent and largest tombs of the Longshan culture and the fact they were most likely placed there (in larger numbers, in rows and between the internal and external timber-lined tombs) seem to indicate an emblematic role. They could symbolize a high social position: writings of the 1st millenium BC testify to the role of the bow and arrow as a male attribute and symbol of public authority. During the Western Zhou period, the king empowered his representative by handing his bundle of arrows to him. Royal gifts of bows and arrows to aristocrats are recorded by inscriptions in bronze vessels from the same period.

The inscription describes the rewarding of Duke Wen of Jin (636–628 BC), following the victory over the state of Chu in the Battle of Chengpu in 632 BC, with a red bow and a hundred red arrows and a black bow with a hundred black arrows.[109] Since the image of the arrow also forms part of the symbol *hou* = "duke, liege lord" also found in the earlier late Shang period, the conclusion can be drawn that the arrow already symbolized at that time the idea of "commanding authority, of superiority, of *potestatis imperii.*"

The drop in the number of funerary objects, their limitation to pottery vessels and exclusive attributes of elite burials – timber-lined burial tombs, *bei* "wine glasses", pig jawbones – points to changes in comparison with the Neolithic situation. Given that a certain type of vessel was consistently found in pairs or fours, or that pig jawbones were found in fours or in multiples of four, we can assume that certain customs regarding the numerical ratios of funerary objects were set.

These ratios seem to indicate an abandonment of a ranked society and the rise of a stratified society, in which social classes had been carved out and the vying for status completed. From this moment there is little doubt about who made up the society's elite: those who had

---

[109] Jakub Maršálek, Sociální analýza pohřebišť pozdního neolitu (cca 3000–2000 př. n. l.) na území provincie Shandong (A social analysis of late Neolithic burial grounds in the Shandong province (ca. 3000-2000 BC)), doctoral dissertation, Charles University in Prague, Humanities Faculty, Institute of the Far East (specialization: The History and Culture of Asia and Africa, supervisor: Prof. Oldřich Král, PhD.), June 2003, p. 80, (the Chronicle of Zuo, 28th year of the Duke Xi).

already acquired a position generally acknowledged and clearly and qualitatively expressed by "tags" in funerary objects.

Should we interpret the drop in the number of jade objects found in the graves here (though the preserved samples found are far more impressive in their craftsmanship) in the sense that rare materials no longer ended with the dead at burial sites, but were instead used ostentatiously at public rituals (or were bestowed to the cult) by the elite of that period to demonstrate their prestige, importance and wealth?

Archeologists have held the view that, in matters of the social arrangement of this period, society had already created lineages that together formed a patulous, complex and hierarchically structured architecture of "conical clans." In these clans the individual lineages mutually assumed positions according to their proximity to the lineage of the clan's founder: the nearer one was to the founder's descendents, the higher the level of social prestige. The central position in the conical clan was assumed by the founder's lineage for ritualistic reasons. This lineage was thought to be closest to the spirits of the clan's ancestors and, therefore, the only ones in the clan to hold a sufficiently strong cult position to activate nature's fertile powers for the benefit of all other members of this social configuration. Owing to their access to the spiritual world's powers, it was actually the clan's ancestors who performed such rituals. The creation of the state then culminated with the representatives of these central lineages, together forming groups linked by political and contractual and even family (e.g. through marriages) bonds. Such groups then acquired public power for the benefit of all members of the original clan, thus becoming a political community. The clan members would then pay for the services of the ruling elite through farm work and military service. One of the explanations of the origin of the symbol *zu*, used for naming the lineage and consisting of the image of an arrowhead under a standard, even assumes that this is a social group constituting the basic unit of armed forces and, therefore, to a certain extent an artificially constructed group.[110] This explanation fits well with the

---

[110] Jakub Maršálek, Sociální analýza pohřebišť pozdního neolitu (cca 3000–2000 př. n. l.) na území provincie Shandong (A social analysis of late Neolithic burial grounds in the Shandong province (3000–2000 BC)), doctoral dissertation, Charles University in Prague,

aforementioned symbolism of the arrow as a symbol of supremacy, of commanding authority and *potestatis imperii*.

Indeed, the renowned Chinese custom of soothsaying using flat bones, most often cattle shoulder bones or turtle shells, dates back to the Longshan cultural complex. The oracle would heat a copper spike in a fire and apply it to the surface of the bone. Cracks would then form on the bone's surface that the expert would interpret. Other innovations of the age include the introduction of the *Taotie*, an ornamental motif of a human or animal mask. This would later be used as a protective and beneficial symbol.

The Longshan cultural complex evidently influenced surrounding groups of the population. Although the Zhukaigou steppe culture in Chinese south Mongolia (on the northern border of present-day China) mainly raised cattle, their material culture reveals a Longshan influence, including the use of smoothed oracle bones. Today we speak of "interacting spheres of culture," the mutual permeation of several cultures, when referring to the Longshan sphere.[111]

## China's Northern Regions during the Chalcolithic Period

The Hongshan culture thrived during the Chalcolithic Period, perhaps as early as the 4th millenium BC, in northeast China to the north of the Bohai Bay northeast of Beijing and in the Liao River basin in lower Manchuria. Use of a heavy plow was already begun in this period. The craftsmen here were skilled in working with clay, jade and bronze.

A temple of some of the local gods with an altar and several rooms was even found at the Niuheliang site in the middle of burial grounds with graves possessing a varied number of funerary objects. This is a remarkable site that deserves more detailed commentary. The entire

---

Humanities Faculty, Institute of the Far East (specialization: The History and Culture of Asia and Africa, supervisor: Prof. Oldřich Král, PhD.), June 2003, p. 80–81.

[111] Norman Yoffee, Myths of the Archaic State, Cambridge, Cambridge University Press 2005, p. 230.

group of sixteen cult buildings is located at the summit, on the slopes and at the foot of the Nulu'erhu massif, and is roughly ten kilometers long and five kilometers wide. The sunken-featured temple of the fertility goddess (?) apparently represents the central place of worship. Totaling 75 m² in area, this building was originally constructed from clay and wood in the form of an elongated rectangular space, whose one side was adjoined by a partition, and with a trilobate-structured end. The temple, situated on an extended north-south axis, is over 25 meters long and 2–9 meters wide. The building's ruins revealed fragments of six terracotta sculptures of the goddess, of which one was larger than life-size, while the others were roughly the size of humans. Terracotta figurines of dragon heads and bird claws were also found here. The interior may have even originally featured a fresco.

The temple is situated atop a mountain ridge; a circular "sacrificial altar" built from stone and surrounded by a wall is apparently part of it.

The graves here, situated on the northern and southern mountain slopes under the temple, are mound-like in shape with a large burial containing an abundance of funerary objects surrounded by poorer and even secondary burials. The survivors built for the deceased elite a total of five square-shaped tombs of stone and enclosed them in a wall. The deceased received a number of funerary objects for their journey to the next world, including jade ornaments and weapons and painted pottery vessels. The central tomb no. 1 provided an abundance of rare finds of jade, ornaments and rings, one of which bears the depiction of a mythical creature with a pig's head and dragon's body, while others feature dragon-head images.

The bearers of the Hongshan culture maintained contact with hunter-farmer strains of the Fuhe culture on the northern border.

The Lower Xiajiadian culture, situated along the northern border of China stretching from the sea to the border with Mongolia, became the Hongshan culture's successor in 2500–2000 BC. The population here sustained itself through the cultivation of various species of millet. Master craftsmen were already skilled in working with bronze.

The bearers of the culture lived in villages consisting of sunken-featured adobe houses clustered closely together. Most of the houses were round, though the larger houses could also be rectangular and the village was protected by stone or clay walls surrounding it. There is evidence that these walls were already made using the process by which clay was packed into frames. Graves of the more affluent can also already be distinguished here at burial sites, and the battle axe, appearing only at large male burials, is clearly emblematic of a warrior.

Oracle bones, usually with holes drilled through, appear here, and the culture's art is represented by discoveries of *taotie* masks.

It seems that the Chalcolithic culture complexes presented at this time a very diverse mosaic of variously organized social bodies that maintained vigorous contact, through which tangible and intangible goods were mutually exchanged. Slowly but surely a unifying base was formed that the first Chinese state would later be built upon.

# THE BEGINNINGS OF THE STATE

## The Traditional Interpretation of Chinese History

Chinese tradition interprets the dawn of the country's history in mythologized form as a succession of three royal dynasties: the Xia, Shang (or Jin) and Zhou. The Shang leader Cheng Tang dealt the Xia state (traditionally dated as 2205–1760 BC) a fatal blow in defeating its last ruler, King Jie. The Shangs then dominated (1760–1122), until they themselves succumbed to the surge of the Zhou dynasty. The Zhou representatives would rule in China until 770 BC, from which point only the eastern part of the country would be under their reign (Eastern Zhou, 770–256 BC). During the ensuing Spring and Autumn period (770–476 BC) the central government disintegrated and a number of conflicts broke out between the individual regional powers (the Warring States period 475–221 BC). It was the First Sovereign emperor (Qin Shi Huangdi) who finally put an end to these endemic civil wars, completely removing the then merely symbolic rule of the Zhou Dynasty and uniting the entire land under his rule (221–210 BC).

The fact that traditional Chinese historiography describes quite accurately the creation of the state body is noteworthy. According to this version, the Great Yu, the first lord of Xia, summoned all other Lords of the nation and got them to agree that, after his death, Yu's first born son would assume the highest office. He managed to do so despite the disagreement of the previously designated successor, and thus the dynastic principle of rule was established. From this moment forth, instead of the former title of lord *(hou)*, the highest Chinese political figure was now called king *(wang)*.

We must, however, proceed carefully with the information derived from ancient Chinese history. Modern research has reached the conclusion that the oldest Chinese historical records currently known, the

"Bamboo Annals," were written only later during the Eastern Zhou period, and that for the oldest period they reveal discrepancies with authentic historical records of that period.


## The Erlitou Culture

While doubt has never been cast on the historical existence of the Shang and Zhou dynasties, experts have been somewhat perplexed in assessing the credibility of the interpretation of the first Chinese state and its Xia Dynasty rulers. Attention has been repeatedly drawn in this regard to the Erlitou site on the upper part of the Yellow River (Huang He). This site is 3 km² in size and the population is estimated to have been 18,000–30,000.[112]

The site itself provides proof of a five-phase settlement. Artificial terraces made from packed clay appeared in the second level, while extensive buildings and tombs were found in the third level. The fourth level yielded evidence of numerous supply pits. Radiocarbon dating tells us that the site was settled at approximately 2100–1800 BC.

The foundations of at least two palace buildings were found in the third layer. The first of these was built on a terrace with an area of 108 × 100 m. The 1–2 m high terrace was filled with layers of clay that were roughly 4.5 cm thick and along whose circumference ran a 45–60 cm thick clay wall. A rectangular 36 × 25 m area was created on the northern end of the terrace and excavators documented on its surface a group of post holes that formed the outline of a large hall measuring 30.4 × 11.4 m. This hall was evidently constructed by pre-historic builders using organic wickerwork suspended from the beam structure and covered with a saddle roof. This district was entered from the south through a pillared gate.

A smaller but better preserved second palace was located approximately 150 m northeast of the first. The foundation terrace measured 73 × 58 m and it also contained a hall in the northern part of its central section. With an area of 33 m² the hall consisted of three main parts

---

[112] Norman Yoffee, Myths of the Archaic State, Cambridge, Cambridge University Press 2005, p. 43, Table 3.1.

and its outer walls were surrounded by verandas. To the north of the hall was a large in-ground tomb with its upper pit 5 × 4 m in size; the prehistoric gravediggers dug a smaller burial pit in the bottom of this part and, after placing the funerary objects in the grave, carefully filled everything in with packed layers of clay. Other burials here were, however, completely void of funerary objects. This district was entered through a pillared gate from the south.

Residential homes were clustered around both palaces. Some of these houses were sunken-featured, others built on ground level. In the 3rd and 4th layers we find what are probably many ash-filled waste pits, pottery kilns and even crucibles for bronze melting.

As far as basic subsistence activities are concerned, as previously mentioned no important innovations were introduced here in comparison with the prior period.

Skilful potters supplied the population with Erlitou pottery of grey or dark material that was mixed with sand and handmade or wheel spun.

The basic raw materials used still included stone, bone and shell, from which farmers made hoes and sickles. Other tools and weapons – axes, adzes, chisels and arrowheads – were also made from stone. Ritual objects, however, were made from jade.

For the time being, bronze was only used to make a very small number of tools; a bronze knife, a bodkin, chisel and an adze made more from copper than from alloy (98% copper, 1% tin) were found here, as were arrowheads, fishhooks and small discs of an unknown purpose from the new material. Bronze was mainly used to make ritual vessels, weapons and musical instruments. Bronzes from the Erlitou period are still considered the oldest objects of this type found in China.[113]

Some of the deceased in the Erlitou period were buried in varnished coffins. They were buried with numerous valuables to accompany them to the next world – both bronze and jade objects. It seems that jade commanded particular respect here, since jade objects were always placed inside the coffin, while other artifacts, even those with the same

---

[113] For details on bronzes from Erlitou in a cultural context see Sarah Allan, Erlitou and the Formation of Chinese Civilization: Towards a New Paradigm, The Journal of Asian Studies 66/2, 2007, pp. 461–496.

functions as the jade ones (such as weapons) were found outside the coffin.

An important find at the site consisted of a large number of oracle bones – especially the shoulder bones of pigs, sheep and cattle – though these still did not have inscriptions. Temples were also found here in which tablets, bearing the names of the ancestors of the ruling lineages, were possibly stored. Sacred districts, enclosed by walls, were also discovered.

## In the cities and peripheral areas of the first state

In most cases, Chinese cities played the role of social and military centers, mainly performing tasks posed by state administration. Cities therefore very much resembled each other and possessed an almost obligatory, "model" appearance. The rectangular layout featured a fortification of clay walls pressed into frames *(hangtu)*. The walls entered through gates with the main gate usually the southern one. The technique of packing clay into wooden frames was also used for the residences of the Chinese elite built on raised terraces.[114] Members of a single lineage or clan generally dwelled within a single city, thus creating an organism bound primarily by factors of kinship.

The results of new research on the Sanxingdui site, 40 km northwest of Chengdu, the capital of China's Sichuan province, provide a quite explicit example of the urbanism of China's earliest cities at the dawn of ancient history.

The site covers a total area of 17 km². The city's development took place over four phases, of which the first (2700–2000 BC) falls under the Longshan culture of the Chalcolithic period. Researchers date the site's second and third phases roughly to 1700–1500 BC. The city centers were already in place at that time with the city walls enclosing buildings, sunken-featured structures and tombs. The construction of the city walls, delineating a rectangular plot with a total area of 2.6 km² and positioned adjacent to the river bank, began during the

---

[114] Charles K. Maisels, Early Civilizations of the Old World, London and New York, Routledge – Taylor and Francis Group 2001, p. 222.

site's second developmental phase, sometime after 1700 BC. Urban life dissipated at the end of the fourth developmental phase here (ca. 1500–1000 BC) sometime around 1000 BC. In its development, the site thus depicts the fate of China on the path from prehistory to the historical period of rule by the first three Chinese royal dynasties.

We know of no metal-made objects that date back to the site's first two phases; mainly clay pottery decorated with string imprints was found here.

Excavations revealed at the site the foundations of 18 houses, three ash pits, two places of sacrifice (?) and four tombs, in which, unfortunately, neither the remains of the dead nor funerary objects were preserved.

Pottery fragments, objects of jade, gold, stone and bronze, as well as cowry shells, were found in the sunken-featured buildings of Sanxingdui. There were also over 60 elephant tusks and over 3 m³ of burnt and broken animal bones. The conclusion can be drawn from this that these sunken-featured buildings served a still unknown ritual purpose.

One of these pits "with treasures" (pit I – the "place of sacrifice") is 1.64 m (depth) × 3.48 m (width) × 4.64 m (length) in size. They were filled with layers of soil and over 300 handmade artifacts were found here. The middle layer of this fill contained a substantial number of bones that had been burnt and broken before being deposited there, perhaps of animals that were burned in sacrifice. A number of jade ritual objects were found at the bottom of the pit, including a group of "scepters," as well as ritual bronze objects, semblances of human heads and masks made of bronze and a few pottery vessels. Some of the bronze objects feature a gold-leaf overlay. The pit most likely dates back to the very end of the site's development (13th century BC).

The second place of sacrifice (pit II) possesses very similar dimensions: 1.68 m (deep) × 2.3 m (wide) × 5.3 m (long). Over 600 artifacts of bronze, gold, jade, ivory, stone and pottery were unearthed here. The pit's fill had a yellowish soil and finds were made in three layers. The highest level contained over 60 elephant tusks. Excavators found massive bronze objects in the middle layer: the rendering of a standing human figure, depictions of human heads, a mask, three depictions of a tree and ritual vessels. Finally, at the bottom of this place of sacrifice, jade and stone tools were found, as were jade blades and discs, small animal masks, bronze figures of birds and animals and even seashells.

Renderings of trees made from bronze warrant special attention here. Following their reconstruction they reached heights of 1 m, 2 m and 4.2 m and were thus monumental sculptures. Each tree has nine branches with nine pieces of fruit, leaves and with nine figures of birds sitting on them. The birds were made to resemble toucans with large arched beaks, feeding on the fruit, and wholly unlike the eagle heads that were also found here. Human figures kneel around the trunk of the largest tree. This could very well have something to do with the image of the "tree of life."

The two pits contained over 40 renderings of human heads, some of which were decorated with gold-wrought plating. They featured different types of hairstyles, including braids and even headdresses. The large-eyed faces were each made to be very unique: sometimes

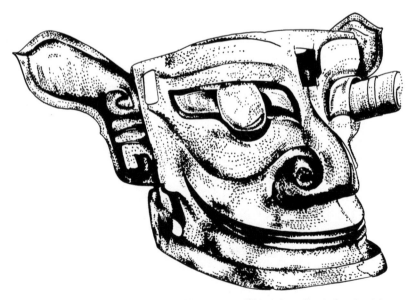

Fig. 45 The bronze mask of a deity or divine ancestor. Place of sacrifice in Sanxingdui, 17th–11th century BC.

with giant ears, sometimes with cylinders instead of eyes or with a trunk-like nose [44].

One exceptionally important find is a bronze human sculpture from Sanxingdui. This figure, standing 172 cm high with his elbows at his chest and hands at the height of his face, raises his arms, perhaps in an act of carrying an elephant tusk (which, however, was not found). The figure, dressed in a long close-fitting robe with tight sleeves, stands on a decorated foot stool with four feet resting on a pedestal – all totally 90 cm in height. The sculpture thus reaches a height of 262 cm and weighs over 180 kg.

Other renderings of bronze bird heads accompany the human sculpture. One of them is 43.3 cm tall and has a socket for mounting as well as openings to attach it to a handle. Another head was made in the form of a bell. These heads, staring wide-eyed, also threaten with their powerful crooked beaks. Even a miniature 12-cm high bronze rendering of an entire bird of prey was preserved.

Given that some of the bronze objects stored here evidently passed through fire, this find could testify to the "burning ceremony"*(liaoji)*, known from the oracle bones of the Shang period, by which the hills, rivers and earth were appeased and venerated.

Similar places of sacrifice were also found at other Chinese sites from that period. These sites revealed jade ritual objects (disc- or lozenge-shaped), as well as axes, spear or lance heads, knives or bronze tablets with an animal mask or geometric marquetry made with turquoise (Gaopianxiang, Mayangxiang in Sichuan).

## Zhengzhou

This site most likely consists of the older seat of the Shang Dynasty that preceded the more recent Anyang. Zhengzhou is located on the southern bank of the Yellow River, some 150 km south of Anyang. The city's founders demarcated between two rivers a walled district that was 1.75 km (north-south) × 1.5 km (east-west). The creation of the city was undoubtedly influenced by the location on the Yellow River at the place where it leaves the area at the foot of the western mountains and flows into the eastern plains. The total expanse of the agglomeration here can be estimated at 25 km²; the inner city alone covers an area of 3.25 km². Up to 100,000 people are thought to have lived here.[115]

Since the ancient center is located underneath the present-day industrial city, archeological research here is limited. Nevertheless, a number of interesting finds have been made.

The palace district is situated in the northeast quarter of the city and covers an area of roughly 300,000 m². A large number of foundation terraces made from packed clay have been found here ranging in size from roughly 1000 m² to buildings measuring dozens of square meters. Structurally speaking, these buildings again featured beam supports with walls from organic wickerwork and inner pillars 30–40 cm in diameter that were positioned every two meters or so and supported the veranda that extended to the edge of the foundation terrace. The palace district may have been surrounded by a 5–6 m wide moat.

Burials with modest funerary objects were found in the vicinity of these buildings. The deceased received mainly bronze ritual vessels and ornaments (bronze and jade hairpins).

Even in Zhengzhou the central quarter was accompanied by workshop districts (bronze, pottery, bone, etc.) and the residences of service personnel.

The discovery of thirteen bronze objects, mainly vessels, made outside the city's southeast corner is a remarkable find from this site. Four cube-like, four-legged *fang ding* vessels used to prepare food offerings were found here; one of the vessels measures 1 m in height and weighs 86.4 kg, another, round and three-legged, is 87 cm tall and weighs 64.3 kg. The other two were 81 cm in height and weighed 75 and 52 kg.

## Anyang

This was an extensive agglomeration of settlements with a total of 17 sites spread over an area of approximately 24 km² (a different cal-

[115] Norman Yoffee, Myths of the Archaic State, Cambridge, Cambridge University Press 2005, p. 43, Table 3.1.

culation gives 19 km$^2$) and inhabited by some 120,000 people.[116] The area in the immediate vicinity of one of the more recently established cities of the Shang Dynasty had the form of an elliptical region with a longer axis that did not exceed 200 km.

With a size of approximately 10,000 m$^2$, Xiaotun was most likely Anyang's administrative center. Research has revealed what is considered to be three phases of the social center, progressing chronologically from the north to the south (districts A, B and C). District A has the form of fifteen parallel rectangular buildings constructed on foundations of packed clay.

These buildings with beam frames and walls of organic wickerwork possessed pillars standing on stone foundations and probably supporting thatched roofs. District B consists of eleven rectangular or square buildings on these kinds of foundations and arranged in three rows with a north-south orientation. The middle row contains three large buildings and five gates. Burials with horses and battle wagons with wheels and numerous spokes (18–28) were found in their vicinity arranged around a modest-sized terrace with walls of organic mesh. The more recently established district D features 17 buildings on packed-clay foundations with burials nearby. Sunken-featured dwellings about 4 m in diameter and housing service personnel (?) with large rectangular or round storage spaces stood in its vicinity. Shops working with bronze, stone, bone and pottery were located here.

One noteworthy find in Anyang was that of two elephant skeletons.[117] The site of Yinxu has also recently been subject to excavations as part of the research done on the agglomeration here. Excavators also encountered here palace architecture, royal tombs and regular residential quarters.[118]

---

[116] Norman Yoffee, Myths of the Archaic State, Cambridge, Cambridge University Press 2005, p. 43, Table 3.1.

[117] Jakub Maršálek, Sociální analýza pohřebišť pozdního neolitu (cca 3000–2000 př. n. l.) na území provincie Shandong (A social analysis of late Neolithic burial grounds in the Shandong province (3000–2000 BC)), doctoral dissertation, Charles University in Prague, Humanities Faculty, Institute of the Far East (specialization: The History and Culture of Asia and Africa, supervisor: Prof. Oldřich Král, PhD.), June 2003, p. 68.

[118] Norman Yoffee, Myths of the Archaic State, Cambridge, Cambridge University Press 2005, p. 96.

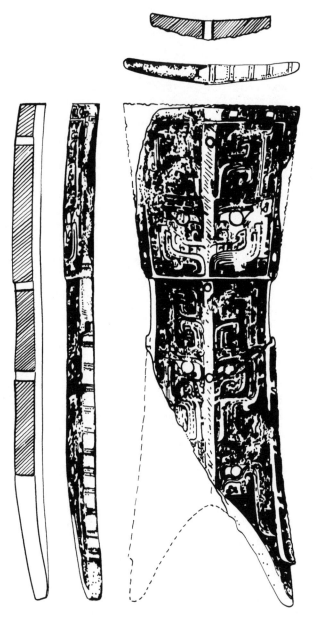

**Fig. 46** Bone tablet featuring a carving of a vertical row of three *Taotie* masks from Anyang.

An Anyang burial site was discovered on the northern bank of the local river. Eleven royal tombs and over 1,000 ordinary burials were revealed here. Dwellings of service personnel and workshops were also found here. The eleven royal tombs are divided into a western group of seven and an eastern group of four burials. This corresponds in number to the eleven kings that ruled from Anyang. These tombs were kept in deep and spacious pits that were entered by long ramps with a north-south direction and shorter ramps in an east-west direction. Buried with the deceased were objects made of stone, jade, shell, bone, antler, dentin, pottery and bronze. The deceased were accompanied to the next world by several human sacrifices, sometimes with their heads severed from their bodies. A written record on human sacrifices made to ancestors on orders of the King Wen Ding of the Shang Dynasty was found here. Many of these objects are crafted at the highest conceivable artistic level of that period [45].

## Western Zhou

Even though we have the least amount of archeological information available to us on this dynasty, which chose to position its power base furthest west of the middle section of the Yellow River, it is relatively well known from inscriptions on bronze artifacts and from later historical sources. Inscriptions on oracle bones from that period were also found.

This appears to have been an originally nomadic group that gradually settled and adopted many of the customs and traditions of the agricultural population.

New objects made of burnt clay – roof tiles, bricks and façade plates – were also produced during this dynasty's rule. Otherwise, however, the changes in the content of the material culture are only in form, not in quantity.

An example of a residence for this dynasty's elite can be seen in a building excavated at the village of Fenchu in the Shaanxi province [46].

This residence also stands on a pounded-earth platform with a height of 1.43 m and 45 m (north-south) × 32 m (east-west) in size.

The focal point of the building positioned along a north-south axis consists of a ceremonial hall with an open courtyard to the south side and two enclosed symmetrical courtyards on the north side. The southern courtyard was entered through a gate to the entire premises with a partition wall blocking a view of the courtyard from the outside. The walls and rooftops were protected by plaster and we even find sewage lines using terracotta pipes.

We also know that the Zhou had central residential agglomerations surrounded by workshops (bronze, pottery, bone) and residences for service personnel, as well as by burial grounds.

Research of one of the "service settlements," the village of Zhangji-apo (near Feng and Hao, two of the dynasty's first capitals), yielded remarkable results. Fifteen sunken-featured dwellings, both shallow and deep, were documented here by excavators. The floor space for the shallow dwellings measured 2.2 × 4.2 with a depth of 1.4 m under the surface. A central pillar and wall built of packed clay supported a round

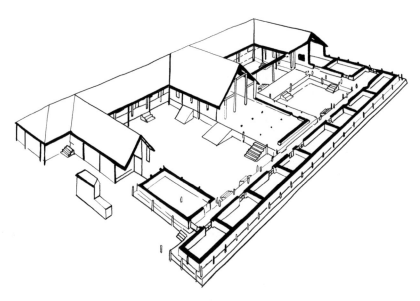

**Fig. 47** Reconstruction of elite residences in the village of Fenchu in the Qishan district, Shaanxi, late 2ⁿᵈ millenium BC, Zhou Dynasty.

thatched roof. The structure was entered by a ramp and the interior contained a fireplace, sleeping area and storage niche. Although the walls and floor bore traces of fire burns, it was usually damp inside when it rained. The deeper homes could be up to 3 m deep beneath the surface and were usually oval in shape with a diameter from 7.8 m to 9.5 m. The interior could be divided by a partition wall with doors about 1.2 m in size. Narrower and deeper supply pits and wells accompanied the dwellings.

The villagers made a living by farming or as craftsmen. A total of 65 tools with mainly stone blades were found here, as were 51 axes, of which seven bore traces of honing. Other finds included ten honed stone chisels, a bronze hatchet and 15 bronze knives with handles that had ring-shaped eyelets. The farmers here used spades of bone; 82 pieces of them made from the shoulder bones or lower jawbones of horses or cattle were found here, as well as 23 made of stone and seven from seashells. Harvesting tools found included 246 reapers and 90 sickles, mainly made of seashells. Massive mowing blades were honed from stone into rectangular single or double-cut blades, and sickle blades usually had holes bore through them on the back side so that they could be strapped to a handle as is still the custom in China today.

The people of the village made bodkins and needles from bone; such implements were also found made from bronze or horn. A total of 310 arrowheads found here were made from deer antlers and bone. Clay molds used for casting round objects from bronze and pottery implements for potters and weavers were also discovered here.

These findings show us that the technological profile of the period's main manufacturing sectors did not change all that much from prehistoric times and thus that the political development most likely did not reflect the transformations in the economic base.

Information provided by reports on the legitimization measures taken by the rulers of the Zhou dynasty to justify their move toward empire rule and away from the sovereignty of the previous dynasty is extremely interesting. Their line of reasoning is primarily based on a rebuke of the arrogance, incompetence and inability of the rulers of the preceding Shang dynasty who had neglected to carry out that the very

**Fig. 48** Lamellar armor, Qin Dynasty period (221–210 BC).

acts they had assured their subjects they would: the flawless execution of cult rituals. It is due to these lapses that the heavens stripped them of the mandate to rule and entrusted the Zhou with it.[119]

This ideological construct was apparently so convincing that the Zhou even won over some of the experts who had previously served the "old regime." Some experts of the *shi* class, of no blood relations to the royal family and referred to in Shang writings on oracle bones, even climbed higher on the social ladder.[120]

We will later read of the first "ministries" that were created in the courtyard of the new rulers. Aside from employing experts, the royal court of the Zhou rulers also enlisted archivists (*zuoce*), whose tasks ranged from preparing ceremonial texts to writing historical records.

Not only is a relatively crystallized and even consolidated public authority system perceptible during the Zhou dynasty, we can also detect its symbolic correlations. According to the ceremonial regulations valid towards the end of the dynasty, the king was supposed to possess nine kettles (*ding*) and eight vessels (*gui*), his lieges seven *ding* and six *gui*, higher nobility and court dignitaries five *ding* and four *gui* and the lower nobility three *ding* and two *gui*.[121]

The tomb of Lord Guo Ji, the ruler of the Guo estate under the dominion of Western Zhou in the province of Henan, provides us with a good idea of the dynasty's funeral rituals. A total of nine large graves and four burial places with the remnants of wagons and horses and over 17,000 funerary objects were found here. The ruler Guo Ji departed to the next world with his face covered by a material onto which his survivors stitched the image of his face using jade discs. A number of jade ritual objects, including marquetry in the form of animals, were

---

[119] Norman Yoffee, Myths of the Archaic State, Cambridge, Cambridge University Press 2005, p. 99, in citing the following: "Heaven instructed us, favored us, selected us, and gave us the mandate of Yin (Heaven) to rule over your numerous regions."

[120] Norman Yoffee, Myths of the Archaic State, Cambridge, Cambridge University Press 2005, p. 99.

[121] Jakub Maršálek, Sociální analýza pohřebišť pozdního neolitu (cca 3000–2000 př. n. l.) na území provincie Shandong (A social analysis of late Neolithic (ca. 3000–2000) burial grounds in the Shandong province), doctoral dissertation work, Charles University in Prague, Humanities Faculty, Institute of the Far East (specialization: The History and Culture of Asia and Africa, supervisor: Prof. Oldřich Král, PhD.), June 2003, p. 87, note: 283.

also discovered here. Bronze objects were found in the tomb, as were iron swords with jade handles and golden belts.

In Western Zhou, rituals to honor ancestors took the form of feasts in which the living members of lineages contacted their ancestors in the next world. These feasts not only strengthened the solidarity of elite social units, but also internally divided them and established degrees of subordination and submission in them. Both intoxicating (alcoholic) drinks and the meat of sacrificed animals were consumed at these feasts. This meat represented a rarity of high prestige and significance. In the 1st century BC, the rulers of the feudal states who belonged to the same clan as the emperor received from him gifts of meat as an exceptional honor. The right to consume meat from offerings thus became one of the attributes of the ancient Chinese aristocracy, which reserved for itself the privilege of offering sacrifices.

Following the decline of the central government during the Eastern Zhou Dynasty (771–256 BC), a fight for sovereignty broke out among the seven states: Yan, Zhao, Wei, Qi, Qin, Han and Chu. As previously mentioned, the Qin state emerged as the victor and its ruler, the First Sovereign Emperor (221–210 BC), united all of China under his rule [47].

# THE ECONOMY OF THE FIRST CHINESE STATE

One important finding was that the creation of the first Chinese state did not yield any novelties in production and production technology. It therefore came into being as a social and political phenomenon, making use of an economic base that had already been formed. Hence we will not find here any traces of a revolution in production means that official pseudo-Marxist orthodoxy had sought in researching the period prior to the dawn of the state. The intensification of work methods apparently led to the introduction of the mass production of cast iron in the 7th to 6th century BC.

A certain degree of innovation is, however, evident here. These advances include the wheel and axle, which, surprisingly enough, we do not find proof of until the late Shang period, i.e. the 13th to 11th century BC. It appears that this invention made its way here from the Central Asian steppe as a reflection of the contact with the nomadic nations there. The reader is most likely aware that the most famous Chinese export, silk, is known to have come from this period.

Chinese civilization always took care to ensure that the economy was running smoothly and providing the population with all necessities, and the Chinese thus deservedly acquired and maintained a reputation as an industrious and diligent people. The very size of the community of serfs, unimaginable in the West, already had state elites to perform this role. We know from numerous sources that already in the 5th century BC the Chinese tax-paying community consisted of 12,000,000 individuals and that, by the onset of modern times, this number had reached an unbelievable 54,600,000 taxpayers. The need to sustain and supply such a large mass of people naturally placed considerable demands on the productivity of Chinese agriculture, crafts and trade.

# SOCIETY

## Characteristics of the Oldest Chinese State

The first written sources of Chinese history, inscriptions on oracle bones from the Shang Dynasty, provide us with a view of the activities of the early Chinese state.[122]

These writings mainly tell us the chain of hierarchical subordination: if the king gave someone an order, he also had to tell that person to carry out the order. The fact that the formulation "he who receives the order accepts the king's matter as his own" appears in the oracles texts tells us that the hierarchy of power still fell well short of constituting a coherent chain of commitments, obligations and automatic duties. The individual receiving the order then enlisted the relevant managerial and service staff and carried out the king's order. Such tasks generally consisted of expeditions, hunting (e.g. elephants), capturing game and the likes. The task recipient then notified the king or the king's subordinate that the order had been successfully carried out.

As for the Shang king's relation to the land of his subjects, oracle bones describe royal activities undertaken in allied towns (hunts, inspections, etc.) for the purpose of moving the king and his court around his territories. It seems that upon moving to one of the allied towns, the ruler would set up his "camp," where he would conduct his activities (prophecy). Yet the king could also have dispatched his staff to the allied town for some reason or ordered them to travel there (or declare such an order as a prophecy).

After arriving to the allied town, the king either ordered his subjects or mobilized their collective or collectives to undertake an activity. In

---

[122] Superbly covered by David N. Keightley, The Late Shang State: When, Where, and What?, in: David N. Keightley (ed.): The Origins of Chinese Civilization, Berkeley – Los Angeles – London, University of California Press 1983, pp. 523–564, on pp. 528–529.

doing so, he would sometimes assign a leader for them who could even come from a different allied town. The king may have even assigned official titles to his subjects at his temporary residence. According to some of the writings, the king cared about the health of his subjects and initiated a prophecy ceremony to find out if the sick would recover.

The king received at his seat in the allied town material supplies to run his court, e.g. animal (shoulder) bones, seashells, turtle shells or other necessities.

The king or his dignitaries sometimes set out with an allied town or towns on war campaigns. Naturally, the questions appeared in prophecies of whether the king and the allied town would win in battle and this query was usually answered affirmatively. Sometimes, however, the prophecy also mentioned that losses would be suffered by the allied town's troops. Generally, the prophecy ceremonies were performed to ascertain the course of the military conflict – how far the enemy would go, whether it would attack the allied town and how successful such an attack would be, whether the king's side would receive assistance or reinforcements and whether it would win, etc. In some cases, the allied town and royal "camp" could become the target of an attack by the enemy or individuals not ruled by the king. Prophecies concerned not only military conflicts, but also other political events, such as new alliances bound by marriages.

Royal experts (or the king himself) often prophesized in allied towns and would have the necessary equipment transported there for this purpose. The king would also make sacrifices to the deities and perform ceremonies – sometimes to benefit specific individuals or all their relatives. Pigs were apparently often chosen for sacrifice. These ceremonies were attended either by individuals or entire collectives from allied towns. The king or his masters of ceremony would recite incantations for the good of allied towns. Cult activities included farming rituals, of which, unfortunately, these inscriptions tell us very little. We only know that during the prophecy rituals the king inquired into whether there would be enough rain or a bountiful harvest. In certain allied towns, sacrifices or other rituals could even be organized with other friendly allied towns. It appears that the names of the oracles themselves and the scribes recording their results repeated in various regions, leading us to believe that these experts accompanied the king from region to region. An analysis of written sources shows, among other things, that the entire sphere of ritualism and prophecy was gradually professionalized and bureaucratized.

It was most likely the veneration of the royal dead in the Shang dynasty that held the entire federation of lineages together. For it was through the ancestors of the royal family that the Shang kings were to reach further and more intensively the spirit world than anyone else. The king's monopoly on communication with ancestors via bronze vessels and manipulation through the wealth of the individual lineages intensified the effect of this factor. It was the rituals that bonded the alliance and solidified relations.[123]

A still very open, unstable and essentially unfinished form of the oldest Chinese state is apparent from this information. The fact that the territory ruled by its kings was not connected, but formed "islands" separated by countries under other dominion, relates to this. David Keightley's research efforts have even provided us with a map that perfectly shows this disjointed, mosaic-like state complex – the predecessor of the actual territorial state [48].[124]

The ceremonial communal feast retained its importance at this time. Sets of bronze vessels (*gu* drinking vessel and *yue* drinking or pouring vessel) were frequently found in graves of the Erligang culture. Two and even four sets of these vessels were buried with the deceased.[125]

---

[123] Norman Yoffee, Myths of the Archaic State, Cambridge, Cambridge University Press 2005, p. 97–98.

[124] Superbly covered by David N. Keightley, The Late Shang State: When, Where, and What?, in: David N. Keightley (ed.): The Origins of Chinese Civilization, Berkeley – Los Angeles – London, University of California Press 1983, pp. 523–564, on p. 544. Map 17.3.

[125] Jakub Maršálek, Sociální analýza pohřebišť pozdního neolitu (cca 3000–2000 př. n. l.) na území provincie Shandong (A social analysis of late Neolithic burial grounds in the Shandong province (3000–2000 BC)), doctoral dissertation, Charles University in Prague, Humanities Faculty, Institute of the Far East (specialization: The History and Culture of Asia and Africa, supervisor: Prof. PhDr. Oldřich Král), June 2003, p. 88, note 285.

# A state arises from kinship

The basic family units forming the skeleton of the Chinese state were lineages *(shi)* and the clans created from them *(xing)*. The king *(wang)* could then award a domain under the individual lineages, or award the income from their corvée or military services, to a member of the elite, to the queen, prince or to a nobleman of high status. The king could even decide to move whole clans to strategically important (though

**Fig. 49** The main areas of late Shang state according to inscriptions on oracle bones. The map's shaded areas show the main sites of the Upper Erligang and Anyang phase. The disjointed, "mosaic-like" nature of the early state centers' authority is captured nicely here.

remote) lands to ensure the unhindered possession of these lands. Usually, however, the founder of a new province obtained the right to rule the people who had already settled there. Moreover, lineages of expert craftsmen and masters of ceremonies that traditionally dealt with these professions, and passed them down from father to son, were made available to serve his new court. The symbolic handover of regional rule was expressed by an investiture ceremony in which the candidate received robes, standards, horses and battle wagons.

One Chinese text *(Zuo-zhuan)* even directly describes this way of establishing a provincial government. The Duke of Lu underwent the above-described investiture and received for it a large and ancient bow; to accompany him his received six *zu* (family units) who were originally from Yin. The chieftains of their clans were ordered to "have the leaders of their families gather from near and far their generations of relatives and to lead these multitudes" to accompany the duke to his new province.

What did one holding such a mandate do in his new territory? He first established a fortified settlement, a *guo*, from where he intended to govern the land. He had the right to build temples at his residence to honor the dead and request that they provide protection, assistance, support and their blessing. Then he surrounded his seat with a regional network of service settlements and operations, thereby creating a "city-state", a formation also called a *guo*. The entire process was therefore essentially carried out as an act of the initiator and of the family groups assigned to him to perform special tasks and duties. Although the local peasantry was obliged to pay taxes and perform corvée, they otherwise were not burdened with requirements and obligations. The new lords let the farmers stay where they were and did not meddle that much in the life of their communities. Thus, this was a social act performed on the basis of general consent basis, respect for socially acknowledged conventions, trust in a promise given and obedience. Force seems to have played an imperceptible role here.

Yet it is clear that, in addition to these "feudal" bonds based on personal honor, ancient China was also familiar with state formations of an utterly bureaucratic nature. The Chu state located in the valley of the Yangtze River was governed by centrally controlled administrative bodies called *xian* (probably meaning "district," *xiancheng* means district town). These bodies were lead by experienced officials whose jobs entailed moving from place to place. The Chu state long enjoyed independence until the First Sovereign Emperor joined it with the united empire in 223 BC. It seems, however, that the First Emperor used the model of the Chu state in dividing his entire empire into lower administrative units.

During the Zhou Dynasty, rule was passed from eldest son to eldest son, thereby creating a "great lineage" *(da zông)*. Brothers, younger sons and allies were entrusted with inherited positions in the royal court or received "fiefs" (farming estates) in remoter towns. The sons of such favored dignitaries then inherited rule from them in the provinces, thus creating "lesser lineages" *(xiao zông)*, regional "replicas" of royal rule and of the court. Even younger sons obtained important positions in the courts of their fathers, or they were given "lots" in even remoter towns and thus the entire network was constantly expanding.

The average population of such a city district with adjacent farmland ruled by a single member of the elite reached 5,000 people.

However, it was during the Western Zhou Dynasty (1122–770 BC) that the first three governing bodies appeared in charge of specific state departments. These were the "ministries" of agriculture *(situ)*, public works *(sikong)* and justice *(sikou)*.

## What followed?

Major social transformations then occurred in China in the Spring and Autumn periods (770–476 BC). Since these do not fall within the timeframe dealt with in this book, we will merely summarize them. Specialists of the *shi* class, originally administrators and warriors of the lower order began to study, along with the art of war, literature and ritual. In becoming officials, they began to offer services to the lords of the Warring States (519–222 BC). A committee of intellectuals was then formed that guarded and guaranteed the survival of Chinese spirituality and culture. Under the First Sovereign Emperor (221–210 BC) this group supported imperial rule in the form of a moralized orthodoxy sanctified by political authority. It was at this time that this kind of committee, augmented by the principles of meritocracy, took root. Its task was to formulate and introduce a comprehensive and structured view of the world and attitude toward it that was unburdened by group interests. These intellectuals defended the view that the state's primary task was to constantly rectify the reality around us, suffering from imperfection and corruptness, in accordance with the dictates of a higher moral order.[126] They thus became the collective bearer of dynastic legitimacy and came up with the idea that always only one ruling dynasty legitimately governed. The finishing touches were thus made to the state system in which the spiritual foundations were imposed by the rulers of the Shang Dynasty.

China is a land of hierarchies *par excellence*, and the traditional five or even four subordinations – serfs to kings, sons to fathers, wives to husbands and younger brother to elder brothers (friendships belong here as well, though this is not considered subordination)[127] – created, at least in theory, a clear and transparent system of decision-making authorities.[128] In more recent historical times, the figure of the emperor and his plenipotentiaries dominated the area above the blood-relative bonds. Not only was the emperor the highest representative of state power, who named all officials, he was also the highest judge, the supreme commander of the military and also performed other exceptionally important cult and ritual functions. Important acts in space and time fell to him: he determined the design of the capital city, of other important city centers and of settled rural areas according to the cult ideals. He also defined the start of the individual calendar periods.

He determined, in accordance with the religious interpretation of climatic and natural phenomena, the color of courtly attire, which became the official imperial color, and also decided on the form of the court rituals and court music according to the cult ideals.

---

126 Norman Yoffee, Myths of the Archaic State, Cambridge, Cambridge University Press 2005, p. 99–100: the task is "to present a comprehensive view of the world, not merely of any particular group, and argue that the main task is to remake present reality, corrupt and imperfect as it is, in accordance with the dictates of a higher moral order."

127 See the writings of Confucius cited in the appendix.

128 Jinhua Jia, Kwok Dang-fei: From Clan Manners to Ethical Obligation and Righteousness: A New Interpretation of the Term *yi*, "Journal of the Royal Asiatic Society," 3rd Series, vol. 17, Part I, 2007, pp. 33–41 (p. 39 on social bonds, namely on the five subordinations).

The situation for the emperor of the Middle Kingdom (as China has been called since ancient history) was made substantially easier by the reflection of the divine light that had shown on his position since time immemorial. Ever since prehistoric times, the ruler of the Chinese state had been an individual invested with extremely potent religious and extensive supernatural powers. More than any other ruler from ancient history, the symbolism of the Chinese emperor also permeated the cult sphere: The Chinese world has four sides – black north, blue-green east, red south and white west – which hold together and lead the yellow center, i.e. the emperor, into harmonic relations (the emperor's exclusive claim to the yellow or gold color is derived from this). The emperor is the lynchpin of celestial order; he combines earthly bliss with celestial harmony and thus guarantees that life on earth progresses as it should. The rituals that the emperor celebrated were essential for initiating the phases of the year, the new seasons and all events occurring in nature. The emperor therefore cannot be anything else but the highest ruler, judge and commander, the source and provider of order, law and justice. If it were not for the emperor, the world would fall into chaos, anarchy and into an everyone-for-himself fight. This very strong ideology of the emperor naturally had an effect on both representatives of regional authorities and on foreign aspirants to the Chinese imperial throne, almost all of whom would accept this ideology. This is also why, despite the fact that throughout its history China was frequently humbled, humiliated and exposed to the cravings of the power-hungry within China and of foreign conquerors, the Chinese culture was never threatened. The shine of the emperor's grandeur overwhelmed all those aspiring to the throne so that, with the transfer of central power, they also accepted the way by which the figure of the emperor infused and helped create the spiritual structure of Chinese society.[129]

A proverb from one of the classical writings well captures the redistributive nature of Chinese society: "Dukes live on tribute, ministers on their estates, *shi* ['gentlemen'] on the land, and peasants on their toil."[130]

---

[129] For more on the nature of the highest Chinese office see Joan Ching, Son of Heaven: Sacral Kingship in Ancient China, "T'oung pao" 83/1–3, 1997, pp. 3–41.

[130] Charles K. Maisels, Early Civilizations of the Old World, London and New York, Rout-

## What the elite took with them on their journey to the next world

The fourth king of the Shang Dynasty, Wu Ding, also married Fu Hao from the Tzu clan. Lady Hao embraced public life, leading ritual sacrifices and even taking part in battles. Exceptional power was concentrated in the hands of royal couples – a fact tellingly reflected in the funerary objects that accompanied Fu Hao in her grave on her journey to the next world.

A grandiose tomb (M5) was built for her in the city of Anyang after her death. This is the sole burial site from the Shang Dynasty for which we know the name of a historical figure actually buried here. The burial pit is 5.6 × 4 m in size with a depth of 7.5 m. A total of 1,928 objects were placed in the grave by survivors of the deceased. There were 460 bronze objects, 750 made of jade and 74 of precious stones. Sixty-three stone tools were found here, 11 pieces of pottery, 560 objects made of bone, 3 ivory bowls, 15 river shells and 6,800 other shells. The funerary objects included bronze weapons and ritual vessels, over 20 bone arrowheads, more than 490 bone hairpins and 3 clay whistles.

The queen's service set of bronze vessels also featured an opulently decorated wine glass (*xiaozun*) in the form of an owl, a four-legged kettle (*ding*) in the form of a mythical animal (*kui*) and another similar vessel in animal-like forms, a cooker with three steaming pots (*yan*) and a twin wine carafe shaped like a palace (*oufangyi*).

The jade objects accompanying her to the next world included carvings featuring birds, perhaps phoenixes, and in another case an owl, possibly worn as decorations or sewn to clothing. A smallish, though fascinating figure of a kneeling servant with his hands on his knees and a second kneeling human figure with bird's head were also found here.

One of the wine glasses, carved from ivory with real and mythical animal forms, features turquoise marquetry.

It should be mentioned here that non-elite classes continued to be buried at common burial grounds depending on the lineage classifica-

ledge – Taylor and Francis Group 2001, p. 332. On the duties of the peasants during the Zhou Dynasty see Hao Jitao, Peasant and State in Classical Athens and Zhou China: A Comparative Survey, "Journal of Ancient Civilizations" 8, 1993, pp. 78–104.

tion *(zu)* they belonged to. Customs included the burial of individuals who had not yet reached adulthood, often children, outside the main burial site, e.g. in containers in residential areas.

## The spiritual world

Let us first use the sources available to us to inquire into the belief systems of the first Chinese state of the Shang Dynasty.[131]

The Chinese had the highest reverence for the god Di, also called "Shangdi" or "Celestial Emperor," as the supreme deity of the Shang pantheon. We have no idea if this name applied to a single being or to a whole group of deities. Di was the celestial deity, though sometimes his name was added as an honorary title to the name of Shang rulers and a special liturgy was performed in his honor. The cult customs linked to this deity are quite similar to the veneration of the dead, though it seems that the offerings to Di were not made directly from worshippers of the Shang Dynasty, but vicariously through their divine ancestors. A cosmic deity, Di controls natural forces such as the clouds, wind and storms. He sends drought and other calamities and approves (or disapproves) major societal acts such as the founding of cities or the commencing of military campaigns. The four cardinal points fall under his jurisdiction and he may have emerged as an astral deity, perhaps inspired by observation of the North Star.

Other beings worshipped during the Shang Dynasty were most likely natural forces and their personifications – the Sun, Moon, wind and storms, as well as the Earth and even the cardinal points. The appearance here of female guardians (and not male guards) of the East and West is noteworthy and may be an incarnation of the goddess Earth.

It is clear that the veneration of the dead already represented in this ancient period one of the pillars of the Chinese spiritual world. The dynasty's genealogy gives a total of 35 historical ancestors – both mythical

---

[131] Aptly described by Wang Tao, Shang ritual animals: color and meaning (Part 1), in: Bulletin of the School of Oriental and African Studies of the University of London 70/2, 2007, pp. 305–372.

and real; their spouses and sometimes their courtly dignitaries were commemorated during ceremonies. The ancestors were called by their "temple names" *(miaohao)* and regular sacrifice rituals were performed in their honor. Mythological figures, the "High Ancestors" *(gaozu)*, also appeared in inscriptions on oracle bones. Their names were inscribed using pictorial symbols – e.g. using a picture of a bird – without a set order of symbols, and they were not known by their "temple names."

Temples and altars were built in honor of all of these beings. Regular ceremonies determined by the liturgical calendar (e.g. a weekly ritual to honor the dead) were performed there, including burnt offerings *(liao),* libations and invocations. Food and wine were most commonly offered at this time, though domesticated animals – bulls, pigs, sheep and dogs – were also sacrificed.

Human sacrifices were also offered, often decapitated.[132] Shang kings enjoyed hunting as an edification of early statehood's ideology; they would then offer the hunted game – wild pigs, deer, tigers and wild birds – to their deities. Sometimes jade objects, such as weapons, and gifts of (white) textiles, most likely silk, would be brought to rituals [49].[133] Bronze vessels in the form of mythical creatures took on special importance, since only through them could a mystical connection be made with the dead. This is why bronze had an exceptional, cult significance during the Shang Dynasty.[134]

The offerings were chosen according to how they compared with the powers attributed to them. Animals sacrificed to the *yang* force were supposed to be red, while the *yin* force required that animals of dark colors be sacrificed.

Prophesy using oracle bones was among the most renowned customs and traditions of the Chinese spiritual sphere. Bovine or sheep bones, especially cattle shoulder bones, were most often used for

---

[132] Wang Tao, Shang Ritual Animals: Colour and Meaning (Part 1), in: Bulletin of the School of Oriental and African Studies of the University of London 70/2, 2007, pp. 305–372, p. 310, note 18 and p. 326, note 87.

[133] Wang Tao, Shang Ritual Animals: Colour and Meaning (Part 2), in: Bulletin of the School of Oriental and African Studies of the University of London 70/3, 2007 pp. 539–567 and p. 548, note 23.

[134] Norman Yoffee, Myths of the Archaic State, Cambridge, Cambridge University Press 2005, p. 96.

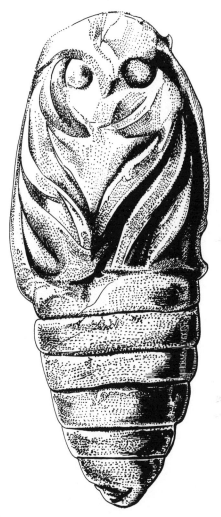

**Fig. 50** Amber pendant in the form of a silkworm's cocoon that silk was made from; 10th century AD, from tombs of the Liao Dynasty.

this. Turtle shells were apparently used later in the eastern coast and Yangtze regions (Dawenkou culture). Before being used for prophetic purposes, the bones first had to be cleaned, dried and shined and had all organic content removed from them, any remaining cartilage cut

**Fig. 51** Oracle bone from the Shang/Yin period. The inscription gives three acts of prophecy performed in intervals of three decades. The prophecies concerned the blissful and ominous nature of the upcoming decade. Cracks formed on the left side of the bone at the middle when a red-hot implement was applied.

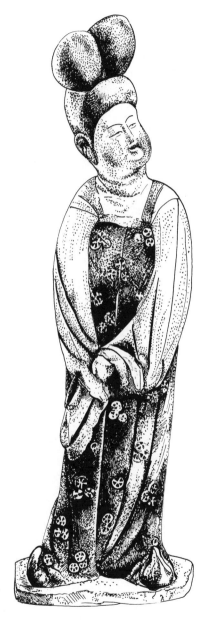

**Fig. 52** A noble lady, a funerary sculpture dating to around the mid-7th century AD.

away. The prophecy was carried out so that the oracle (or king) applied a burning hot implement to the bone's surface, cracking it. The experts then interpreted these cracks as prophetic signs, whereupon the prophecy was inscribed in the surface of the oracle bone [50]. Even cases in which the prophecy was not fulfilled or proved to be wrong were recorded. The services of dream interpreters were also resorted to for these purposes if, for instance, they wanted to explain a king's dreams. Written records of acts of prophecies even seem to indicate different "prophecy schools" and experts entrusted with interpreting prophecies. It was also revealed that, besides the king, the elite of the first Chinese state could also initiate prophecy ceremonies, though these individuals were most likely members of a royal house, the king's relatives or courtiers [51].

Specialists of that age also attempted to influence natural forces, e.g. to magically summon rain. They performed ritual dances and brought burnt offerings for this purpose, sometimes even drowning their sacrificed creatures in the river.

This leads to a debate on the extent to which the first Chinese religion can be considered shamanistic, or whether it was a spiritual system created by a society that had already entered statehood and which, through the veneration of the royal dead, helped to maintain the social hierarchy and forge loyalty toward the ruling dynasty [52].

**Fig. 53** A pair of dancers, a funerary sculpture dating to around the mid-7th century AD.

Information is just now emerging on how the Chinese perceived the form and nature of this world and the people's place in it. The Earth was square shaped and each of its cardinal points probably already had its own symbolic color as well as its own guardian deity with a special name. The winds blowing from the four cardinal points were sent by the gods, and the borders of the Middle Kingdom were perceived in the direction of the four cardinal points. The extent to which this symbolism of the four cardinal points and of their symbols was already present in Chinese prehistory is debated.[135]

Let us now discuss the Chinese people and how they imagined humanity's idyllic (as well as proper and ideal) state. The following piece of writing from the late Western Zhou period (10th–9th century BC) offers insight:

*Anciently, humans and spirits did not intermingle. At that time there were certain persons who were so perspicacious, single-minded, and reverential that their understanding enabled them to make meaningful collation of what lies above and below, and their insight to illumine what is distant and profound. Therefore the spirits would descend into them.*

*The possessors of such powers were, if men, called* xi *(shaman), and, if women,* wu, *(shamanesses).*

*Those who supervised the position of the spirits at the ceremonies, made the vases (used to) present victims, and appropriate clothes, made the descendants of the past saints glorious, knew the (sacred) names of mountains and rivers, the principal ancestors, (dealt with) all the affairs relative to the ancestral temple, (were in charge of) the difference between father and son (in the ritual), the enforcement of respect, the proper order of ceremonies, the principles of respect and justice, the proper physical behavior, the control of fidelity and trust, offerings and purifications and manifested respect to the luminous deities, were the* zhu *(invocators).*

*Those who established family and personal names, who knew what plant should be cultivated for each season, the color (of the hairs of) sacrificial animals, the different kinds of jade and textile, the different colors of (ritual)*

---

[135] Gabriele Fahr-Becker (ed.), The Art of East Asia, p. l.: Tandem Verlag GmbH 2006, p. 16 upper left: grave M45 from Xishuipo, the Yangshao culture, the deceased among forms of the tiger and dragon made from pebbles. However, the date of this grave is debated.

*clothes, the (proper) quantity of (ritual) vessels, the rules (concerning) the order of ancestral tablets, the proper positions during sacrifices, mounds and swept soil (for sacrifices), deities of above and below, the origin of the clans and abided by the ancient rules were the* zong *officers.*

*Therefore, there were officers for Heaven, Earth, the spirits and the different things, who were called the five officers, who ruled their own domain (of competence) and did not intermingle (with each other's domain).*

*So the people were trustful, the spirits had a luminous virtue and the people and spirits had their own realm. There was respect and no untoward familiarity. As a consequence, the spirits sent down blessing on the people, and accepted from them their offerings. There were no natural calamities.*[136]

We have here an illustrative and detailed description of the relationship between the human world and the spirit world that was considered by ancient Chinese sages to be proper, desirable and just. This text actually seems to show a very ancient attitude toward life. There is no mention here of gods; only people and "spirits" appear. The harmonic relationship between man and everything that transcends him is then considered the criterion of all order of the human and spirit world, just as it was understood in the other early civilizations of the Old World.

This is actually an idealized picture of a "golden age" that is still void of priests and lords and where the classless society is ruled by officers appointed by the "people" and the "spirits" based on their moral, intellectual and ethical qualifications. There is still no distinction made between the spiritual and social sphere, both blend into one. It matters little if this is an authentic text or an interpolation from later periods: for us it represents a reflection upon the original idyllic state of humanity that grew from the roots of Chinese thought. Only later did there appear the central office of ancient China, the king and the emperor, which gradually became the guarantor of heavenly and earthly order.

It is important to point out, however, that changes occurred during the Zhou Dynasty that distinguished it from the situation under

---

[136] The *Guoyu*, probably from the Warring States period: G. Boileau, Wu and Shaman, Bulletin of the School of Oriental and African Studies, University of London 65/2, 2002, pp. 350–3076, on p. 357.

the Shang Dynasty. Research has already shown that, although the basic ritual and ceremonial components of religion did not differ all that much between the Shang and Zhou dynasties, changes can be seen in the periods' dogmatisms (?) as expressed by differences in the customary colors used for cult purposes.[137] During the Shang Dynasty, a preference was expressed for white and multicolored (animal) offerings, often chosen for sacrifices to the most important ancestors, for fertility rites and for invocations. The spirits of the earth and cardinal points were at that time remembered through animals of yellow color and dark shades; this also applied for the ritual summoning of rain. Offerings of a red-yellow color prevailed toward the end of the Shang Dynasty. The cult profile of the Zhou Dynasty, traditionally linked to the color red (just as the Shang Dynasty was linked to white), was probably in part derived from this. There is also proof that ceremonies began to occur at a set frequency (a weekly cycle) and that certain types of ceremonies were attached to specific worshipped beings.

The extremely influential factor of the ruler's spiritual legitimacy, which has yet to be mentioned here, must also be figured in the social processes. The Chinese king and later the emperor, the Son of Heaven *(Tianzi),* had to possess the power of *de* to undertake the Way of Heaven *(Tiandao).* Only in this way did he secure for himself the Mandate of Heaven *(Tianming).* As previously mentioned, the rulers of the Zhou Dynasty had already used this line of reasoning to justify their takeover of power through two factors: They declared themselves the lawful successors of the first Xia Dynasty and they insisted that the previous Shang Dynasty had lost its Mandate of Heaven due to the incompetence, ineffectiveness and oppression of its rule.

Though the origin of Chinese writing can be attributed to cult aspects, there soon appear lists of various goods on perishable materials such as silk or pieces of bamboo.[138] Possible predecessors of the system

---

[137] There appear in bronze inscriptions from the Zhou Dynasty toward the end of the 10th century BC some 20 various types of rituals, of which 17 had already been referred to on oracle bones from the Shang Dynasty: Wang Tao, Shang Ritual Animals: Colour and Meaning (Part 2), in: Bulletin of the School of Oriental and African Studies of the University of London 70/3, 2007, pp. 539–567, pp. 560–562, note 43.

[138] Charles K. Maisels, Early Civilizations of the Old World, London and New York, Routledge – Taylor and Francis Group 2001, p. 224.

of writing here continued to be discussed by researchers inclined to see them in the symbols and engravings on Neolithic or Chalcolithic pottery. While it still seems that these symbols do not form a continuous and arranged system providing us with the sought testimony, attempts are made to see in them emblems of lineages, families or clans.[139]

Chinese writing has still essentially preserved the traits it acquired in the first centuries of its existence. The famous Chinese endeavor to systematize and describe the entire visible world has even provided us with definitions that the learned doctor and scribe Xu Shen (30–124 AD) gave in the epilogue to his dictionary *Shuowen Jiezi*. He classifies script characters as the results of a process consisting of six basic steps:

1. deictograms – relating to their metaphorically conveyed meaning (i.e. indexes or symbols);
2. pictograms – indicating conveyed meaning through a simple depiction of the relevant thing (i.e. icons);
3. morphophonograms – dual-component characters, in which one component indicates the semantic field that the character belongs to while the second indicates the pronunciation of the entire term (indexes or symbols);
4. syllogigrams – the logical joining of multiple originally independent characters, referring to metaphorically conveyed meanings (i.e. indexes or symbols);
5. iterative characters – created by the graphic modification of an original character accompanying a semantic modifications (icons, indexes, symbols); and, finally,
6. homophonic ("derived") characters – working with homophony in which a spoken word represents a character depicting existence symbolized by another, similarly sounding word (symbols).[140]

The first two categories – deictograms and pictograms (the only character retaining their original graphic form) – only represent 4%

---

[139] Norman Yoffee, Myths of the Archaic State, Cambridge, Cambridge University Press 2005, p. 94.
[140] Jean-Jacques Glassner, Écrire a Sumer – L'invention du cunéiforme, p. l.: Editions du Seuil 2000, pp. 166–167, in the English version of the book (Jean-Jacques Glassner: The Invention of Cuneiform, tr. Zainab Bahrani, Marc van de Mieroop, Baltimore and London, The Johns Hopkins University Press 2003) on pp. 124–125.

of all the characters. The rest of the writing system is made up of the other four categories of characters.[141]

This is clearly a system of icons, indexes and symbols that is mainly supplemented by phonetic complements, i.e. symbols that help to disambiguate when a multiple interpretation is possible. We are also familiar with combinations of visual and sound symbols that precisely determine which term is being used. There also appear symbols that, in speaking the given term, refer to another similarly sounding term. Semantic complements, symbols determining the category of terms which the character in question belongs to, are used to specify the meaning of a character in the event of ambiguity.[142] This extremely complicated system of writing (a minimum of 1,500 characters must be known for basic reading) is still used today.

Later, under the rule of the Western Zhou Dynasty (1122–771 BC), bronze vessels frequently bore public inscriptions. Rulers and those in positions of power at that time built temples of immortalized ancestors that were opened with grand ceremonies in their honor. Commemorative inscriptions of these events were recorded on bronze vessels in which offerings were made at these temples.

Since prehistory, the Chinese calendar has been a combination of the moon and sun calendar with a relatively free and flexible system of months that takes into account seasons, temperature, vegetation growth and animal behavior and the possible inclusion of leap months. The calendar conformed to the movement of the stars and also contained information on when agricultural and cultural customs were to be carried out. According to the traditional interpretation, one of the most ancient Chinese emperors entrusted two families with overseeing the calendar and time information. The Chinese state had, since prehistory, set up and maintained calendar offices in charge of determining the period of important holidays and significant dates during the year.

---

[141] Jean-Jacques Glassner, Écrire a Sumer – L'invention du cunéiforme, p. l.: Editions du Seuil 2000, p. 186, in the English version of the book (Jean-Jacques Glassner: The Invention of Cuneiform, tr. Zainab Bahrani, Marc van de Mieroop, Baltimore and London, The Johns Hopkins University Press 2003) on p. 142.

[142] Norman Yoffee, Myths of the Archaic State, Cambridge, Cambridge University Press 2005, pp. 94–95.

These offices published almanacs for the people that contained the exact dates of such holidays.

As previously mentioned, the main components of Chinese spirituality always consisted of the cult of personified natural forces and the veneration of the dead; the oldest Chinese religious customs can perhaps be characterized by their affinity to Shamanism.

The deities of the age descended on the shamans of ancient China, resulting in the latter acquiring extraordinary skills, knowledge and power: They were able to invoke rain, purify places of sacrifice or summon the deities to a sacrifice. The Chinese have possibly, since prehistoric times, understood nature and the cosmos around them as an eternal cycle of the universe's primary forces inscribed in the system of the four cardinal points leading out from a common center. This fundamental pair of all cosmic forces, known as yin-yang and depicted by the familiar symbol of a circle divided into two "tadpoles" (black and white), represents the nature of world events in the Chinese understanding. Yin is characterized as cold, wet, dark, diffuse and passive and incorporates femininity. Yang, by contrast, is hot, dry, light, sparse and aggressive, and is associated with masculinity. Both forces are inseparably joined and the one cannot exist without the other. Together they create a dynamic, ever-turning balance in which one side's predominance is counterbalanced by the other. Neither of the sides can, however, dominate forever, and each contains in it traces of the other (the "eyes" in the tadpoles).

Along with architecture and perhaps painting, the works of which unfortunately have not survived, monumental sculpture dating back as far as the Shang Dynasty should also be mentioned. Sculptures from the royal tomb M1001 at Xibeigang in Anyang depict an array of mythical creatures: a tiger-man, pig-man and frog-man were among those found here.

# HOW THEN IS A STATE BORN?

# FIRST, A BRIEF REVIEW

We shall now try to recap what we know of the entrance of the state into human history.

Since roughly the 1970s, the attempt to explain the state's inception and the stabilization of factors of an economic nature has predominated in its research. Frequently arising in this regard are terms such as *surplus product, craft specialization, trade development, surplus mobilization* (generally meaning its output from direct manufacturers and redistribution managed by social elites) and the ideologically conditioned stabilization of social structures including controlling and controlled groups. Symbolic and metaphysical aspects of the development are generally understood as, if not complementary to, then at least a sanctification of this socially new economic phenomenon.[143]

This approach, at one time so stimulating and innovative, has recently run up against the limits of its interpretive possibilities. For historical research and archaeology in particular have reached conclusions that quite convincingly point to problematic aspects of this interpretation. This primarily consists of findings that cast serious doubt on the subsistence possibilities of prehistoric, and especially Paleolithic and Mesolithic populations.[144]

Notions of ancient human collectives as groups living in conditions of extreme existential danger and poverty and constantly threatened by famine, have proven to be, for the most part, unsubstantiated. Scholars

---

[143] I am using here terms such as "metaphysics" and "metaphysical" in the sense of the classification by the editors of Aristotle's works in which they called "metaphysics" the writing that was beyond his works on physics. Both in Aristotle's works and in this text it involves an intellectual activity that is the object of one's interest in a reality "beyond" the world that can be grasped by our senses and experiences, a group of ideas concerning the arrangement of this part of the world that we are unable to comprehend with our senses or experiences.

[144] See in particular Marshall Sahlins, Stone Age Economics, Chicago, Aldine 1972.

now see the earliest times of human existence as a period that, though it was in no way idyllic, was relatively well supplied; one in which there was virtually unlimited food to be had from natural resources.

Thus the primordial period of human existence can be justifiably viewed as one of "paradisiacal" abundance.[145]

This finding has rebuked the generally held assumption that social movement toward more structured forms of social life, to technical progress, to social stratification and intellectual maturation is mainly bound to human fear of a lack of food and to the satisfaction of man's basic subsistence requirements. This also casts a doubt on the assumption of a purely subsistent, material basis of human life as the impetus for social progress and development.

Archaeological and ethnological research of the earliest and pre-industrial forms of human society also soon ran into phenomena that, although their reality was impossible to deny, completely contradicted generally held evolutionistic ideas of the firmness of the bond between the subsistence methods of human collectiveness and the technical and intellectual means at their disposal. It is enough to recall here the "Mesolithic city" of Jericho surrounded in 10,000–9000 BC by a rampart and moat carved out of the cliffs, with an area of 4 hectares and an estimated population of 2,000. Archaeological exploration of the Göbekli Tepe site has substantiated the ability of early Neolithic artists to turn massive stone blocks into pillars of colossal architecture adorned with relief decorations. The technological know-how and skills of early farmers have also been attested to in a similar manner. Only recently did it come to light that our familiar and currently most cultivated compact wheat *(Triticum aestivum/compactum)* has no direct wild ancestor, and that the very first evidence of its existence appears at the beginning of 7000 BC when it was cultivated by hybridizing Emmer wheat *(Triticum dicoccum)* with a wild grass. Prehistoric growers thus demonstrated not only a deep knowledge of the life cycles of relevant plants, but also showed that they were adroit in the practical use of this knowledge.

---

[145] Aggregate numbers can be found in: John Peoples, George Bailey, Humanity – An Introduction to Cultural Anthropology, Saint Paul – New York – Los Angeles – San Francisco, West Publishing Company 1988, p. 161, Box 82.

Ethnological research in the same period in numerous areas of the world proved the existence of groups of hunters and gatherers that, under certain natural conditions, inhabited stabile settlements, divided their hunting grounds according to set "hunting rules," and thus had, to a certain extent, private ownership of production means, as well as stratified societies in that they owned slaves.

In short, ancient societies did not rise according to the rungs of the evolutionary ladder that we've attributed to them.

The extent to which the old Childe-Braidwood paradigm based on the primacy of man's economic base and subsistence activities vis-à-vis the entire sphere of human social life should still apply is, therefore, a valid question. Hitherto research has enabled these original axioms to be significantly modified.

Indeed, it has become apparent that the economic sphere is not alone in driving historical development, although its importance for the history of mankind certainly cannot be denied. Instead, we come across here something to the effect of a three-phase engine in which the guiding force of the engine of human history alternates between economics, the socio-political sphere (including that charming trait that the ancient Greeks called *thymos,* i.e. the desire for recognition and the respect of one's neighbors) and the area of spiritual and cultural works. Let us now view the state's entrance into human history as an example of a sweeping social transformation, in which the new scientific findings that we've amassed on the previous pages can help us grasp the mechanism of human society's development.

# SUBSISTENCE

## Agriculture

There is little doubt that agriculture formed the economic backbone in the development of the early state, and that this consisted of sedentary farming and not shifting cultivation (e.g. grass-field or fallow rotation), even though it was still present in the economic life of these lands. It was this type of agriculture that had, even before the inception of the state, not only sustained its people, but also enabled them to create a surplus product, a tangible output for which the economic necessity of immediate consumption did not apply. In this sense, the early state had a relatively easy task: to convince the people to relinquish the surplus product to the elite so that they could invest it in a way considered beneficial for the entire society. So instead of the people consuming the surplus product over the course of various celebrations, it would, by exchanging it for alliances, be invested into ensuring social peace and stability or be divided among relatives or other groups as deemed appropriate.

Agriculture of the pre-state period in the examined regions was characterized by two production-technological processes that we customarily (and inaccurately) call "revolutions": the "secondary products revolution" and the "simple machines revolution." The term "secondary products revolution" was introduced by English archaeologist Andrew Sherratt in the early 1980s.[146] This term is understood to mean the further innovations in agricultural production processes that provided early farmers with other, hitherto unknown crops. This mainly consisted of yields from gardening and orcharding activities that were

---

[146] See Andrew Sherratt, Plough and pastoralism: aspects of the secondary products revolution, in: I. Hodder, G. Isaac and N. Hammond. (edd.), Pattern of the Past: Studies in honour of David Clarke, Cambridge, Cambridge University Press 1981, pp. 261–305.

particularly developed following the sedentarization of the Neolithic population, i.e. after the stabilization of human settlements in space and time. It was only with the definitive sedentarization in prehistoric communities that people were able to fully devote themselves to intensive agriculture such as gardening and orcharding.

Although these were work-intensive processes that required a relatively high level of energy output, they also introduced new vitamins into the diet and enabled farming to be carried out even in areas where the nature of the terrain did not allow for classic field cultivation. Such places included valley slopes between mountains or even bodies of water (the *chinampas,* the Aztec floating gardens, come first to mind). Besides fruit and vegetables, garden cultivation also provided wine and, given the high sugar content in some fruits, created the prerequisites for the successful management of fermentation processes, thereby transforming sugary juices into high-percentage alcohol from which intoxicating drinks could be distilled. Though priests and shamans of ancient cultures made more use of this than the public at large, these new types of edibles could have been also gradually consumed by a broader circle of people. The Chalcolithic "secondary products revolution" enriched the diet of our ancient ancestors with essentials foods still considered important, such as grapevine, dates, figs and olives.

Another impact of the "secondary products revolution was the improvement of livestock production, especially the more efficient use of milk and dairy products. With society's division into sedentary farmers and specialized nomads, livestock became increasingly important as a source of food, and ancient herdsmen began to make better use of the nutritious milk of their animals and to prepare other foods from it. This process was also facilitated by the exploitation of the economic resources of a land more suited to nomads than farmers – semiarid or even desert conditions. This change also led to enrichment in people's diet, but more importantly it allowed for further development of human settlement and population of areas that were not conducive to supporting the agricultural population. The population quickly increased and the people sought a livelihood anyway they could. Development toward pasturage also led to important social transformations: The new economic base ushered in a specific social structure, the way of life and spiritual world of the nomadic pastoral population. All this would have a lasting effect on the future of human history.

The second revolution, which facilitated the work of pre-state farmers, was a process that can be called the "simple machines revolution." This actually involved the technical use of the simplest machines that people discovered through the ages: the first- and second-class lever, the inclined plane, the wedge or wheel and axle. These machines were used in all facets of the Chalcolithic economic sphere and facilitated farm work. Of high importance was the appearance of ards, the first plowing tools – implements that broke up the soil, but still not the kind of plow that would break it up and turn it over – that applied attributes of the first-class lever. This enabled a larger area of soil to be cultivated, requiring that cross-plowing techniques be employed in which the soil is tilled twice at right angles to the original direction. Farmers utilizing ards and plows also began to feel the need for draft animals to help them better control the new machine. Their first choice for the job was probably cattle, but to subject milk-providing cows to exhausting toil hitched to a yoke probably did not make that much sense to them. This is apparently how the castrated form of cattle came to be – the bull was turned into an ox. As true experts in the matter have informed me, a bull is too wild to harness to a yoke, but an ox is not. Prehistoric farmers must have also figured this out at some point.

Cereal cultivars, already developed in Neolithic times in an attempt to maximize the crop, were now grown by Chalcolithic farmers in soil that was better tilled thanks to the plow. Other simple machines were also used to help assist them in their work. Applying the wheel-and-axle principle, the cart, a means of transportation, was created. This invention led to an increase in the size of cultivated land and meant that the crop did not have to be carried home on backs and heads like before. The Neolithic farmer harvested as much as he could personally take home; the Chalcolithic farmer stored in the granary everything that he and his family managed to grow using plowing tools and then took the crop home using a carriage drawn by animals (further proof of the increased need of draft animals). There is even reason to believe that the principle of an inclined plane was used in unloading the crop from carts and possibly even in its other movements.

Two circumstances must, however, be emphasized. First of all, these new work methods did not at all replace the older agro-technologies that had been in use for thousands of years. Shifting cultivation methods such as the grass-field type in which only part of the land is cultivated while another part is left to lie fallow to reacquire nutrients were applied and became a set part of the age's economic makeup. The families of sedentary farmers using the shifting fields system would often increase their yield by employing similar methods on the outer edge of the farmland surrounding the village settlements. Shifting cultivators then had to also allow for the presence of shepherds, whose herds grazed in pastures either very close to the crops or sometimes even in fields that had already been harvested or were lying fallow. It was therefore important in early states using basic subsistence activi-ties (i.e. crop cultivation and the raising of livestock) that principles concerning the shared use of cultivated and otherwise exploited land be agreed to within the broader collective of producers, each of whom required a different farming strategy. These are the very circumstances that still constitute an important social component in the lives of sed-entary farmers and nomadic Bedouins in the Near East, and could have contributed to the beginnings of state life in the basin of the large rivers where farmers, shepherds, hunters and gatherers all sought a livelihood.

It should also be noted that the creation of the state did not bring with it any substantial transformation in agriculture's production base. All basic farming innovations had already taken place in the Chalco-lithic Period, and from the information available to us it seems that the birth of the state did not in itself lead to improvements in agriculture. New agricultural inventions were used sporadically by the lords of ancient states instead of being systematically deployed in farming. We know, for instance, that gardens, orchards and vineyards very soon became the property of the Egyptian pharaohs.[147] This logically stems from the fact that these intensive farming operations can be relatively simple to set up and operated, providing that there is a large enough work force. The harvest from such operations then enriched people's

---

[147] Muhammad Abdarrazik, Die altägyptische Weingarten (k3nw/k3mw) bis zum Ende des Neuen Reiches, Mitteilungen des Deutschen Archäologischen Instituts in Kairo 35, 1979, pp. 227–247, on page 227.

diet in terms of flavor and energy value. Yet in other cases the bearers of the ancient cultures were reticent and even critical toward new inventions. The Sumerian disputation "The Debate Between the Hoe and the Plow" ends with the hoe winning since it is always ready to be used, while the cumbersome plow, which requires special handling and servicing and has a propensity to break down, can only be used for certain kinds of work.

## Craft

In order to avoid the disputes and difficulties accompanying the definition of the term "craft," we should, strictly speaking, confine ourselves to the processing of natural materials. Here, too, the aforementioned "simple machines revolution" was already in full stride in the Chalcolithic period. Work with clay and stone was influenced by the invention of the wheel and axle, which led to the creation of both the potter's wheel and the mechanical drill for working with harder kinds of stone. All of these inventions influenced the extraction of raw materials, compaction, the smelting of the first metals and work with them. Another "simple machine" (though more an element) should be added here to the repertoire of Chalcolithic manufacturers – fire.

The Chalcolithic period saw marked development in pyrotechnical methods, including pottery production, metal processing and creating the first artificial materials in human history: glass-like faience and later, when the stated had stabilized, glass itself. Along with pyrotechnology came the need for fuel; already in the Chalcolithic period these products must have had a considerable impact, at least in areas around the focal points of the societies, on the natural landscape. Specifically, this would have involved deforestation for fuel purposes, while in the basins of large rivers bundles of reeds would have served this need.

Yet production activities would have also been influenced by non-economic factors in the Chalcolithic period. While craft activities were originally located without distinction within the various villages of a given culture, social polarization and the onset of regional centers resulted in the movement of craft operations to their vicinity. We see this in all focal points of the early state. This concerned providing services to important social centers using nearby settlements whose people specialized in crafts. Pre-state Hieraconpolis in Egypt, Mesopotamian settlements of the late Uruk period and urban settlements of ancient India and China were all familiar with and used these specialized service organizations.

It should also be pointed out that a number of the craft operations reveal influences of a non-economic nature. This mainly consisted of materials that had no direct economic significance, but which played an important role in the social and even spiritual sphere. Egyptian palettes, requiring a certain degree of stone-cutting specialization, skill and ingeniousness to be made, served mainly as attributes and "indicators" of social position. The first Mesopotamian faiences that appeared during the middle Uruk Period at Tepe Gawra were probably imitations of impressive and socially valued gems made, for instance, of imported lapis lazuli, the originals of which many people would have been unable to afford. Earthenware bracelets, i.e. objects of an explicitly decorative nature, were even made using quite complex technology at extremely high temperatures in the workshops of Mohenjo-daro. Furthermore, it seems that this production was somehow controlled by one of the central offices (the find of a pair of fire pots sealed across the contact point of the two vessels). Such a trend was distinctly evident in the bronze work found in China, where the ancient elite believed that only bronze vessels enabled effective communication with the world of the dead. We see here that the world of Chalcolithic craft was not solely governed by economic aspects. The social and spiritual questions in it played such a significant role that they probably even directly brought about certain types of production. Some kinds of craft were also made possible here by embleming activities related to the elite's need for legitimacy, or directly to the cult or even liturgical apparatus that arose from the axioms of the age's spiritual systems. The production of stone vessels, for instance, was monopolized by the royal court in early dynastic Egypt.[148]

---

[148] Petra Vlčková, Kamenné nádoby s nápisy – Prameny k poznání správního systému Raně Dynastického Egypta (Stone vessels bearing inscriptions – sources providing an understanding of the Administrative System of Early Dynastic Egypt), in: Ľubica

# Trading

A somewhat complicated situation is apparent in trading activities and the long-distance contacts of the early state societies. The long-distance exchange of material and intellectual goods had, of course, been going on since at least the Middle Paleolithic Age (Eastern Anatolian obsidian in the Shanidar Cave in northern Iraq). The Chalcolithic Period still did not have trade in the sense of profit-oriented activities using generally accepted currencies. Instead, these were forms of exchange found in pre-industrial societies based on reciprocity and redistribution. Reciprocity, the mutual and direct exchange of material goods between individual producers as an activity geared mainly toward establishing friendly relations between the recipients, was clearly a routine matter in the world of the first state centers. Not only did it concern the everyday life of the public at large, but also the elite of the given societies, who elevated the exchange of gifts (*keimelia* in Hellenic) to an act of great social importance, even ceremonial in nature.[149] In contrast, we see the birth of redistribution in the formative period of the early states. Society already had in place at this point a coordination center that received goods from direct manufacturers and supplied them to consumers who were generally not the same as the original manufacturers. Redistribution is a relatively important social process and its occurrence, to the extent that it can be recorded, is unquestionably linked to the birth of early statehood. The most familiar example is still offered by Sumerian Mesopotamia, where the transition from reciprocity to redistribution is evident in the archeologically quantitative decrease in portable containers (baskets, sacks, packages, vessels, etc.) and an increase in the presence of storage area seals – from the Uruk Period until the peak of the early dynastic period (ca. 3500–2700 BC).

---

Obuchová, Petr Charvát (ed.), Stát a státnost ve starém Orientu (The state and statehood in the ancient Orient), a series of studies by the "People and the Land in History" work group, Prague, The Czech Society for Oriental Studies 2006, pp. 8–25, on page 8–9 and 24.

[149] See Ian Morris, Gift and Commodity in Archaic Greece, Man 21/1, 1986, pp. 1–17.

In pre-dynastic Egypt the redistribution of edibles is evident in the central processing plants supplying goods such as beer in large quantities. The results of new research in Gilund seem to indicate the existence in India of the centralized collection of material goods and perhaps their ensuing redistribution.

The trading realm was influenced less emphatically by the Chalcolithic "simple machines revolution," although, along with the first wheeled vehicle, river and sea boats appeared here for the first time as extremely effective means for cheaply transporting large loads great distances.

Non-economic factors were obviously present as well. Many goods and especially opulent materials used by the elite of the age to indicate their privileged position had to be acquired elsewhere at a considerable expense without the importer expecting significant profit. Lapis lazuli, mined with great difficulty and in the extreme conditions of mountainous Badakhshan in present-day Afghanistan and imported great distances to Sumerian Mesopotamia and pharaonic Egypt, offers a striking example. New customers, the inhabitants of prehistoric princedoms in central Asia, also gradually appeared on this route. Their interest caused the branching off of new distribution routes for this highly sought mineral. Thus the stone's significance was apparently not linked only to the milieu of early state centers. As every visitor to British Museum in London will attest to when seeing for themselves the wondrously impressive jewels, weapons and fashion accessories of lapis lazuli found in royal tombs in the Sumerian town of Ur, the ancient manufacturers knew how to make ornaments from them that were indeed worthy of royal courts. A similar role was played in China by jade, which is not native to this land and must have been imported from areas near Lake Baikal.

The economy of the early states did therefore not only follow purely economic reasoning: factors of a social and, evidently, spiritual nature also entered the arena of material goods.

## Settlements

During the creation of the early state an increasing majority of the population settled in villages and single dwellings, or in temporary nomadic and hunter-gatherer camps. Nevertheless, a correlative to the creation and development of more constitutive and deeper layered social bodies is actually the differentiation in settlements that frequently reveal the professions of those who established the settlement, or at least of their important inhabitants.

The first factor that emerged distinctly enough from the prehistoric darkness for excavations of the settlement to detect it consists of cult and religious activity. These are the buildings that begin to stand out from the common Chalcolithic settlement in the areas we are dealing with and that take on characteristics distinct from the usual residential structures. A central temple, clearly of considerable importance, was built at Hieraconpolis in Egypt, probably before the middle of the 4th millenium BC. Differences in the appearance of settlements also began to appear relatively early in Mesopotamia where cult edifices were built even before the secular centers (Tell el-'Oueili 3), which even replaced them in some cases (Tell Awayli 4). "Peace under the palm trees" finally set in right before the state emerged, when there appeared atop a giant *haute terasse* in Susa of present-day Iran a "temple" and a "palace" and, quite tellingly, a single, and thus most likely shared warehouse complex, i.e. a supply center. Settlements with a markedly more assertive cult function had already appeared in the early Harappan period, after 3000 BC (the Amri culture in the Mohenjo-daro vicinity). We also know of a temple of one of the fertility goddesses at the Niuheliang site that is representative of the Chinese Chalcolithic culture of Hongshan.

It is clear then that spiritual and religious factors played an exceptionally important role in the creation and development of early statehood, and that patronage (in the sense of supporting the construction of cult buildings) represented not only an element that welded together the various layers of society, but was also an important viability and solidarity test for these early states. The construction of temple architecture meant there were considerable demands placed on the numbers, output and organization of the workforce employed here and, consequently, also on the performance of the organizational and logistics apparatus in charge of managing the project. The acquisition of cult inventory often represented a significant investment into procuring rare and valuable materials from remote regions, which may have led to purely economically focused endeavors that were, at least from our perspective, a "noble waste." This, however, was not the view held by the inhabitants of the early states: participation in similar construction enterprises may have represented for them a certain form of achieving a very specific social consensus, in which the entire society "from lord to commoner" came together to perform a shared task *ad bonum publicum*. The fact that the temples and temple communities often represented a "third power" that was significantly involved in finding common ground between the ruling and the ruled is apparent from, for instance, the history of ancient Mesopotamia.

Although the secular elite appeared later on the scene of the early state's impressive and exceptional architecture than their sacral colleagues, they certainly did not neglect representing their offices.

Their presence is indicated in Egypt's Hieraconpolis by a "fort" most likely built sometime at the very beginning of the Egyptian state just before the end of the 4th millenium. Over time, the stature and prestige of the pharaoh's position fully prevailed in Egypt, so that at the end of the 3rd millenium royal administration took over the religious institutions.[150] After initial battles were fought out between the sacral and secular sectors of society, the situation resembled more of a truce than outright peace. Nevertheless, the lay administration bodies there acquired (as some colleagues conclude) palaces, perhaps even as early as during the late Uruk culture period. The location of the assembly (UKKIN) of greater Uruk community, of whose existence written sources provide eloquent testimony, is a question of great interest. Though the Mesopotamian temple entered the 3rd millenium BC side

---

[150] Petra Vlčková, Kamenné nádoby s nápisy – Prameny k poznání správního systému Raně Dynastického Egypta (Stone vessels bearing inscriptions - sources providing an understanding of the Administrative System of Early Dynastic Egypt), in: Ľubica Obuchová, Petr Charvát (ed.), Stát a státnost ve starém Orientu (The state and statehood in the ancient Orient), a series of studies by the "People and the Land in History" work group, Prague, The Czech Society for Oriental Studies 2006, pp. 8–25, on page 21.

by side with the Palace, latent tension soon once again grew into an open conflict that was briskly resolved by the "reformer" Uruinimgina of Lagash (2352–2342 BC), who simply confiscated all temple property and placed it under the control of the secular ruler Lagash. Researchers in India are somewhat confounded in attempts to prove the elite's participation in such an advanced and refined way of life that would be unimaginable today without some form of state organization. There is little choice but to view the entire realm of the proto-Indian *ecumene* as a united whole whose central bodies and elite groups are evident at all sites – primarily at Mohenjo-daro, but also Harappa and other extraordinary sites that shed significant light on the cultural level of the secular elite of ancient Bharat. In contrast, it seems that for the area of Chinese civilization the religious administration soon passed into the hands of a secular ruler – the emperor – who perfectly joined the sacred and profane aspect of the Chinese world view.

In terms of the structure of settlements, the rise and development of the early state can thus be characterized as a fracturing of society into socially distinct groups of the sacral elite and secular elite accompanied by the mobilization of social forces towards "generally beneficial" projects. The degree of success with which the early states' elite were able to construct, organize and stabilize new social bodies in space and time then depended on the persuasiveness of the arguments made by the elite, but also on their credibility, i.e. their ability to support all their claims to society through their own behavior and lifestyle.

For clarity's sake, we should also add that the settlement systems of ancient states were quite permeable structures whose fabric was penetrated by social groups not building permanent settlements. These were mainly groups of people living within a hunter-gatherer economy. Another similar example is provided by nomads, generally shepherds, who not only passed through the territories of these states, but also left and returned to them as they pleased. Unfortunately, archaeology generally fails in the cases of these groups and the considerably sketchy and meager information comes from a wide range of sources.

Sources dating back as far as the early Sumerian Dynasty (ca. 3000–2334 BC) have provided details on what are most likely groups of hunters and fishermen living in the marshland areas of present-day southeast Iraq. The administration of the city-states at that time imposed specialized tasks (e.g. military service) upon them and attempted to force them to accept a settled way of life and agriculture-based livelihood.

Researchers rely mainly on archeology for their information on nomads.[151] Though on the one hand it seems that the nomads have maintained their customs and lifestyle over thousands of years, researchers rarely get the opportunity to support this finding through more extensive investigation. A Sumerian narrative from the 19th–18th century BC on the engagements and marriage of the god Martu, the personification of the nomadic and hunter-gatherer way of life, is the mythical correlative of the absorption of nomadic groups by the Mesopotamian majority society. Martu's request to marry the daughter of the city god Numushda is granted by the "civilized" father, even though Martu has no permanent home, does not know how to prepare food on a fire, is constantly traveling through the desert and does not even find a permanent final resting place after death.

## Burials

It is generally assumed that excavations of burials provide archeologists with information on the social stratification of the people in question, as well as of their spiritual world and thinking.

In fact, it is more prosaic than that. After the final comprehensive and extremely generalizing work on burials[152] fell into oblivion and

---

[151] See Roger Cribb, Nomads in Archaeology, Cambridge, Cambridge University Press 1991, and more recently Stefan R. Hauser (ed.), Die Sichtbarkeit von Nomaden und Saisonaler Besiedlung in der Archäologie, Multidisziplinäre Annäherungen an ein methodisches Problem, Mitteilung des SFB "Differenz und Integration" 9, Orientwissenschaftliche Hefte herausgegeben vom Orientwissenschaftlichen Zentrum der Martin-Luther Universität Halle-Wittenberg Heft 21/2006, Halle (Saale), OWZ 2006, and Benjamin Adam Saidel & Eveline J. Van der Steen (edd.), On the Fringe of Society: Archaeological and Ethnoarchaeological Perspectives on Pastoral and Agricultural Societies, BAR International Series 1657, Oxford, Archaeopress 2007.

[152] Lewis Binford, Mortuary practices: their study and their potential, in: J. A. Brown (ed.), Approaches to the Social Dimensions of Mortuary Practices, Memoirs of the Society for American Archaeology No. 25, 1971, pp. 6–29.

vanished with the murmuring of post-processual debates in archaeology that occasionally escalated to a roar, research in this area returned to an essentially neo-positivist position and ceased to attempt a bolder methodical approach. This resulted in an adherence to the belief that the quantity and quality of funerary objects were to be considered the criterion for judging the deceased's social position in that "the more the society had and the richer they were, the better off they were." The universal validity of this rule still has yet to be proved, and findings from the areas examined here show that the whole matter is much more complex. We are also faced with quite complicated research tasks when considering reflections of the spiritual world in burials.

The extent to which we can substantiate burial sites in the early states of the Old World is an important and extremely interesting question, and yet this question does not seem that difficult in Egypt or China. In the Hieraconpolis area in Egypt, excavation has revealed some 8,000 graves with the total number of deceased buried in them estimated at 20,000. The same applies for China, whose overall archeological picture is necessarily fragmented and incomplete given the size of the country. China offers a relatively large number of high-quality excavated and documented burial sites. In contrast, the Mesopotamian and proto-Indian civilizations can be seen as wholly atypical in this. Let us begin with a quite provocative example: Neither primordial nor Sumerian Mesopotamia has offered a sufficient number of burial sites that would provide an opportunity to portray even a fragment of the original populations. Ancient Mesopotamia's largest burial site, in Eridu of present-day southern Iraq, provided 193 excavated graves with the original number estimated at around 800 burials. The famous city cemetery in Ur represents in ancient Mesopotamia the largest number of excavated burials. Here the roughly 2,500 deceased were buried over a time span of a thousand years during the 3rd millenium BC. A considerable discrepancy arises when comparing the Hieraconpolis number with this.

Though documentation on finds from Mesopotamian burial sites does exist, it is meager at best. We have already examined the prehistoric period here and know that there have only been a few dozen burials documented from the period of the Uruk culture and that even after 3,000 BC (already in the historic period), the number of burial sites, including those near large urban centers, is surprisingly small.

Let us compare this with the aforementioned information from the Sumerian writings on the life style of nomads.

The proto-Indian civilization is only slightly better in this regard. Although Harappa is surrounded by cemeteries, they are not overly abundant (hundreds of burials) and the culture's metropolis, Mohenjo-daro, is practically completely void of burial sites. This then represents quite a serious discrepancy in our data that needs to be explained.

We should first ask what the burial sites in the world's early states have in common. In all cases providing data, we see that since the Chalcolithic Period the deceased have been buried in a uniform position, generally on one of the pairs of cardinal points, facing a single direction with their heads all pointing the same way. In my view, this indicates that all of these groups already had an idea of how the worlds of both the living and the dead were arranged, and that they buried their dead so that the coordinates of their final resting place cohered with the order of the universe. This is a rather banal finding, for the attempt to imagine "what would happen if" and "what will happen when I die" is what distinguishes man from animal, at least as far as we know. In cases in which control material is available to us from settlements, we often find that orientation aligned with the cardinal points is also evident in prominent public buildings (e.g. the orientation of important buildings with their corners aligned with the cardinal points in Mesopotamia). All this indicates a quite pronounced formulation of man's fundamental attitude toward the events around him, to the universe surrounding him and to his fellow humans and is already evident in the Chalcolithic Period.

Another rather remarkable characteristic of the finds from the burial sites is the extreme abundance of funerary objects found with deceased adult women. We have already seen a similar situation in Egypt and China. The thorough distinction in Mesopotamia of the male and female deceased only becomes evident in the historical period, though female burials are not that much more equipped with funerary objects than their male counterparts; the same applies for burials in

India.[153] Here the discrepancies begin to accumulate according to the region, and the whole matter thereby gains significance.

Let us now try to satisfactorily interpret the findings. The Egyptian and Chinese findings evidently attest to a more or less normal situation in which, although the deceased depart from the world of the living, they maintain access to their underground dwellings where they can, if necessary, be sought and continue to form, along with the living inhabitants, part of their native community. Both the exceptional role of the veneration of the dead in Chinese culture and the extreme attention devoted to funerary objects in Egyptian culture would be consistent with this.

In both civilizations the somewhat macabre French proverb can be applied: *"le mort saisit le vif"* (death seizes life).

How do the Mesopotamian and Indian civilizations differ? We will start with the Mesopotamian sphere, which is the closest part of the Near East to us. This region provides us with a clue that could explain the whole situation to us. A Soviet archeological expedition excavated a multi-layered settlement of the prehistoric Halafian culture (6500–4000 BC) at the Yarim Tepe II site in northern Iraq. Archeologists have noticed that dwellings at the sites also contained, in some cases beneath the floors, a wide variety of burials: that of entire bodies, of their parts and of cremated bodies. It is also worth noting that cremation burials were concentrated in the settlement district where fire was worked with and where excavation has revealed several pottery kilns. With this in mind, let us consider if this is a case of identifying the essence of human beings (or at least part of it) with a certain element – in our case fire – which the individual returns to after death or crosses through to the world of the dead. The elements do indeed frequently constitute the boundary between the living and the dead in ethnological cultures. Burying the deceased in graves dug in the ground quite simply indicates that the individual is relinquished to the element Earth; while cremation means that the body is given over to the element Fire (or passes through that element to the next world). The concept of the

---

[153] Jean-Daniel Forest, Les pratiques funéraires en Mésopotamie au début du 3ᵉ millénaire avant Jésus Christ, étude de cas, Paris, ERC 1983 (Chapter: Ur cimetière Jemdet Nasr).

river Styx, across which the mythical ferryman Charon transports the deceased, tellingly illustrates Water's role. Finally, we even have proof attesting to the element of air in this kind of "border" role for the people of pueblo settlements in southwest America. In large subterranean rooms called *kivas*, the survivors of the deceased worshipped spirits called *kachina*, the souls of the dead, who lived underground but who could also take the form of clouds.

Could then the absence of graves in the culture of ancient Mesopotamia mean that the deceased were relinquished to elements other than the Earth? We cannot rule this out. The most telling testimony on the Sumerian afterlife was provided by graves with an abundance of finds from the city graveyard in Ur. In some cases of lavishly arranged burials, funerary objects were found that were typical for men and women.[154]Rather than drawing conclusions of hermaphroditism, we should recall the Sumerian writings describing the journey of the deceased in the afterlife which entails presenting honorary gifts, the very objects they took to their graves, to the deities residing in the world of the dead.

These findings support the Sumerian idea of the afterlife as a journey that could very well include the notion of a kind of supernatural "gate" that (each) deceased must pass through and that could consist of one of the elements.

Findings from the Indian subcontinent indicate a similar view. The Tamil epic poem *Manimekalai* from around AD 1 provides us with a thorough description of the cemetery on the city's outskirts, albeit from a much later time. Four columned entrances with brightly painted facades lead into the perpendicularly walled cemetery. Inside, however, the walls are strictly whitewashed. The visitor is welcomed at the entrance by fired clay sculptures of a deity holding a sacred thread and trident. In entering through one of the gates the visitor is presented with a view of patulous trees, from whose branches hang the heads of those who fearlessly sacrificed their lives. The cemetery has places of sacrifice, altars and shrines of the goddess of the burial groves, where

---

[154] For a more in-depth examination of these questions see Susan Pollock, Ancient Mesopotamia – The Eden that Never Was, Cambridge, Cambridge University Press 1999.

the survivors of the deceased bring rice offerings. Other tomb-chapels distinguish places where the meritorious were buried. The cemetery's guards, who lived there, helped in different ways to prepare the dead for their final journey: cremation at the edges in the corner of the cemetery, laying the bodies in graves or burial tombs, interring the remains in urns or exposing the bodies to the elements.

Here we stumble upon something that could explain the whole matter: the custom of treating the body of the deceased in a way commensurate with their status and according to how they died.[155] It is this differentiated treatment of the deceased that could result in a situation familiar to us in excavating Mesopotamian burial sites: the documented cases always only capture part of the actual state.

In reviewing the ancient history of Mesopotamia, we find one more possibility of explaining this surprising phenomenon. This is the fact that the people of the Mesopotamian cities often buried their dead in burial tombs in the courtyards of their homes. After the bodies were laid to rest, the tomb was walled up until the next burial, when the remains of an earlier corpse were heaped in a corner to make room for another body.

This could be repeated several times with the oldest remains then completely succumbing to decay.[156] Nevertheless, the ancient Mesopotamians commemorated the deceased with a special ritual, so by no means did they neglect honoring the dead.

We will therefore conclude that the veneration of the dead is apparent in burials at all early state centers and that, one way or another, they reflect the attempt to include them in the life of the living community.

---

[155] See Lewis Binford (Mortuary practices: their study and their potential, in: J. A. Brown (ed.), Approaches to the Social Dimensions of Mortuary Practices, Memoirs of the Society for American Archaeology No. 25, 1971, pp. 6–29) where he stipulates six factors that can be used to distinguish burials in ethnological cultures: age, sex, place of death, circumstances of death, immediate social personal and broader social persona.

[156] See Paolo Brusasco, The Archaeology of Verbal and Nonverbal Meaning, Mesopotamian Domestic Architecture and Its Textual Dimension, BAR International Series 163 1, Oxford, Archaeopress 2007, and Andrew C. Cohen, Death Rituals, Ideology, and the Development of Early Mesopotamian Kingship – Toward a New Understanding of Iraq's Royal Cemetery of Ur (Ancient Magic and Divination VII), Leiden – Boston, Brill – Styx 2005, especially page 106 on the *kispum* ceremony commemorating the dead (this ritual contained *shumma zakàru*, invoking the name and *me naqu*, pouring water).

This was done in Egypt and China using quite standard procedures involving rituals over the dead body. Mesopotamia and India offer a somewhat different picture and differentiate the commemoration of the dead (e.g. according to their merit) in placing an emphasis on acts of a spiritual and ritual nature concerning the cultures of the dead.

# SOCIETY

The Chalcolithic period represents the beginning of the breaking up of human society into groups distinguished by their livelihood, social role and position in the universally acknowledged arrangement of the visible and invisible world. Humanity had already amassed at this level of historical development such an abundance of findings, experience, knowledge and skills that completely controlling it was no longer within the powers of the individual and the social division of labor became absolutely necessary: in other words, a system in which "this one does this and that one does that."

Human society was then confronted with the need to deal with a wide range of complications, predicaments and problems that it had never had to face before. If everyone did not do everything, but this person did this and that person did that, how would they agree on the demand for their goods, how would they ensure that asymmetric production does not occur? If some people made one specialized product while others supplied goods demanding different skills and energies, would this not lead to a breakdown in supplies – to shortages, poverty and hunger? How would they ensure that the contradictory demands of the individual specialized production groups were made adequately compatible and at least minimally met? Clearly, everything did continue down that path. Which of these new "partial production" groups of human society had prioritized demands and why? Were farmers, shepherds, hunters and fishermen, craftsmen, merchants or shamans more important? Why? If two specialized groups of the populations came into conflict, who was to settle the matter and what criteria and rules were to be used? Most importantly, what would the ancient gods and goddesses think of all this and how could they even allow for it to happen? If a beautiful fairy sits on the rocks at the bend in a stream by a forest pool on quiet summer evenings, what right does some stranger with a hammer and hoe have to break open the rocks, clear a little area and impose mill wheels on the stream under the pretext that raw materials are located there that could be used to make metal tools? If our deity (e.g. the fire god) commanded us to conquer all others with force, who would prevent us from doing so and why should we be prevented? If our fields were regularly spoiled by groups of hunters and gatherers who considered them to be sources of especially tasty grasses, who would prevent us from waiting for them to come again and shooting every last one of them – men, women, children and the elderly?

Based on these and other social contradictions arising from economic, social and spiritual specialization, human communities living in the Chalcolithic Age began to feel the need for coordination centers that would bring at least some kind of order to the precarious balance of interpersonal relations and that would acquire sufficient authority to instill a system of universal coexistence. Not, mind you, a just and unflawed system: Justice is a human invention, and that which is human is fleeting, and therefore imperfect and incomplete. The system would have to be simple, clear and legible so that every member of the communality in question would know how to act in certain situations and, most importantly, what he or she should not do under any circumstance. Even more precisely, it would have to be a system that did not place at the dawn of human history a special emphasis on the ethical aspects of human coexistence (ultimately each member community would govern itself by tried-and-true laws and customs that were thousands of years old), but that clearly and distinctly approved of certain acts and punished others. This would change the social reality of the Chalcolithic world into one much more varied, intense and complicated. Our French colleagues sagaciously called their recently published anthology that deals with this area "The Chalcolithic Age and the Construction of Inequalities."[157] The word "inequality" may be hard for us to swallow, yet for the rather smooth run of Chalcolithic societies inequality represented the only solution. At least no one has yet to come up with a different solution that would pass the thousand-year test.

---

[157] Jean Guilaine (ed.), Le Chalcolithique et la construction des inégalités, t. II., Paris, Editions Errance 2007.

## Organizational centers of the Chalcolithic societies and their facilities

In setting up coordination centers, the Chalcolithic societies observed time-tested principles and relied on institutions proven effective
through the ages. Groups of hunters and gathers already recognized
two permanent and periodically occupied "offices": the chief and shaman. During the Chalcolithic period these two had the unenviable task
of creating from the anthill of conflicting human interests a "simple
machine" that would not make human life "poor, brutish, nasty and
short." These were the individuals who gradually assumed a status that
enabled them to manipulate the social mechanisms and to remold the
existing social structures.

This did not entail "organized force"; if the chieftains of the pre-
state period committed such ineptitudes and tried to assert their will
through brute force, they would lose their lives or at least their taxpayers. The afflicted people would certainly take to their heels; just go
ahead and try to catch the escaped farmers, shepherds or craftsmen in
the wooded mountains, on the open steppe or upon the waves of the
endless sea, when you have hardly fifty soldiers at your disposal and
about 3-months worth of supplies for them. Instead, another route was
taken: For the early elite to by trustworthy, they could not take, but had
to offer. They had to offer something that people had been unfamiliar
with up until then; something that would enrich the people's lives in
a way never before seen or heard. Alfred Gell nicely characterizes the
situation in writing that the original elite's efforts were directed towards
"a collective social other, whose gaze must be met and whose sensibili-
ties must be captured and entranced."[158] Here and elsewhere I try to
answer the question of what this was.

Since the first shamans had enough problems of their own communicating with the powers of the spiritual world, and the performance of
their office required long and painstaking preparations often detached
from human societies, the decisive role in creating the balanced system

[158] David Wengrow, The Archaeology of Early Egypt – Social Transformations in North-East Africa, 10,000 to 2650 BC, Cambridge–New York–Melbourne–Madrid–Cape Town–Singapore–Sao Paulo, Cambridge University Press 2006, p. 154.

of Chalcolithic inequality fell to the chiefs (or however contemporary ethnology calls them), the leading figures of the period. For the sake of clarity and brevity, we will take the liberty to use this relatively general term in referring to the socially active elite of the pre-state period. The chiefs were indeed the ones that the people of the Chalcolithic communities turned to most often with their concerns and troubles, and those chiefs, who did not think only of their prestige and stature, but took into consideration the long-term prosperity and benefits of the communities that they led, were the first to begin contemplating rules to introduce at least basic order to the Chalcolithic chaos. We will attempt to determine in this chapter how they acted.

## Courtiers of the first rulers: clever, resolute and foresighted

Performing one's social obligations was extremely important to the elite since it consolidated their social status. It was already undoubtedly true at this time that the stronger the position of socially prominent figures, the stronger the people believed that not only did their leaders not lie, but that they practiced what they preached and that their actions benefited the entire society. To meet their social obligations the early elite needed two categories of assistants who were indispensable to them.

They first had to acquire assistants that were intelligent enough to control the increasingly complicated Chalcolithic social bodies and loyal enough not to be put off by the fact that their entire lives would be devoted to occupying the position "of the number two man or woman (or number three, four or twenty-nine as the case may be)." In other words, they needed adept managers and skillful administrators. These individuals included military leaders who were extremely useful in the armed conflicts accompanying the birth of states. The use of organized force during this historical period has been greatly reflected upon, yet there is a scarcity of actual materials on this. The information we do get from such sources lead us to believe that the leaders of the early states used organized force prudently and always with a specific purpose. Once this goal was achieved, the military actions were brought to an end.

Unfortunately, measuring the organization abilities of the early states represents one of the most difficult tasks that historical research faces. In general, the progressiveness and managerial proficiency of the architects of early statehood is often measured by aspects such as the number and quality of the first ancient buildings, the degree of proficiency in craft technology, the level of artwork and the size of the territory that archeological testimony tells us the ancient rulers were capable of uniting under their leadership. Most of these criteria, however, consist of past testimony telling us the high level of organizational progressiveness achieved, but not providing us with knowledge of how it was obtained.[159] We have already expressed the view that early statehood did not arise in connection with sweeping innovations in production, and that the first state centers were created based on redistribution. It was the gathering of the surplus product from direct manufacturers and its distribution to consumers with other manufacturers which represented one of the basic organizational tasks that managers of the early states had to master.

In this sense, only sources of prehistoric and early ancient Mesopotamia illuminate the historical dynamics involved in the managers of the early states developing organizational skills. We have already said that the seals in clay that originally sealed portable containers (baskets, sacks, chests, vessels, packages, etc.), can be socially interpreted as reciprocity, the mutual exchange of material goods, whose purpose is usually the social benefit of both participants of this kind of transaction.

---

[159] Very informative documents on the redistribution of foods from royal sources to cult institutions are provided, for instance, by writings from early dynastic Egypt (early 3$^{rd}$ millenium BC): Petra Vlčková, Kamenné nádoby s nápisy - Prameny k poznání správního systému Raně Dynastického Egypta (Stone vessels bearing inscriptions - sources providing an understanding of the Administrative System of Early Dynastic Egypt), in: Ľubica Obuchová, Petr Charvát (ed.), Stát a státnost ve starém Orientu (The state and statehood in the ancient Orient), a series of studies by the "People and the Land in History" work group, Prague, The Czech Society for Oriental Studies 2006, pp. 8-25, on p. 21-24, especially table 9 on p. 23.

We find in this case traces of movement in only one direction – from the supplier to the consumer, who opens the package and breaks the seal (and who usually reciprocates by providing different goods or services, the traces of which archeology still needs to reveal). In contrast, seals taken from the doors of storage rooms represent a two-phase, bidirectional movement: You first store something inside and then you monitor when, why and by whom it is brought outside. This movement there and back can already be interpreted as *redistribution*. A social process of this nature points to the existence of a social coordination center that controls and regulates the movement of material goods – i.e. a body that undoubtedly emerged in the early state's center, if it was not already there. Early historic Mesopotamia provides us with relatively telling and abundant information on society's path from reciprocity (= the sealing of portable containers) to redistribution (= the sealing of entrances to storages rooms) that can be summarized in the following tables.[160]

The developmental trend from reciprocity to redistribution, and therefore from the socially managed movement of goods led by wholly spontaneous mechanisms to the deliberate offtake of surplus goods by the center, which distributes them for consumption as it deems appropriate, is quite clear here. In observing the forms of the socially relevant exchange of material goods, the creation and stabilization of the early state becomes apparent. We are literally making history out of lumps of clay here.

Unfortunately, we lack similar studies from other centers of early statehood. In time, archeologists will undoubtedly present them in the field of the early history of ancient Egypt, which offers relatively abundant sphragistic material from the 3rd millenium BC when Pharaoh's state administration was established and stabilized.[161] The results of

---

[160] Once again I am including results of my past work here: Petr Charvát, Mesopotamia Before History. London and New York, Routledge – Taylor and Francis Group 2002, p. 202, and also The backs of some seals from Nineveh 5, "Iraq" LXVII Part 1, Spring 2005 (Papers of the XLIXe Rencontre Assyriologique Internationale London, 7–1 1 July 2003, Part Two), pp. 391–397, see p. 394–395.

[161] This path was taken by e.g. Jochem Kahl, who noticed that writings on funerary object of prominent Egyptian tombs of the first two dynasties are the signatures of the senders rather than the address of the recipient: David Wengrow, The Archaeology of Early Egypt –

| Site | Period (BC) | % of seals from portable containers of goods | % of seals from entrances |
|---|---|---|---|
| Late Uruk and Jemdet Nasr – all finds | 3500–3000 | 96.99 | 3.01 |
| Jemdet Nasr – new excavation | 3200–3000 | 91.66 | 8.33 |
| Susa (Early Dynastic Period = ED) | 3000–2700 | 80.96 | 19.04 |
| Ur, "City League" seals (ED I-II) | 3000–2700 | 31.00 | 69.00 |

| Site | Period (BC) | % of seals from portable containers of goods | % of seals from entrances |
|---|---|---|---|
| Ur, specimens of 52 seals from layers SIS 8–4 (ED I-II) | 3000–2700 | 65.77–46.15 | 44.23–53.85 |
| Nippur, Innana's temple, layers ED I | 3000–2700 | 76.34–67.44 | 23.26–32.56 |
| Fara or Shuruppak (ED I) | 3000–2700 | 8.72 | 88.17 |
| Abu Salabikh waste heap, (early ED III) | 2600–2500 | 43.56 | 56.44 |

recent excavations in Gilund indicated that a similar approach could be taken here as well.

Different criteria will be necessary for measuring the level of organizational and managerial skills and the ingenuity of those founding the civilization there. It is perhaps again worth mentioning the proverb from one of the classical writings that adeptly captures the redistributive nature of Chinese society: "Dukes live on tribute, ministers on their estates, *shi* ['gentlemen'] on the land, and peasants on their toil."[162]

Social Transformations in North-East Africa, 10,000 to 2650 BC, Cambridge – New York – Melbourne – Madrid – Cape Town – Singapore – Sao Paulo, Cambridge University Press 2006, p. 235. An Italian archeology expedition had already found storage room seals during a review excavation of Petrie's "South Town" in Naqada: Claudio Barocas, Rodolfo Fattovich, Maurizio Tosi, The Oriental Institute of Naples expedition to Petrie's South Town (Upper Egypt), 1977–1983: An interim report, in: Lech Krzyzaniak, Marek Kobusiewicz (edd.), Late Prehistory of the Nile Basin and the Sahara, Poznań, Poznań Archaeological Museum 1989, pp. 295–301 (p. 301 – a total of ca. 300 seal impressions from the doors of storage rooms, but only six have impressions of cylinder seals).

[162] Charles K. Maisels, Early Civilizations of the Old World, London and New York, Routledge – Taylor and Francis Group 2001, p. 332.

## Courtiers of the first rulers:
## Those who speak with the gods

The second, and probably most important group of the early states' elite, were specialists in spiritual matters, the successors to the afore-mentioned Shamans. These individuals were in charge of overseeing social order in accordance with the widespread understanding of the visible and invisible world and man's place in it. It should again be emphasized that this was not a simple ideological justification for the existence of socially superior individuals; these "engineers of the human soul" had to contemplate, propose and justify a social order that would integrate social innovations, not disturb the bases of the generally shared understanding of the world's arrangement, and yet provide everyone in this new social structure with human worth and a socially dignified place. The role of the priests in the formation of the early states was never easy and they often had to choose whom to serve: the secular lord, or the one who "commands for one to even give his life for the love of his fellow men." We are dealing here with a barely comprehensible area that can hardly be made sense of without taking into consideration sources from later periods. These sources can give us at least a basic idea of how the priests of the early states understood the role of the social centers, from which law and order spread through the new society.

### Egypt

On the whole, findings from ancient Egypt, which we have already dealt with in depth, offer a clear view of the situation. Part of the Egyptian pharaoh's being was consubstantial with the gods of the Nile Valley and surrounding regions, and another with all the people of the "Black Land." The divine impulse could thus only flow to Egyptians via the pharaoh, who occupied a key position on the path of the most sacred substance from the heavens to mortals. It originally seems that the Egyptians imagined this "flow of sacredness" in an extremely con-crete way as the activated fertility power.

Therefore, all the fertility power of water and the soil, of livestock and wildlife, and even of people flowed from the gods and passed exclusively through the pharaoh. This was indeed a very strong argument for the pharaoh's central position in Egyptian society.

The constitutive role of the pharaoh "establishing" or "re-establishing" Egyptian state institutions is very graphically illustrated by a bas-relief located in the underground spaces beneath the famous step pyramid of Djoser in Saqqara (after 2650 BC). The pharaoh, shown running while performing the jubilee of the thirty-year anniversary of his rule *(sed)*, holds a cat-o'-nine-tails as a sign of his power, and most likely a legal document called "that which establishes a house." Since, in performing this ceremony, the pharaoh evidently ran around the shrines of all Egyptian deities set up in a special courtyard in the pyramid district, this is quite clearly interpreted as their re-establishment following the closure of the thirty-year cycle of the pharaoh's rule. This evidently represented a moment in which the end of the organized world and the onset of primitive chaos threatened. By performing this ceremonial act, as depicted and immortalized by the sculpture, the pharaoh is obviously trying to prevent this.[163]

Moreover, Egyptian written documents provide important proof of one of the basic parameters of the ancient kingdom that should be mentioned here. As early as the 1st dynasty (at the threshold of the 3rd millenium), Egyptian sages were keeping records of the ancestry of their kings and had a firm grasp of their historical chronology. This is, in fact, the very beginning of historiography.[164]

## Sumer and Akkad

A quite remarkable situation is found in ancient Mesopotamia owing mainly to the fact that, at least in the first thousands of years of the Sumerian states' existence, there was a lively debate on the nature of central power. We have already described how during the late Uruk and Jemdet Nasr period (ca. 3500–30000 BC) the high priest EN and

---

[163] David Wengrow, The Archaeology of Early Egypt – Social Transformations in North-East Africa, 10,000 to 2650 BC, Cambridge – New York – Melbourne – Madrid – Cape Town – Singapore – Sao Paulo, Cambridge University Press 2006, pp. 131–132, Fig. 6.3 on p. 132.

[164] David Wengrow, The Archaeology of Early Egypt – Social Transformations in North-East Africa, 10,000 to 2650 BC, Cambridge – New York – Melbourne – Madrid – Cape Town – Singapore – Sao Paulo, Cambridge University Press 2006, pp. 229–231, Fig. 10.2 on p. 230.

high priestess NIN infused the Sumerian land with fertile power and everything which that entailed. As leading theocratic figures or, better yet, heads of society's temple life, both were apparently officials of a lay, yet still unclear nature, who bore the title of NAMESHDA.

We know that this figure assumed a very high, perhaps even the highest position within his scope of authority, and that he was a top official in Sumer. Yet we do not know the exact essence of his position. Perhaps he was the highest secular ruler; the form of the symbols used to write his title – a basket or beater, a wooden block and a stretch of land with two irrigation ditches – could lead us to believe that his authority was somehow related to the division of the grain crop on the thrashing floor, though this is pure speculation. At the start of the 3$^{rd}$ millenium BC (ca. 3000–2600 BC) the situation changed insofar that the place beside NIN, originally occuppied by EN, was assumed by an officer named LUGAL, who ensured fertility; LUGAL and NIN then became the "Lord" and "Lady" of ancient Sumer's city-states. NAMESHDA continued to hold at this time a very honorable position, and we even know that he enjoyed the same respect as the entire "league of cities," whose legal acts he co-sealed. Substantial change then occurred in the 26$^{th}$–25$^{th}$ centuries BC. NAMESHDA completely disappeared from the social life; "*lugal*" and "*nin*" became the king and queen. Sumerian and later Mesopotamian society was, however, already so used to the duality of the highest secular and spiritual position that, even through in time the only one remaining was the lay head – the lugal, *sharrum*, king – society would fill the void by proclaiming its ruler a god.

What was the deification
of the Mesopotamian rulers like?
We should stop here and spend at least a moment on this question. Beginning in the ancient period the deification of the Mesopotamian rulers provoked the indignation and rage of all fanatics who did not or refused to see the true essence of the matter. Verdi's opera *Nabucco* offers a telling example. Watch and listen carefully the next time you go! First and foremost, the very fact that the Mesopotamian ruler had to declare himself a god proves that it was commonly understood that his essence was perceived as purely human. Contrary to the Egyptian

pharaoh or Chinese emperor, who dealt directly with divinity and had it in their "work descriptions," the lords of the Mesopotamian society were merely shepherds and nothing more.

The rulers of ancient Sumer declared themselves gods relatively rarely in the 3rd millenium, doing so only in times when society strongly expressed doubts about the legitimacy of his rule. The first such case of this can most likely be found in the gold, silver and jewels placed with the deceased in the famous "royal tombs" of the city cemetery in Ur (27$^{th}$–26$^{th}$ century BC). This immoderate "noble waste" of social wealth, skill and ingeniousness was apparently carried by the Ur society to emphatically convince everyone that Ur's "lords" and "ladies" were, in fact, incarnations of the death and rebirth of the gods Dumuzi and Inanna. This essentially entailed a lavish and dramatic ceremony most likely aimed at confirming the legitimacy of Ur rulers facing a power threat from the northern kingdom in Kish. This kingdom had grown so powerful in this period that it had wrested power from the hands of the Ur rulers throughout practically all of Sumer. The second case concerning the history of the Akkadian Empire is apparent with its fourth ruler, Naram-Sin of Akkad (2254–2218 BC). Writing has been preserved that can be seen as a kind of "baptismal certificate" of Naram-Sin's divinity and explains the circumstances under which this ruler obtained divine status. The inscription states that, following a general uprising in Sumer and Akkad and the ensuing attack on the empire by the enemy, Naram-Sin fought and won nine battles in a single year. In protecting the country from civil war and suffering at the hands of the foreign usurpers, the grateful subjects then pleaded with the deities of the empire's individual member communities that divine status be bestowed upon their ruler and the gods complied with this request. We see here evidence of a "democratic" deification based on social consensus in acknowledging the exceptional worth of an individual to the entire society.[165] This is not at all the same as the haughty ruler whose pride tolerates nothing short of divine status. We are also quite sure in our assumption that Naram-Sin's period represents a time in which significant doubts were cast on the legitimacy of the Akkadian

---

[165] See Walter Farber, Die Vergöttlichung Naram-Sîns, Orientalia N. S. 52, 1983, pp. 67–72.

Dynasty's rule. Not only did Naram-Sin have to withstand a major uprising, but the "hometown" of his own dynasty, the city of Kish, where the Akkadian kings came from and whose royal title they bore at the beginning of their reign, even gathered in a "great assembly" and, rejecting Naram-Sin's sovereignty, chose their own ruler. To commemorate this occasion this ruler received that name "Kish-Assembled" *(Ipchur-Kish)*. We also know that the empire's military forces weakened under Naram-Sin to the point that he was forced to form an alliance with his eastern neighbor, Elam, which was unprecedented in the history of the Akkadian Empire. It therefore seems that Naram-Sin's deification represented a quite desperate attempt at self-preservation that, however, did not last long. Not long after the death of his son, the ancient Akkadian Empire disintegrated, departing to a subterranean world awaiting excavation.

The next and final deification of Sumerian rulers occurred under the reign of Shulgi, the king of the Third Dynasty of Ur (2094–2047 BC).

After the fall of the ancient Akkadian Empire and its disintegration into individual city-states that were apparently plundered from time to time by marauding nomadic Gutians, Sumer recovered and set itself to forming an empire under the Uruk ruler Utu-hengal, who led a victorious fight against the Gutians. Hardly had he rested on his laurels, however, when a putsch orchestrated by his loyal aley, Ur-Nammu the king of Ur, stripped him of power. Ur-Nammu then went on to rule the entire empire alone without any serious opposition. Ur-Nammu (or Ur-Namma as he is sometimes referred to) devoted his life to consolidating his new monarchy and left the questions of legitimacy to his successor, namely to his Shulgi. His "deification," clarified by a number of written records and glorifying the perfection of the king's physical and spiritual powers, once again demonstrate remarkable traits. In indirect, yet strong disagreement with Naram-Sin's divinity, Shulgi's ideologists maintained that the king did not need to rely on a god to proclaim his divinity, since he had already become a god in his mother's womb. This womb had been fertilized by the semen of his divine father, who had taken the form of the ruler's earthly father. Shulgi was thus born a god and related to numerous divine and heroic figures of Mesopotamia's distant past, include the legendary Gilgamesh. As

such, Shulgi is a being of divine essence, supremely perfect, characterized not only by an athletic prowess, before which any present-day
Olympian would pale with envy, but also by incredible intellectual
capabilities. One cannot help but think of Alexander the Great, who
nearly two thousand years later would similarly justify his claim to rule
the civilized world. It should also be noted that Shulgi carried out his
own daring feat the moment the legitimacy of the new dynasty had to
first be established. After Shulgi's death (his departure the way of all
flesh seems to have been interpreted as an "ascension," even depicted
in artworks), his dynasty's rule over his father's domain did not even
survive two generations.

### India and China

We have already lamented the fact that our inability to read the writing
of proto-Indian civilization has prevented us from learning more about
the spiritual cultural of the first center of the Indus-Sarasvati civilization. There is no other choice than to resort to the relatively crude and
blurred testimony offered by archeological sources. There is evidence
that some production activities were even under central control. For
instance, for the manufacturing of earthenware bracelets, fired in a pair
of crucibles (which fit together) in a reduction atmosphere and at a temperature of ca. 1200°C we can refer to the pair of crucibles (officially?)
sealed. The monumental architecture and urbanism of proto-Indian
city centers provides more than a wealth of evidence of the ability to
coordinate extensive and complex public works *potestas imperii*. Some
pictures seem to show that high officials of the proto-Indian civilization
performed religious ceremonies and perhaps even made offerings to
their deities. The central offices or office thus undoubtedly assumed an
important role within this civilization, though that is the extent that
can be safely assumed.

The sages of the early Chinese state created one of the most complex structures, anchoring the role of the social centers in the life of
the whole society. The Chinese emperor appointed all officials and
was the highest judge and commander-in-chief of the military. He
also performed other important cult and ritual roles. Constitutive acts
concerning space and time fell within his sphere of authority: he de-

termined the plans for the capital city, for other important city centers and for settled rural areas according to cult principles. He also defined the beginnings of the individual calendar periods. He determined, in adhering to the religious interpretation of climatic and natural phenomena, the color of courtly attire, which became the official imperial color. He also set the form of the court rituals and court music according to cult principles.

The situation for the emperor of the Middle Kingdom, as China has been called since ancient history, was made substantially easier by the reflection of the divine light that had shown on his position since time immemorial. More than any other ruler from ancient history, the symbolism of the Chinese emperor also permeated the cult sphere: The Chinese world has four sides – black north, blue-green east, red south and white west – which hold together and lead the yellow center, represented by the emperor, into harmonic relations (the emperor's exclusive claim to the yellow or gold color is derived from this). The emperor, the lynchpin of celestial order, combines earthly bliss with celestial harmony and thus guarantees that life on earth progresses as it should. The rituals that the emperor performs were essential for initiating the phases of the year, the new seasons and all events occurring in nature. The emperor cannot, therefore, be anything else but the highest ruler, judge and commander, the source and provider of order, law and justice. If it were not for the emperor, the world would fall into chaos, anarchy and into an "everyone-for-himself" fight. This very strong ideology of the emperor naturally had an effect on both representatives of regional authorities and on foreign aspirants to the Chinese imperial throne, almost all of whom would accept this ideology.

## Three social estates and the birth of the state

The points that we have just described strongly support the conclusion that societies of the first states already included representatives of all classical "three estates" – those who pray (spiritual), those who fight (in other words, those who organize and lead – namely the king, his court and subordinate leaders) and those who work (meaning those who supply – farmers, shepherds, craftsmen and merchants).[166] Society's dispersion into specialized group must have occurred even before the creation of the early state centers, as the conclusions from the archeological interpretation of settlements clearly show. Cult-specialized sites already appear in the prehistoric period and most even earlier than secular sites, or more or less contemporaneously with them.

The development of this initial social differentiation represents a very important factor in the rise of the first states. Only through the dispersion of society into functionally specialized groups, consisting of a cohesively functioning body under the auspices of the central authority, were the prerequisites created for the development of supraregional political units that were able to administer, control and protect larger and more organic social units, and do so with a long-term perspective. But then, even representatives of one of these "estates" were able to build powerful empires – the empire created by the rulers of South African Zulus in the 19th century AD is a case in point. Their kingdom, however, did not last long, while the first state centers, able to fill the power-created form with spiritual content, endured in one form or another for thousands of years.

Once a political body develops a structure composed of original "estates," whose activities are organically in synchrony and harmonically complement each other, it begins its expansion phase. This does not merely entail a power struggle with, and occupation of neighboring lands; the elite of the given society impose their world view and try to ensure that all classes of citizens accept them. The process of this "civilization mission" carries on if the natural environment allows for it and the people on the system's periphery are willing to accept the underlying cultural model carried by the expanding center.

Clearly this primarily cultural and spiritual expansion cannot continue interminably. In moving from the center to the system's periphery, this cultural model takes on increasingly original and locally colored traits that are more or less perceived to be distinctive. Nevertheless,

---

[166] Georges Dumézil elaborated on this theory for Indo-European history, see Robert Schmitt, Dumézilsche Dreifunktionentheorie, in: H. Beck et al. (edd.), Reallexikon der germanischen Altertumskunde, Band 6, Lieferung a Berlin – New York, Walter de Gruyter 1985, pp. 276–280 (including bibliography).

the territorial size of the first state centers is an important criterion of success of the ancient elite's spiritual work – a gauge by which the credibility of views and attitudes offered to the neighboring populations is measured. Clear differences emerge in this respect in examining the first state centers. Egyptian civilization originally represented for Nubia a wholly acceptable model, as attested to by the cemeteries of Nubian elite figures buried with Egyptian artifacts and containing symbolic statements fully compatible with the Egyptian conceptual apparatus. Following the creation of the Egyptian state, this early Nubian culture apparently succumbed to Egypt's reckless expansion and did not recover until much later. Yet the Egyptian cultural model represented for the Nubian elite the only possible solution, as demonstrated by the history of the 1st millenium BC. Hardly anything remained by then of Egypt's ancient glory and the role of preserving Egyptian culture was assumed by the Nubian states, from which there even emerged one of the Egyptian dynasties of that period. Nothing provides better testimony of the power of the Egyptian spiritual legacy than the fact that in the 7th century BC the Nubian-born pharaohs faced Assyrian expansion into Egypt.

Both the elite of Sumer and of Akkad failed to fully maintain the political sphere of their influence. Already at the start of the 3rd millenium BC the Elamite civilization (today southeast Iran) had probably deliberately broken away from the Sumerian cultural model, which, nevertheless, had strongly inspired the Elamites, though only after they had created their own writing and perhaps even numerical systems. The historical relations between Sumer and Elam are characterized by a paradoxical dichotomy that is similar to that of Egypt and Nubia: although both lands were politically at extreme odds, in spiritual matters they shared the same underlying cultural model. This later led to the famous edict by Cyrus the Great from the 6th century BC written in cuneiform on a clay cylinder found in Babylon and considered "the world's first manifesto of religious and spiritual tolerance and civil liberty."

In contrast, the proto-Indian and, in particular, Chinese elite were evidently able to maintain their sphere of influence more or less unscathed. While the proto-Indian cultural sphere, with all its variety and diversity, seems to give the impression of political, spiritual and administrative unity, it is clear that this system did not withstand the test of time and faded away even before the arrival of the Indo-Iranian Aryans, who gave India a visibly different civilization. It is of great regret that, given our inability to read the written records of the proto-Indian culture, we are denied the chance to ascertain which aspects of the Mohenjo-daro and Harappa cultural legacy survived until the arrival of the Aryans and which may have penetrated their civilization and culture. Experience tells us that good and useful inventions hardly ever disappear, thus the Aryans theoretically could have built upon the culture proto-Indian cultural legacy. This, however, is purely speculation that the current perspective can neither confirm nor refute. It was the Chinese center that showed true prowess in building an early state's united, syncretistic culture. We have already witnessed the adeptness with which the Chalcolithic leaders of China were inspired by the inventions and achievements of many cultures there, and how they amassed this knowledge and know-how and experience so that they could later create a uniform system of ideas and attitudes based on a uniform scale of values that arose from the set underlying cultural model.

Finds from the Chinese culture nicely show us who the bearer of this cultural model really was. They were the empire's intellectuals, "the group of sages", who determined the standards, the scale of values, and offered advice and recommendation and, if necessary, also rectified and even protested.

# METAPHYSICS

We will now attempt something slightly risky that may even seem absurd: a brief and general description of the spiritual factors that may have had an effect on the creation and development of early state centers of the Old World.

The chapter on burials already examined the propensity to position the bodies of the deceased according to a uniform ritual. It can be assumed that this regularly observed custom bears witness to a formulated and shared idea of the principles and arrangement of visible and invisible components of the world, and on the relationship of the deceased to entities that were important for them and whose spatial position was defined. We are, therefore, confronted here with a world view that had already refined the notion of this world and man's place in it. The distinguished German scholar Alwo von Wickede eloquently expressed this in his work on structures in painted works made by potters of prehistoric Mesopotamia: While for the oldest style of ceramic painting from the Samarran culture (6000–5000 BC) the decoration was necessarily created from a single point, in works of the Halaf culture (6000–4000 BC) the basic component of artistic decoration is an axis. For the Ubaid culture (5000–3500 BC), it was the "glide reflection" (in German *Gleitspiegelung*).[167]

## The human world, space, time and their nature

We can logically assume that it was the transition from the Samarran point to the Halaf axis that marked a radical transformation in world

---

[167] Alwo von Wickede, Die Ornamentik der Tell Halaf-Keramik, Ein Beitrag zu ihrer Typologie, Acta Praehistorica et Archaeologica 18, 1986, pp. 7–32, particularly pp. 29–30.

view. This would also play a role in the development of the early state centers. For without a conceptual system working with a total grasp of the inhabited area (in Greek *ecumene*) in the form of a center and periphery through which the significance of a horizontal axis as an organizational element reveals the system, it is impossible to build a state unit that necessarily involves the delegation of authority and the spatial scaling of uniform administration.

Yet that is not all: Positioning the axis vertically, we can formulate ideas regarding the organization of the world with its image that is no longer merely two-dimensional, but a hierarchically three-dimensionally principled image. The idea is thus forged of a visible world and a spiritual world, the sphere of forces ruling the visible world and controlling it, however inaccessible to the human senses and experience it may be. Another question is what occurs in the underworld, which for the people of early statehood was not, as it seems, an exclusively negative place. In this way the original unit, clearly working with a two-dimensional idea of space supplemented by an afterlife in which powers inaccessible to our senses lived on the level of the visible world, developed into an elaborate three-dimensional concept of the spatial coordinates of human existence.

In their understanding of visible space, it seems that the idea of the world divided into four cardinal points prevailed from a very early period among the people of early statehood. A world organized in this manner represented a "civilized" and thus universal human space for the early state centers. Beyond its borders was the non-world, a non-space (and evidently also a non-time), not subject to human activity and, therefore, untamed, inhuman and, consequently, potentially dangerous, the haunt of beasts, wild non-human creatures, heinous demons and evil powers. For the people of these early states, the term "world" meant exclusively the area that they themselves had populated and civilized; the terms "world" and "people, i.e. my people" meant the same thing. The synonymity of the terms "land" (later KALAM) and "people" (later UN) in ancient Sumerian writings support this. The people of early statehood were aware that something existed outside their world, but they had a very difficult time conceptualizing this non-world. In the 15th century BC, the Egyptians noted with wonder that the great river (Euphrates) did not flow from south to north as the properly behaving Nile did, but from north to south! The ancient Chinese, with their traditional sense for order, dealt with this situation by calling all inhabitants of the four cardinal points beyond the Chinese borders "barbarians" (northern, southern, western and eastern barbarians).

The people of early statehood also dealt with time in a remarkable way. At first, they did not understand it as a separate entity, but incorporated it into space as one of its properties. This principle once again clearly expresses a Chinese way of thinking. Chinese cosmology assigns four seasons to the four cardinal points – black north, blue-green east, red south and white west: north is assigned to winter, east to spring, south to summer and west to autumn. Furthermore, the entire system includes a rotating equilibrium between the universe's principles of composition through yin (cold, wet, dark and female) and yang (hot, dry, light, ascending and male). Winter possesses the greater principle of yin, while spring has the lesser principle of yin. Summer holds greater yang and autumn lesser yang. It occurs this way since the principles of yin and yang are interlocked; one means nothing without the other and together they create a ceaselessly turning equilibrium in which they each prevail for a while. This is, however, a dynamic equilibrium, so that none of the principles can prevail forever. So time is incorporated into space as its integral part and the whole forms an ideal enclosed system, repeating the same action through the ages in observing its own laws. Since Chinese civilization supplemented the cardinal points with a fifth element in the form of a golden empire located in the middle of the entire system, the primary ruling office also became an eternal, mythically embedded principle of the universe. Yet Chinese civilization was also familiar with the principle of time's linear movement (noticeable in its historiography in the form of the chronological succession of the rulers' dynasties).

We expect that something similar occurred with the early Sumerian civilization in which the cylinder seal incorporates the ideal unity of space represented by the seal's image and of cyclical and linear time. At least traces of time's incorporation into space can be found in ancient Sumerian writings from the 4th millenium, in which the same expressions represented the times of the day and wind directions, which were probably the same as the cardinal points ("midday wind" = south, "midnight wind" = north). The ancient Egyptian conceptual system apparently had a similar outlook, though with proto-Indian civilizations we once again come up against a lack of written records.

## The non-human world

Though the world of the people was subject to the laws dictated by the deities, what was it like with the animate, albeit non-human world? Sources exhibit a certain ambivalence to the creatures of the animate world in this regard. On the one hand, there extends beyond the borders of the *ecumene* the world void of people; a world untamed and, therefore, dangerous, full of beasts of prey and threatening powers. In order to reduce the threat that the human world from this side is exposed to, the lords of the civilized world were obliged to expand the sphere of the human civilization and decrease the area that was unpopulated, the *an-ecumene*. This was generally done by hunting wild and dangerous animals, whose death helped bring peace and order to the human world. This motif is described in practically all four centers of the Old World, though most conspicuously in the already degraded form on the reliefs of Assyrian kings' palaces. We can even find there that service personnel brought the wild animals to the king in a cage so that his Highness could shoot or stab it without overly exerting himself.

On the other hand, a respect for animals as for forms and "disguises" of the divine world is certainly apparent in the formative phase of the early state centers. The people of ancient states often considered some animals to be incarnations of gods: Mesopotamian fish as an aspect of the water deity Enki has already been noted here, and there are many other similar cases as well. We are naturally already familiar with the concept of animals as a form of deities from ancient Egypt. After all, Horus, in his falcon form, provided the pharaoh ideology with one of the most effective symbols of Egyptian royal power. A crown decorated with animal horns was a symbol of Mesopotamian divinity.

Creatures composed of part-human, part-animal bodies appeared on proto-Indian seal images and, although we do not know what exactly these creatures were, it can be assumed that there was a connection to the Aryans' religion ("proto-Shiva"). We even find parts of animal bodies on bronze busts of human heads from the ancient Chinese site of Sanxingdui.

The belief that some creatures from the animal kingdom are as close to the gods, if not closer than people, is evident both in the reverent animal burials found in prehistoric Egypt and in the nature of the names of animals in Sumer. Linguistic research has revealed that cows were given names used by people, and even the names of gods for the sake of protection.

In the civilizations of the early states, the non-human component of the human world is thus evidently included in the general context of ideas on the principle of the world. As with people, animals also represent the gods' creations – sometimes good, sometimes evil. The animal world did not differ all that much from the human world: they, too, were created by the gods and subject to the laws chosen for them. Just as with people, animals can be proponents of evil, in which case they must be opposed. Yet other animals embody or represent deities and, as such, deserve honor and respect. They can even apparently be ancestors or protective "totems" of human lineages. The pharaohs of ancient Egypt revered the sacred white baboon as their ancestor.[168] Early phases of Egyptian and Mesopotamian history reveal instances of rulers whose names denote animals.[169]

In the Sumerians' case it was Dog, Lamb or Scorpion, while the Egyptian Narmera's name means "Furious Catfish."

---

[168] Peter Kaplony, Der Schreiber, das Gotteswort und die Papyruspflanze, Zeitschrift für ägyptische Sprache und Literatur 110, 1983, pp. 143–173, on p. 158.

[169] This might consist of the type of state built by a "king-foreigner," coming from beyond the borders of the established society. See David Wengrow, The Archaeology of Early Egypt – Social Transformations in North-East Africa, 10,000 to 2650 BC, Cambridge – New York – Melbourne – Madrid – Cape Town – Singapore – Sao Paulo, Cambridge University Press 2006, p. 217, note 34.

## Is the world around us composed of the elements?

We have already learned that the people of the early states viewed the visible world as one divided into the four cardinal points and filled with divine, demonic, human and animal creatures. Let us now ask how they perceived the nature of this material world. This question is extremely complicated and any response to it needs to be made in a hypothetical spirit. We pointed out in the chapter on burials the spatial similarities in work conducted with fire and cremation burials at the prehistoric (Halafian) at the Yarim Tepe site in Iraq. It was in this context that I expressed the assumption that this could concern the notion of departing to the next world via the element of Fire. The question is to what extent this line of thinking can explain the marked differences in the burial customs carried out in the various centers of early statehood. Egypt and China would represent areas in which survivors commended their deceased to the element of Earth. These views would not be shared by India and Mesopotamia. We simply do not have remnants of the deceased in Mesopotamia that would provide us with answers on why this is so. This appears even more conspicuously at the very time Sumerian statehood and writing systems were emerging, during the late phase of the Uruk culture (3500–3200 BC). In examining Mesopotamian cuneiform writing we find that the journey to the next world was made over water. For the hero to visit the immortal Utnapishtim, he had to cross the Waters of Death, which was usually traversed in the boat of the ferryman Urshanabi, the "Mesopotamian Charon." One of the versions of the myth of the dying and rebirth of the god Tammuz describes how, accompanied by everyone who died during his stay on earth, he leaves for earth without returning across Khubur, the river of the dead. This tells us that the ancient Mesopotamians commended the bodies of the deceased to the element of Water, which, naturally, is quite difficult to verify through archeological research. India provides evidence of a markedly different treatment of the dead, as the aforementioned Tamil epic poem *Manimekalai* describes for a later period. We can neither confirm nor refute whether this indicates a familiarity with the theory of the world composed of the elements. We do not know exactly how it was in the proto-Indian case.

Chinese teachings on the principles of yin and yang clearly offer an early example of an imaginative theory on the elements. Only two elements are described here, but there is little doubt of their nature as the universe's primary principles of composition. We have already stated that the Chinese theory of yin and yang might date all the way back to the Yangshao culture in the Neolithic period, though we do not have conclusive evidence of this.

It is therefore better to consider the theory that the people of early statehood were familiar with the elements as hypothetically possible, but not fully proven.

## Powers of the overworld

How did the people of early statehood imagine the creatures occupying the area above the upper end of the Earth's vertically positioned axis? We have no idea, since the civilizations that we are examining here essentially did not portray their deities. Portrayals were usually made at this time of people, most often rulers. If ancient artists felt the needs to refer directly to a divine being, they did so through symbols or emblems. Such emblems could be a natural or artificial creation, and even a living being. The oldest representation of the name of the Sumerian sky god Anu is the picture of a star, though the ancient Sumerians had long before written the name of Enlil, the god of atmosphere and of everything between heaven and earth, in a reed-matting picture featuring an interwoven checkerboard pattern. A symbol of the goddess of the passionate aspect of human nature, of love and war, Inanna, is a picture of a veiled bride. Although it was originally assumed that this was a depiction of a loop-shaped bundle of reeds (the German expression *Schilfringbündel* aptly describes this), more recent research seems to point to the interpretation given here. It is also extremely convincing: what better symbol for a goddess than a radiant, veiled bride?

Ancient Egyptian sources offer extremely meager information on the nature and appearance of ancient divine beings.[170] We must therefore

---

[170] David Wengrow, The Archaeology of Early Egypt – Social Transformations in North-East Africa, 10,000 to 2650 BC, Cambridge – New York – Melbourne – Madrid – Cape Town –

rely on information derived from ancient Sumerian writings. These tell us that Sumerians perceived their deities as creatures that changed their appearance and abode at will, that were omnipresent beings. The symbol used to transcribe the ancient name of the god of water and wisdom, Enki, also means a kind of fish, and the city of Eridu.[171] The forms of Enki's divine essence thus also consisted of these entities.

The gods resided – if they felt like it, sometimes they simply left their homes and returned to them at will – in temples in the form of their sculptures or symbols that their priests and worshippers had to make accessible in advance through a special "mouth-opening ceremony."[172] A fundamental misconception of these emblems as (possible) houses of the gods that the deities may or may not come to as they please, is presented by the Old Testament contention against what is called "deaf blocks and stones," which the 14th-century Czech translation of the Latin "Alexandreid," a life of Alexander the Great, eloquently summed up in speaking of a pagan, who, despite "having a long-eared owl as a god," is the hero. Although we assume that even the most ancient deities were perceived as eternal and omnipotent, both Sumerian and Egyptian records attest to not only the death, but also the eating of divine bodies by mortals, i.e. by the pharaoh who was thought to belong among the deities.

---

Singapore – Sao Paulo, Cambridge University Press 2006, p. 190, note 13, and pp. 195–198 on the probable portrayal of the god Min.

[171] This may seem strange, but there is a Czech myth in this context from the Czech-Moravian highlands, the realm of the mountain spirit Huráň. Apparently, the farmer Daněk once went out to catch crayfish and caught an especially large one. Suddenly a wild wind arose, the forests howled and a thundering voice called: "Where are you, Huráň?" A second, similarly thundering voice answered: "I'm in a jug at Daněk's house." Daněk immediately emptied the jug in the nearest brook and rushed home. I find it fascinating that the concept behind the Sumerian and Czech thinking is the same.

[172] Not to be confused with the eponymous Egyptian ceremony that in this way made the mummified human body accessible to its soul. See David Wengrow, The Archaeology of Early Egypt – Social Transformations in North-East Africa, 10,000 to 2650 BC, Cambridge – New York – Melbourne – Madrid – Cape Town – Singapore – Sao Paulo, Cambridge University Press 2006, pp. 225–226.

# Art

Art was an integral part of the spirituality of the Old World's ancient state centers. This included the performing (rhetoric, music and singing, dance) and fine (architecture, sculpture, painting, crafts) arts. Obviously, we cannot prove that the people of early statehood introduced the "great" arts. For instance, the work of Paleolithic Europe, the level of their refinement and the assumption that their artists underwent systematic and extensive training, has long been discussed. Yet not even in this area are the creators of early statehood seen as primary innovators. They should instead be credited with a significant broadening of the circle of consumers of art and especially with the creation of monumental artworks that we will not hesitate in calling "public." Unfortunately, we find ourselves at a real disadvantage in examining the performing arts, given that the works are of a fleeting nature and defy any attempt at conceptual understanding and assessment. All that we know about these types of art is that they were performed regularly and in a cultivated manner. Music was part of the temple service in Sumer, and probably in Egypt and China too. The playing of musical works, whose structure related to the rationality of the visible and invisible worlds' arrangement and, consequently, expressed the view of Chinese artists on the nature of events around them, was one of the activities used by Chinese civilization to explain the world.

The art of the Old World's early states share one common element: the fine artworks in particular clearly show a refinement of artistic expression and a high level of mastery both in the study of the depicted theme and in the use of technical and expressive means. The highest possible effect of artistic rendering is thus obtained. The depiction of living creatures impress us in the masterful portrayal of the model's external appearance and superb level of artistic representation is clear in both sculptures and reliefs depicting animals or people. Even very simple, everyday works, such as combs in ancient Egypt, take us by surprise with their superbly stylized and controlled silhouette of a bird or animal carved into the handle. The systematic cultivation of art and the establishment of rules of artistic expression led at this time to the creation and stabilization of the first artistic styles. As sculptors and artists of Egypt and Mesopotamia presented their masterworks to their deities and the devout public, "great" art made its way to the administrative and economic spheres (Sumerian cylinder seals, proto-Indian seals). Indian artists also produced outstanding works and artists of ancient China developed means of expression that would not only become dominant features of the Middle Kingdom's artworks, but would also eventually provide a milieu of inspiration for American artists. Although "great" art did not emerge with the birth of the state, it was the state that provided artists with hitherto unknown possibilities to create art on any scale and to broadly apply their works. Art was given the chance to become better organized, to ensure the continuity of creative activities and, through the emergence of a stable system of "state contracts," a decisive step was taken toward forming the first art styles. All this contributed to art's emergence as one of the factors cultivating the public space and enriching public life in the focal points of early statehood.

# CONCLUSION

I no longer intend to keep my readers in suspense. I wrote that the founders of the early states could hardly rely on brute force to coerce the people into subordination and submissiveness. I expressed the assumption that they would have had to go about it in an entirely different way, that they would have had to offer the people something unknown at that time that would have enriched the people's lives. I also promised that I would try to figure out what that "something" was.

First of all, the early state offered its citizens creature comforts. Any citizen of the early state evidently had the right to public assistance if needed, and we also have proof of the distribution of "security allowances" and the use of central resources to supply communities suffering from a poor crop or hunger.

The early state centers also offered safety. Alan Lupton made an extremely perceptive observation: the only difference between the communities on the periphery of the Sumerian *ecumene* in the period prior to contact with the southern civilization and after is that the post-contact society felt the need to fortify itself.[173]

The people in the early state centers undoubtedly also felt great prestige coming from the obvious power of the state and its bodies – a prestige that few would identify with in contemporary society.

Changes linked to the birth of early statehood are perhaps most pronounced in the spiritual sphere. Unfortunately, here we run up against the lamentably barren state of archeological testimony for the earliest phases of existence of the Old World's states, and a lack of such information for the period immediately preceding it.

---

[173] Alan Lupton, Stability and Change – Socio-Political Development in Northern Mesopotamia and Southeastern Anatolia, 4000–2700 B.C. (BAR International Series 627), v. I, Tempvs reparatum 1996.

The priests of the early states mainly ensured the success of basic subsistence activities, the fertility of the soil, of animals and, last but not least, of people. If this faith was active and sincere, it undoubtedly alleviated the people of the earliest state civilizations of the heavy burden of uncertainty.

The people of ancient statehood undoubtedly shared with their communities the conviction that man is not the final link in creation and that he came into being from divine will. It seems that a very strong conviction of the power and even omnipotence of the gods that could be fully relied on prevailed among the people of the first civilizations. All the more painful it must have been for the citizens of the first states when they found out for themselves that the gods did not always have only good in store for their worshippers and disciples.

Yet there is something that the people of the earliest states introduced to the world: Appearing with them on the political scene was the first ζῷον πολιτικον, the "political animal," used to living in a political collective; a man or woman who controlled the most dreadful battle possible – the battle with the dark demons that are inside each of us. In our own age, whose political practice, if not theory, is actually reminiscent of the period prior to the search for a general consensus, and often also reaches back to the irreconcilable spirit of religious wars, luring the demons of rage into the service of political doctrines, let us heed their lesson.

# APPENDIX: THE STATE IN TROUBLE

This marks the end of a long and arduous journey through the focal points of the social development in which humanity's first statehood came into being. A wealth of knowledge and findings from present-day research has been presented. We now know much about it, and yet we cannot shake the feeling that something is missing, that somehow the meaning and intention of the early states elude us.

To rid ourselves of this feeling, we will give the floor to our ancient ancestors. Do not hesitate to stand face to face with them, to sit at the feet of their sages and to hear their words.

This appendix features a selection of writings written at critical times in ancient history, when our ancestors felt as if the state was collapsing before their very eyes. It was at such times that the sages appeared before their rulers so that their words would be heard and could rectify the situation in public affairs. Yet this is a slightly deceptive act on my part, since the texts were mostly written well after the period we are dealing with – in most cases one or two thousand years. Nevertheless, let us keep in mind the age-old tenet that "states are held together by the ideals they were founded on." My hope is that these texts, created as a response to the sudden need to confront an acute social crisis, produce at least a weak echo of the original ideas that their founding fathers had introduced.

## Egypt

We will start with a relatively well known work of literature: *The Admonitions of Ipuwer*, written in the first interim of ancient Egypt's history, ca. 2130 BC. Around 1630 BC two smaller passages were added to it. The text is composed of two parts with the first apparently justifying the legitimacy of the ruling dynasty during the first interim in the city of Heracleopolis, and the second presenting a dialogue between the sage Ipuwer and the supreme creator Re-Atum. Ipuwer indiscriminately describes the social revolution he has witnessed and bitterly blames his god for the complete and utter failure, and for allowing the harshest calamities and woes to beset Egypt.

The below passages were taken from Vincent A. Tobin's book:[174]

*Verily, the offices are opened and their records pillaged;*
*Men who once were serfs have (now) become owners of serfs....* (lines 6–7)
*Verily, the decrees / of the council chamber are tossed aside;*
*Moreover, men walk on them in public,*
*And the rabble smash them in the streets. (...)* (lines 12–14)
*Verily, the children of the nobles are cast into the streets;*
*The wise man says "Yes ! " while the fool says "No ! "*
*And he who understands nothing of it (finds it) pleasing in his sight. (...)*
(lines 19–21)
*Behold now, a fire has blazed up to the height,*
*And its flame goes forth against the land.*
*Behold now, deeds are done which have never before occurred,*
*For the king has been overthrown by the rabble. (...)* (lines 25–28)
*Behold, he who had nothing is (now) the owner of wealth,*
*And the official favors him.*
*Behold, the poor of the land have become the wealthy,*
*And he who owned property (now) has nothing.*
*Behold, cupbearers have become the masters of butlers,*
*And he who was a messenger (now) sends someone else.*
*Behold, he who did not have a loaf is (now) the owner of a storehouse,*
*But his storeroom is stocked with the property of another. (...)*
(lines 76–84)
*Behold, she who had no box is now the owner of a chest,*
*/ And she who used to look at her face in the water (now) owns a mirror.*
*(...)* (lines 88–90)

---

[174] Vincent A. Tobin: Instructions, lamentations, dialogues. Admonitions of an Egyptian sage, in: William Kelly Simpson (ed.), *The Literature of Ancient Egypt*, Cairo 2003, pp. 189–210.

*Behold, a man can be slain in the presence of his (own) brother,*
*And he deserts him in order to save himself. (...)* (lines 127–128)
*[...] As for the commoner, he is watchful,*
*/ So that the day may dawn on him without his fearing it.*
*Men flee (as if driven) by the wind.*
*Those who once worked with fine linen in a house,*
*(Now) all they make are tents like the nomads.* (lines 150–154)
*Behold, why does (God) even consider creating (men),*
*When the peaceful man is not distinguished from the aggressive?*
*Let him but bring coolness upon their passion, / and men will say:*
*"He is the shepherd of all mankind, and there is no evil in his heart." (...)*
(lines 184–187)
*/ The chastiser of crimes is the one who devises them,*
*And there are no pilots on watch.*
*Where is (God) today? Does he indeed sleep?*
*Behold, his power is no more seen. (...)* (lines 197–199)
*Authority, perception, and Ma'at are with you,*
*But it is confusion which you have permitted throughout the land*
*Along with the noise of tumult. (...)* (lines 212–214)
*And it is you who have behaved so that this might come to pass,*
*For you have spoken falsehood.*
*The land is (now) a bitter weed which destroys mankind*
*And none can be certain of life. (...)* (lines 220–224)
*Verily, it is good when men's hands construct pyramids.*
*When pools are dug, and orchards planted with trees worthy of the gods.*
*Verily, it is good when men drink deep,*
*When they drink strong liquor, and their hearts rejoice.*
*Verily, it is good when shouts of joy are in (men's) mouths,*
*When the lords of the estates stand*
*Watching the rejoicing / in their houses,*
*Dressed in fine linen,*
*Their foreheads anointed, and secure for the future.*
*Verily, it is good when beds are prepared,*
*When the headrests of the nobles are well secured,*
*When all men's wants are satisfied by a couch in the shade,*
*And a door is shut (to protect) him who used to sleep in the bushes.*

*Verily, it is good when fine linen is laid out on New Year's Day,*
*(...) on the bank,*
*When fine linen is laid out, and cloaks (spread) on the ground. ...*
(lines 240–254)
*Each man fights only for his sister and protects himself.*
*Are Nubians (the threat)? Then we shall protect ourselves,*
*For the warriors are numerous to drive back the foreign bowmen,*
*is it Libyans? Then we shall route them. (...)* (lines 255–259)
*What Ipuwer said when he answered the majesty of the Lord of All:*
*You have deceived the whole populace!*
*It seems that (your) heart prefers to ignore (the troubles).*
*Have you done what will make them happy?*
*Have you given life to the people?*
*They cover / their faces in fear of the morning!*
*Once there was a man who had grown old and was approaching death,*
*And his son was a child still without understanding.*
*He began to defend (...)*
*But he could not open (his) mouth (to) speak to you,*
*And you robbed him even in the agony of death.*
*Weep (...)* (lines 267–276)

We are tempted to sigh twice in reading this text. First, in lamenting how the history of human suffering has remained the same since time immemorial and how people have enjoyed and willingly committed abominations and barbarities against their neighbors since the very beginning of written history. The second sigh would be in regretting that we were not present at the time to hear with our own ears this magnificent piece of rhetoric. Along with his contemplative skills, wise Ipuver (or whoever wrote this text) clearly demonstrates his exceptional rhetorical gifts, and we should consider here just how many impressive political speeches have not been preserved and subsequently lost through the ages.

But let us return to our question: What does the ancient Egyptian sage then see as the greatest threat to society? He clearly envisioned it as the outright collapse of set social rules and of law and order. The assets of previously established classes fell to ruins; yesterday's slaves became lords and yesterday's rulers turned into beggars. The law is destroyed and rights trampled upon, whatever the sage imagines it is to be. Wisdom weeps in the corner, good is vanquished. There lacks the political will to rectify this situation; society whirls helplessly about like a rudderless boat at sea. A civil war scenario emerged in which "man preys on man." The worst part of it all was that this state of disarray was not brought on by enemies from without, but by the inner weakness of Egyptian society itself. The sage evidently feels that this was caused by the failure of the gods, who created Egypt and are therefore responsible for it, by the ignorance of divine wisdom among people, and, to a certain extent, even by a loss of faith in them.

Let us heed the lesson: The sage does not feel that there is a chance to rectify this by taking political or authoritarian measures. He does not think that defending against inner enemies is an easy task. In conclusion, he draws for the reader an idyllic picture of bliss in properly arranged relations (*Verily, it is good...*) and points out that, in contrast to their present state, there once existed a life worthy of this name. He therefore sees the main task in rectifying public affairs in a return to traditional values consisting of a firm, cohesive, viable and credibly conceived underlying cultural model. Such a return must, however, take place after a critical and ruthlessly thorough review of everything that was erroneous, false or simply just bad in people's relationship to everything beyond them, meaning to their gods.

Yet he would not be a sage with the wisdom of years, if he created an illusion of what is and is not possible to achieve. The entire testimony ends in lamenting that the wisdom of age is entirely useless to the inexperienced young.[175] We are unsure whether the sage's final words mean that he falls silent before those not understanding. Since, however, he used the word "weep," he leaves no doubt of his view of humanity's future fate.

---

[175] The sage would certainly agree with the French saying "*Si la vieiellesse pouvait, si la jeunesse savait...*".

## Mesopotamia

*The Legend of Naram-Sin of Cutha*, which I am introducing here as an example of ancient Mesopotamian thought, is certainly less known to the general readership than the previous text. This is indeed unfortunate since this piece of writing, interpreted by my learned friend and colleague Jiří Prosecký, was for me a real revelation. This was an instructional text, of the kind kept in temples. If sudden and unexpected events occurred, it was found and read so that people knew what they were supposed to do. It therefore begins with the words "Open the foundation box and read the stele." Written in the Akkadian language, it was most likely created during the ancient Babylonian period, i.e. during the 19th–18th century BC.[176] Sometime after 1500 BC, the story found its way to the Hittite Empire in Asia Minor and even into the library of King Ashurbanipal (669–627 BC) in Nineveh. Proof of this text even comes from one of the last Assyrian cities, today the city of Sultantepe in south Turkey, from the very end of the Assyrian Empire at the close of the 7th century BC.[177]

This excerpt was taken from Benjamin R. Foster's book.[178]

*[Open the foundation box] and read well the stela,*
*[That I, Naram-Sin], son of Sargon,*
*[Have written] for all time (...)* (lines 1–3)

*Troops with bodies of "cave birds," humans with raven faces*
*Did the great gods create,*
*Their city was in the earth the gods made.*
*Tiamat suckled them,*
*Belet-ili their mother made (them) fair.*
*Inside the mountain(s) they grew up, became adults, got their stature. (...)*
(lines 31–36)

---

[176] The language in which the cuneiform monuments of the Semitic language were written. The Akkadian language has two dialectics, southern Babylonian and northern Assyrian.

[177] Jiří Prosecký, „Královské knihy" staré Mezopotámie ("The royal books of ancient Mesopotamia"), Prague, The Oriental Institute of the Academy of Sciences of the Czech Republic 1995, pp. 19–23.

[178] Benjamin R. Foster, Before the Muses. An Anthology of Akkadian Literature. Third Edition. Bethesda, Maryland, CDL Press 2005.

*They destroyed the (upper?) Sealands*
  *and invaded Gutium,*
*They destroyed Elam and arrived at the seacoast,*
*They killed the people of the crossing place,*
  *they were thrown to [ ],*
*Dilmun, Magan, Meluhha,*
  *Whatever was in the midst of the sea they killed. (…)*
(lines 56–60)

*I inquired of the great gods, …*
*The latchkey of the great gods did not give me or my dream spirit*
*permission to go.*
*Speaking to myself, thus I said:*
*"What lion observed divination?*
*What wolf ever consulted a dream interpreter?*
*I will go, as I like, like a brigand,*
*I will cast off what belongs to the gods,*
  *I will hold fast (only) to myself. (…)* (lines 75–83)

*When the first year had come,*
*I sent out 120,000 troops against them,*
  *Not one returned alive,*
*When the second year arrived, I sent out 90,000 troops*
  *against them, not one returned alive.*
*When the third year arrived, I sent out 60,700 troops*
  *against them, not one returned alive.*
*I was confounded, bewildered, at a loss, anxious, in despair.*
*Speaking to myself, thus I said,*
*What have I left for a reign? (…)* (lines 84–90)

*When the New Year of the fourth year arrived,*
*At the prayer to Ea, [sage] of the great gods,*
*[When I offered] the holy offerings of New Year,*
*I [sought] the holy instructions.*
*I summoned the diviners and [charged them],*
*Seven extispicies upon seven lambs I performed.*

*I set up the holy reed altars,*
*I inquired of the great gods (...)* (lines 104–111)

*I went after them in great haste and hurry,*
*I overcame those troops,*
*I brought those troops back.*
*Speaking to myself, [thus I said],*
*"Without divination (of liver), flesh and entr[ails],*
    *[I should not] lay [hand on them to kill?]."*
*[I performed] an extispicy concerning them:*
*The latchkey of the great gods [ordered] mercy for them. (...)*
(lines 121–127)

*The shining Morning Star spoke from heaven thus,*
*"To Naram-Sin, son of Sargon:*
*"Cease, you shall not destroy the perditious seed!*
*"In future days Enlil will raise them up for evil.*
*"It (the host) awaits the angry heart of Enlil,*
*"O city! Those troops will be killed,*
*"They will burn and besiege dwelling places!*
*"O city! They will pour out their blood!*
*"The earth will diminish its harvests,*
    *the date palms their yield.*
*"O city! Those troops will die!*
*"City against city, house against house will turn.*
*"Father to father, brother to brother,*
*"Man to man, companion to friend,*
*"None will tell the truth to each other.*
*"People will be taught untruth,*
    *strange things [will they learn].*
*"This city is hostile, they kill,*
*"That hostile city (another) hostile city will capture.*
*"Ten quarts of barley will cost a mina of silver,*
*"There was no strong king [to govern] in the land.*
*"To the great gods I brought (the captives) as tribute,*
*I did not lay hand on them to kill. (...)* (lines 128–146)

*Whoever you may be, governor, prince, or anyone else,*
*Whom the gods shall name to exercise kingship, I have*
*made a foundation box for you,*
    *I have written you a stela, In Cutha in*
*the Emeslam, In the cella of Nergal have I*
*left it for you. Behold this stele,*
*Listen to the wording of this stele:*
*You should not be confounded,*
    *you should not be bewildered, You should not*
*be afraid, you should not tremble,*
*Your Stance should be firm.*
*You should do your task in your wife's embrace.*
*Make your walls trustworthy,*
*Fill your moats with water.*
*Your coffers, your grain, your silver,*
    *your goods and chattels*
*Bring into your fortified city.*
*Wrap up your weapons and [lean] them in a corner,*
*Restrain your valor, take care of your person.*
*Though he raids your land, go not out against him,*
*Though he drives off your livestock, go not nigh him,*
*Though he eats the flesh of your soldiery (?),*
*Though he murders [...],*
*Be moderate, control yourself, Answer them, "Yes, my lord!"*
*To their wickedness, repay kindness,*
*To kindness (add) gifts and gratifications.*
*Avoid them whenever you can.*
*Let expert scribes compose a stela for you.*
*You who have read my stela and so placed yourself*
    *to bring yourself out of [an ordeal like mine],*
*You who have blessed me,*
    *so may a future one bless you.*
(lines 147–175)

Let us first therefore bless the memory of the glorious and mighty Naram-sin so that we too receive the blessing of our descendents.

Yet this quite unconventional text requires some speculation. Its central theme is actually the same as the speech of the Egyptian sage: a betrayal of everything greater than us (here the will of the gods) quickly followed by the warranted punishment. Naram-sin faces a torrent of enemies who plunder and destroy his land. Despite the warning of oracle signs, which he neglects out of arrogance and pride, he wages war with catastrophic consequences: None of his warriors return. It was then that the ruler experienced an "existential shock": He realizes his mistakes, learns from it and decides the next time to adhere strictly to the will of the gods. The country recovers, the ruler's troops are victorious and the captured enemy is pardoned, again in accordance with the gods' will.

This is followed by a charming passage in which Naram-sin is informed that that he does not have to intervene against evil, since this is the competence of the great gods. The gods were to make sure that no "evil under the sun" goes unpunished. Everything that foreign invaders committed in the land would be returned to them in the form of suffering and calamity that the gods would inflict on them in retaliation. Here he describes with obvious pleasure the future woe and misfortune that will befall the offenders and, in doing so, creates the impression that something is being prepared here very similar to the destitution that afflicted Egypt in the previous text. Egyptians and the people of Mesopotamia therefore had first-hand experience with such situations. The same situation is consequently attributed here to the decision of the gods, but with an ethical charge: A country's misfortune is directly linked to the evil that it had previously committed.

The conclusion drawn is then quite Buddhist in ethos, though over a thousand years before the birth of Siddhartha Gautama Buddha from the Shakya lineage who entered into history as Buddha, "the Enlightened One" (probably 566–486 BC). A ruler is recommended to care for earthly possessions, not just their own, but his entire country's, and to face open force, aggression and attacks with a peace-loving approach. The Babylonian sage pondered the woes of his people and drew similar conclusions as the Egyptian sage. The gods are, in the end, responsible for human fates, though the ethos of human harmony, whose effect the Egyptian so longed for, also plays a role. The Babylonian states that man is supposed to firmly confront misfortune and, even if misfortune strikes, not to do anything that would defy the supreme powers. The lesson is similar to that coming from the land of the Nile: Neither the political system nor the fateful losses of life are essential in this land: Once again, the primary factor of man's relationship to the world consists of a scale of values based on the underlying cultural model, which is the most valuable thing that people created in a civilization and carry with them in their journey through life. We are witness here to a remarkable vision of the future political system: The next administrator of public affairs does not have to be a ruler, nor a king, but "someone whom the gods shall name to exercise kingship". Could the Babylonian have a republic in mind?

## India

I am now stretching the limits of historical credibility. If we had comprehensible proto-Indian writings at our disposal, our task would be far simpler and we would not have to stray so far from the thinking typical for the early state's epoch. This, regretfully, is not the case. The "textbook on worldly matters" or *Arthashastra*, attributed to the sage Kautilya, allegedly a minister of Emperor Chandragupta Maurya (end of the 4th century BC), most likely only dates back to sometime around 1 AD. It was therefore written about two thousand years after the events that we are examining here. Nevertheless, it is such an impressive and important document that it certainly deserves mention here. First and foremost, it is the only spiritual Indian writing of this kind, although we know of the existence of other similar treatises. Secondly, the text contains much detailed information concerning the strategies and tactics of the ancient Indian state, as well as instructions to controlling it, written not only *sine ira et studio*, but often with a detached matter-of-factness and rational concreteness that might even make the reader shudder.[179]

---

[179] R. P. Kangle, The Kautillya Arthasástra Part II, An English Translation with Critical and Explanatory Notes. University of Bombay Studies, Sanskrt, Prakrit and Pali, No. 2, 1963.

This excerpt was taken from R. P. Kangle's translation into English.[180]

*Therefore, the king should not allow the special duties of the (different) beings to be transgressed (by them),[181] for, ensuring adherence to (each one's) special duty, he finds joy after death as well as in this life.*

*For, people, among whom the bounds of the Aryan rule of life are fixed, among whom the* varnas *and the stages of life are securely established and who are guarded by the three Vedas,[182] prosper, do not perish. ...* (Chapter 1, p. 12)

*Agriculture, stock raising and trade make up the economy; it is successful because it gives grain, cattle, money, goods and work. With these, through the treasury and the armies, the king controls his and the enemy's side.*

*The means of ensuring the pursuit of philosophy, the three Vedas and economics is the Rod (wielded by the king); its administration constitutes the science of politics, having for its purpose the acquisition of (things) not possessed, the preservation of (things) possessed, the augmentation of (things) preserved and the bestowal of (things) augmented on a worthy recipient. On it is dependent the orderly maintenance of worldly life.* (Book 4, Chapter 1, p. 10)

*In the happiness of the subjects lies the happiness of the king and in what is beneficial to the subjects his own benefit. What is dear to himself is not beneficial to the king, but what is dear to the subjects is beneficial (to him). Therefore, being ever active, the king should carry out the management of material well-being. The root of material well- being is activity, of material disaster its reverse. In the absence of activity, there is certain destruction of what is obtained and of what is not yet received. By activity reward is obtained, and one also secures abundance of riches.* (p. 53)

*The remedy against those principal officers, who live on the king by holding him in their power or who are in league with the enemy, is the employment*

---

[180] R. P. Kangle, The Kautillya Arthasástra Part II, An English Translation with Critical and Explanatory Notes. University of Bombay Studies, Sanskrt, Prakrit and Pali, No. 2, 1963.
[181] Dharma is the basic law of every individual's life in which he keeps to everything that is prescribed by social conventions and habits.
[182] That is first and foremost the nobility.

*of secret agents or winning over of seducible parties, as explained before, or secret instigation or spying, as we shall explain in (the section on) the capture of an enemy's town.*

*But against those treasonable principal officers, who cause harm to the kingdom, (and) who, being favourites or being united, cannot be suppressed openly, he should employ 'silent punishment,' finding pleasure in (doing his) duty.* (Book 5, Chapter 1, Section 89, p. 338)

*A secret agent, after inciting a brother of the treasonable high officer, not honoured by him, should show him to the king. The king should induce him to fight against the treasonable officer by granting the use of the treasonable man's property. When he has acted with a weapon or poison, he should cause him to be executed on that very ground, declaring 'He is a murderer of his brother.' ...* (p. 339)

*Or, a female mendicant (agent), having won the confidence of the wife of the treasonable officer by means of love-winning potions, should cheat (them) by the use of poison. ...* (p. 340)

*Or, he should request the treasonable officer for food by praising 'Your cook or food-preparer is good,' or for a drink, when out on a journey some time. Mixing both those with poison, he should urge the two themselves to taste them first. Having announced that, he should cause them to be slain as poison-givers. ...* (p. 340)

*The king, the minister, the country, the fortified city, the treasury, the army and the ally are the constituent elements (of the state). Among them, the excellences of the king are:*

*Born in a high family, endowed with good fortune, intelligence and spirit, given to seeing elders, pious, truthful in speech, not breaking his promise, grateful, liberal, of great energy, not dilatory, with weak neighbouring princes, resolute, not having a mean council (of ministers), desirous of training, – these are the qualities of one easily approachable.*

*Eloquent, bold, endowed with memory, intellect and strength, exalted, easy to manage, trained in arts, free from vices, able to lead the army, able to requite obligations and injury in the prescribed manner, possessed of a sense of shame, able to take suitable action in calamities and in normal conditions, seeing long and far, attaching prominence to undertakings at the proper place and time and with appropriate human endeavour, able to discriminate between peace and fighting, giving and withholding, and (observance of) conditions and (striking at) the enemy's weak points, well-guarded, not laughing in an undignified manner, with a glance which is straight and without a frown, devoid of passion, anger, greed, stiffness, fickleness, trouble-someness and slanderousness, sweet in speech, speaking with a smile and with dignity, with conduct conforming to the advice of elders, — these are personal excellences. ...* (Book 6, Section 1, Chapter 96, p. 365)

*(Acts) of human agency are good policy and bad policy; of divine agency good fortune and misfortune. For, it is acts of human and divine agency that make the world go. That caused by an unseen agency is the divine (act). In that, the attainment of the desired fruit is good fortune of undesired (fruit), misfortune. That caused by a seen agency is the human (act). In that, the coming into being of well-being is good policy; (its) ruin, bad policy. That can be thought about; the divine is incalculable. ...* (Chapter 97, p. 368)

*Power and success (are to be explained). Power is (possession of) strength.*

*Power is three-fold: the power of knowledge is the power of counsel, the power of the treasury and the army is the power of might, the power of valour is the power of energy.*

*In the same way, success is also three-fold: that attainable by the power of counsel is success by counsel, that attainable by the power of might is success by might, that attainable by the power of energy is success by energy.*

*Thriving with these, the (king) becomes superior; reduced (in these), inferior; with equal powers, equal. Therefore, he should endeavour to endow himself with power and success, or, if similar, (to endow with power and success) the material constituents in accordance with their immediate proximity or integrity. Or, he should endeavour to detract (these) from treasonable persons and enemies. ...* (Section 97, p. 370)

*The king and (his) rule, this is the sum-total of the constituents. ...* (Chapter 2, Section 128, p. 451)

*In the case of unmixed (danger) from the treasonable, he should use against the citizens and the country people the (various) means excepting force. For, force cannot be used against a multitude of people. Even if used, it might not achieve its object and at the same time might bring on another disaster. But against the leaders among them, he should act as in 'the infliction of (secret) punishment'. For it is impossible to use violence against a large number of people, and if it is used, it does not serve its purpose but creates further disaster. Against their foremen, however, let him act as we have described in the chapter on 'silent sentences.'*[183]... (Section 144, p. 489)

Right from the start we find ourselves in a completely different world here. The Egyptian shed tears over the woeful fate of his people and asked the gods how they could have allowed such calamities to happen. The Babylonian already deduced that the gods allowed the calamities to occur. That, however, is not reason enough for people to abandon morality or faith in the gods, since "the gods always act with forethought" and those instigating evil will soon be dealt a similar blow. This is not the case for the Indian, who completely freed himself from the ethos encapsulated in respect for the gods. Very little remained here from the ruler's original mission of mediating between the gods and his people. Yet the king is urged to care for the dharma of living creatures – to maintain the existing social order – but we do not find out anything here about his responsibilities regarding the spiritual world. The world of divine power is completely beyond human reach and cannot be influenced in anyway. In Kautilya's view, public authority is something that the ruler can pragmatically and, in particular, materially perform for the "good of the people." In the interest of the "good of the people," the ruler can certainly perform certain acts discretely for the sake of maintaining public order. For Kautilya, this wholly pragmatic aspect pushes the ethical, if not sacred content of the royal office to the background. We now clearly find ourselves in the company of rulers of the Hellenistic Mediterranean, who in many cases acted very similarly. We are somewhat surprised by the quite lengthy list of virtues that Kautilya attributes to the king. It is not surprising, after all, if in performing his office he often finds himself in situations that must be resolved by means that, for someone else, would undoubtedly

---

[183] See above quotations from chapter 89.

be considered criminal; he must be thought to possess exceptional personal integrity, enabling him to "dirty his hands" while remaining pure. The Indian king was merely a man; for him to maintain his position he needed to be able to think rationally, possess superb tactical skills, impressive personal charisma, a strong stomach and steady nerves.

Moreover, Kautilya insists that the Indian king, despite it all, always act justly and refrain from committing any transgressions, acts of violence or tyranny.[184] The ruler of *Arthashastra* is like a good doctor: he does not harbor any illusions about the bodies or souls of his fellow man, yet is always willing to help them, while maintaining the principles of *primum non nocere* (first do no harm).

## China

I hope the reader forgives my inclusion of two texts into the Chinese section of our documents. Thanks to the Chinese's love for order and respect for history, we have a whole series of unique documents at our disposal. These documents discuss the state and its role and significance beginning in the 6th century BC and provide us with the opportunity to gauge the difference in views held by representatives of China's various philosophical currents.

The author of the first text needs little in the way of introduction. Confucius (551–479 BC) is one of the founding fathers of Chinese thought and is credited with the system that he himself created and still bears his name today. The excerpt given here nicely illuminates Confucius's principles. Let us therefore listen carefully to his words.

The following excerpt is taken from Dun J. Li's translation.[185]

---

[184] "The dharma of everything is not to hurt anyone, to be truthful, pure, to rid oneself of hatred, to be loving and patient" (Arthashastra, Chapter 1, Zbavitel's edition p. 12).

[185] Dun J. Li (ed.), The Essence of Chinese Civilization, Princeton, New Jersey – New York – Chicago – San Francisco – Toronto – London, D. van Nostrand Company, Inc., 1967, pp. 111–113. I am grateful to my learned friend and colleague Lubica Obuchová for this passage.

*Duke Ai asked about government and Confucius replied to him as follows:*

*The prerequisite to the establishment of good government is the presence of good men. A good man follows certain rules in conducting his personal life and is one of these rules is* jen. Jen *deals with man's relationships with other men, and the most important of these relationships is that between parents and children. There is also the rule of righteousness in which one does what is regarded as proper and right. Of all things that one should do, none is more important than honoring the virtuous. To love in accordance with the closeness of the receiving person and to honor in accordance with the amount of virtue the honored possess – therein is the origin from which rites result.*

*A gentleman should devote himself to the refinement of his character. To refine his character, he cannot but serve well his parents. To learn to serve his parents well, he has to know the nature of man. To know the nature of man, he has to know the way of heaven.*

*There are five forms in which the way of Heaven expresses itself, namely, the five relationships among men: Relationships between king and subjects, father and son, husband and wife, elder and younger brothers, and finally, among friends. There are three virtues whereby these relationships can be correctly observed: wisdom, love and courage. In short, action, or the lack of it, is the criterion upon which a man's success or failure in observing these relationships can be judged...*

*"The love of learning is the beginning of knowledge," Confucius continued. "To act in vigor to implement what one believes is close to the meaning of love, and to feel a sense of shame is an act of courage. Understanding the truism of these statements, a man knows how to refine his own character. Knowing how to refine his own character, he knows how to govern other people. Knowing how to govern the people, he knows how to govern the nation and the world.*

*There are nine virtues a king must possess if he wishes to run a successful government for the nation and the world. They are refinement of personal character, honoring the virtuous, love for parents, respect for high-ranking ministers, courtesy to all officials, treatment of all subjects as if they were the king's own children, encouraging artisans from every field of endeavor to come to his kingdom, winning the friendship of foreigners through kindness, and finally, commanding the vassals' fealty via gentleness and magnanimity.*

*His character refined, a king will act according to accepted rules. Because he honors the virtuous, he will receive the best counsels and consequently will not be confused. Since he loves his parents, he will not become a target of complaints from his elders or younger brothers. Showing respect for high-ranking ministers, he will be wisely advised and will know what to do when an emergency arises. Being courteous to all officials, he will receive in return not only courtesy but also gratitude. Treating his subjects as if they were his own children, he will indirectly encourage more people to become his subjects. Encouraging artisans from every field of endeavor to come to his kingdom, he will have articles of all kinds and thus ensure his own economic sufficiency. When kindness is used as a weapon to win the friendship of foreigners, all foreigners will be happy to submit. Finally, when he treats his vassals with gentleness and magnanimity, his authority will be not only feared but also respected. ...*

*Corvée duties are imposed only when people are not busy in the field; tax rates should be kept low at all times. As for the artisans, their products should be inspected daily and tested monthly: let them be paid well so that they can concentrate on and perform well their assigned tasks....*

*In short, it is the king's responsibility to translate these nine virtues into beneficial results....*

*Those who do not enjoy the confidence of their superiors cannot successfully govern the people. Those who enjoy the confidence of their superiors but not that of their friends will cause their superiors to lose confidence in them. Those who enjoy the confidence of their friends but not that of their parents will cause their friends to lose confidence in them. Those who serve their parents well and enjoy their confidence will have to examine themselves as to whether they are truly sincere in their endeavor. If they are not, they will lose the confidence of their parents. No man can be truly sincere if he does not know the difference between good and evil, or right and wrong.*

*Sincerity is the way of Heaven as well as that of man.*

Here the Chinese sage looks back to the times in which the Babylonian spoke to us. To ensure quality state politics means, above all, following the ways to the Heavens, to inquire into the meaning of wisdom given divinely as a guiding principle on the paths of this world. Politics is still not freed here from the general ethical context, assigning everyone the task to incessantly strive for self-improvement during his or her life.

The state and life in the state under these conditions is still a gift of divine powers and, as such, should be charged with ethical value and depend on it. In these conditions, politics, at least as it is defined in Kautilya's *Arthasastra,* does not even really exist. The main goal of the statesman, just like every other citizen, it is to achieve a humanity for which Confucius uses his famous expression – *jen.*[186] To come as close as possible to this virtue, each person should, within the network of the existing social relations defined by the five social bonds, resort to three fundamental virtues – wisdom, love and courage. Wisdom teaches us what is most important on earth – mainly distinguishing between good and evil. Love encourages us to take the path of good, not evil.

Lastly, courage gives us enough strength to carry out our intentions, decisions and resolutions.[187] Confucius preaches ethics, which has not developed into politics as the art of the possible as Kautilya teaches it.[188]

Although the author of the second, substantially different text, Ge Hong (also known as Ko Hung, 284–364), lived much later, he left for us a unique view of the state through the eyes of a Chinese Taoist, a follower of the doctrine preaching universal balance in things, not unlike Mediterranean Pythagoreanism. He came from a clerical family in southern China and was given the opportunity to receive a superb education, but his father died when he was 12 years of age and the family was forced to overcome material hardships. He studied under the master Zheng Yin, with whom he learned both official state literature as well as less commonly known works, including alchemist treatises. He acquired a reputation as a skilled military leader, though he was unable to gain a public office (302–306). He then went into seclusion and devoted himself to the study of the occult sciences in particular and to his writing (ca. 306–314). After a certain period of a new of-

---

[186] Here he concurs with Aristotle, for whom the greatest objective of each person in life is bliss achieved by virtue.

[187] This is close to the sixth part of the Buddhist Enlightened eight-part path – proper virtue, the courage to live in dharma, *samma virya.*

[188] We recall that Kautilya politics allows that which has not been acquired to be acquired, to safeguard what is acquired, increases what is guarded and distributes among the deserving. It is actually, therefore, a gigantic redistribution organism.

ficial career as a court chancellor (ca. 314–331), he asked to be named the administrator of the district on the Vietnamese border, but he was arrested on the journey to his new position and exiled to a hermit's life in the mountains where, at the end of his life, he devoted himself to writing and the occult sciences, and where he also died. He was an expert in Taoism and alchemy and was a prolific writer.

Below is another excerpt taken from Dun J. Li's translation.[189]

*The Confucians say that Heaven creates people and then installs kings to rule them. Can it also be true that the Confucians invoke Heaven to speak out what they themselves wish to believe?*

*The strong oppress the weak who have no choice except to submit. The clever play tricks upon the ignorant who are forced to be obedient. Involuntary servitude characterizes the relationship between a king and his subjects, and the enforcement of obedience is the way whereby the weak – the people – are effectively controlled. In fact, the very relationship between superiors and inferiors results from the successful contest on the part of the strong against the weak and the clever against the ignorant. ...*

*The masses, nameless and thankless, work hard to support the ruling officials. The higher the salary these officials receive, the harder the life the masses have to endure.*

*A man who have been sentenced to death and then receives clemency greatly rejoices; would it not have been better had the death sentence not been imposed in the first place? A hypocrite acquires the reputation of modesty and humbleness by declining the rank and salary bestowed upon him by his superiors; would he not have been more honest had he accepted the honors?*

*Loyalty and righteousness become outstanding virtues only in a turbulent and degenerate society. Filial obedience and parental love become conspicuous and praiseworthy only after harmony has been lost among the members of a household.*

*In ancient times there were neither kings nor ministers. People dug wells to obtain their drink and tilled fields to grow their food. They began to work when the sun rose and rested when the sun set. Being unfettered and carefree,*

---

189  Dun J. Li (ed.), The Essence of Chinese Civilization, Princeton, New Jersey – New York – Chicago – San Francisco – Toronto – London, D. van Nostrand Company, Inc., 1967, pp. 39–41, a selection from the writings of Pao-p'o-tzu.

*they were happy and content. Knowing no such things as competition and aggressiveness, they neither coveted honor nor incurred any shame. It was then that mountains had no trails and rivers carried no boats; even bridges did not exist. Since transportation was impossible via land or by water, people could not annex each other's territories. Warfare became a matter of unfeasibility because there was no concentration of people in any area.*

*Then people had no such concepts as power and profit; consequently they had neither strifes nor calamities therefrom. Weapons did not exist; fortifications were meaningless. All things were incorporeal and yet inseparable; they were lost and yet embodied in the Way....*

*It was only in the later years that cleverness was popularized and craft became the fashion. As the precedence of superiors over inferiors become an established rule, true virtues deteriorated....*

*The further we are away from the days of this unadultered beginning, the more we become base and dishonest. Now people make better and more effective weapons: the more they do so, the longer they prolong the evil or war and conquest. As far as they are concerned, cross-bows can never be too powerful, armor can never be too strong, spear can never be too sharp, and shield can never be too thick. All of these weapons could be easily dispensed with has there been no oppression of one group of people by another.*

*How can a jade tally be made if a piece of raw jade is not cut? By the same token, how can true love and righteousness come about if false values are not abandoned? Evil men like Chieh and Chou did such terrible things as burning their subjects alive, torturing imperial counselors, quartering feudal lords, carving out people's hearts, and breaking men's shinbones. Their arrogance and insolence reached the maximum when they put people to death through the use of hot pillars. Had they been commoners, they would not have been able to commit these wanton crimes even though they might be satanic and sadistic by nature. Why could they do these evil things at the expense of the whole world? It was because they happened to be kings.*

*Evils multiply themselves as soon as the institution of kingship is established. By then it is too late even to be angry. What purpose can anger serve when a person has already been put behind bars and when he has to endure his sorrow and weariness under the worst possible circumstances? While the people suffer below, their ruler trembles above, because every ruler is fearful of his own subjects. He teaches them rites and propriety; he regulates their conduct by the enactment of laws and the imposition of punishment. He tries to stop a great flood with his hands after he has inadvertently broken the dyke. He is bound to fail.*

The circle closes with the above text and, to a certain extent, the development of the ancient state returns to from where it came. Recognition of the "state in trouble" began with the painful realization that the gods for some unknown reason allow woe and suffering to befall mortals. Based on this finding, the wise came to the conclusion that if the gods allow evil to run ramped, humankind has no other choice but to maintain proper ethical principles and faith in the justness of the gods, who eventually punish the wrongful acts, and to humbly and patiently endure evil. This is why everything that happens in the world does so according to the will of the gods and along the path to the heavens. Only slowly and gradually, particularly in the great empires of the Hellenistic period, did *common good* rise to the level of the gods, and politics, freed of its religious and ethical charge, became the art of the possible and passed from the heavens to earth – sometimes, indeed, all the way to mud.

The consequences of this transformation in politics did not take long. In the Roman-controlled West it gave rise to the creation and early development of Christianity, which, though originally started as a movement void of political aims and awaiting the end of the world, later turned to politics itself. In the Chinese-controlled east, Taoist thinkers threw the harshest conceivable accusation into the face of the imperial state and its administration: that the state debases the natural state of humanity, distorts a person and disrupts the natural order of things. They undoubtedly found in the political practices of the day a number of relevant examples supporting their assertion, and thus appear to be extremely clever observers, analysts and critics.

The difficulty obviously lies in the proposed remedial measures. The Taoist Ge Hong comes with the myth favored by all reformers: an idyllic and sunny picture of the "past golden age" when people lived a simple but virtuous life in harmony with nature. The fact that this "golden age" never existed does not have to be pointed out. This is a fiction drawn not from actual sources, but an idea and artificial construction (to put it mildly) construed from antitheses to the current state that the reformer feels to be warped, false and corrupted. In this sense, the Taoists did not provide practical politics with much of a gauge to go on. Yet this was not intentional; they themselves considered the utmost aim of their endeavors to grasp the natural essence of things and the dynamics of their primordial relations, the world as a harmony of mutually antithetical components, as the "Way" (*Tao*).

So the development of the earliest states went back to where they had come from: their pre-state form (at least in theory). For most of the ancient period the people of the earliest statehood lived with the conviction that they were carrying out the gods' will. Yet the gods became more remote, rising even higher, and there were so many people that they gradually began to overshadow the gods, drowning out the gods' voices with their own screams. The wise and perceptive reflected the transformation of state politics into the use of all means to implement the *common good* by shunning practical politics for the religious sphere or through their outright rejection of the state.

One of statehood's developmental epochs thus came to a close. World civilization would have to wait until the Middle Ages for the next one.

# BIBLIOGRAPHY

## Sources

Benjamin R. FOSTER: Before the Muses. An Anthology of Akkadian Literature (3rd Edition), Bethesda, Maryland, CDL Press 2005, pp. 258–270.

R. P. KANGLE: The Kantillya Arthasástra Part II., An English Translation with Critical and Explanatory Notes, University of Bombay Studies, Sanskrt, Prakrit and Pali, No. 2, 1963.

Dun J. LI (trad. et ed.): The Essence of Chinese Civilization. Princeton – New Jersey – New York – Chicago – San Francisco – Toronto – London, D. van Nostrand Company, Inc., 1967.

Jiří PROSECKÝ (trad. et ed.): „Královské knihy" staré Mezopotámie. ("The royal books of ancient Mesopotamia"), Prague, The Oriental Institute of the Academy of Sciences of the Czech Republic 1995.

Vincent A. TOBIN: Instructions, lamentations, dialogues. Admonitions of an Egyptian sage. In: William K. Simpson (ed.), The Literature of ancient Egypt, London & New Haven, Yale University Press 2003, pp. 189–210.

Břetislav VACHALA (trad. et ed.): Moudrost starého Egypta. (The wisdom of ancient Egypt) Prague, Knižní podnikatelský klub 1992.

Dušan ZBAVITEL (trad. et ed.): Kautiljova Arthašástra aneb Učebnice věcí světských (Kautilya's Arthashastra or the textbook on worldly matters). Prague, Arista 2001.

## Bibliography

Muhammad ABDARRAZIK: Die altägyptischen Weingarten (k3nw/k3mw) bis zum Ende des Neuen Reiches. "Mitteilungen des Deutschen Archäologischen Instituts in Kairo" 35, 1979, pp. 227–247.

Cyril ALDRED: Egypt to the End of the Old Kingdom. London, Thames and Hudson 1965.

Sarah ALLAN: Erlitou and the Formation of Chinese Civilization: Toward a New Paradigm. "The Journal of Asian Studies" 66/2, 2007, pp. 461–496.

Alexandra ARDELEANU-JANSEN (ed.): Vergessene Städte am Indus – Frühe Kulturen in Pakistan vom 8.–2. Jahrtausend v. Chr. Mainz am Rhein, Philipp von Zabern 1987.

Anonymous author: Cache of seal impressions discovered in Western India offers surprising new evidence for cultural complexity in little-known Ahar-Banas culture. Ca. 3000–1500 B.C., in: http://www.museum.upenn.edu/new/research/possehl/aharbanas.shtml, cited on Feb 4, 2004.

Joan ARUZ – Ronald WALLENFELS (ed.): Art of the First Cities – The Third millenium B. C. from the Mediterranean to the Indus. New York – New Haven and London, The Metropolitan Museum of Art, Yale University Press 2003.

Claudio BAROCAS – Rodolfo FATTOVICH – Maurizio TOSI: The Oriental Institute of Naples Expedition to Petrie's South Town (Upper Egypt), 1977–1983: An
interim report, in: Lech Krzyzaniak, Marek Kobusiewicz (ed.), Late Prehistory
of the Nile Basin and the Sahara, Poznań, Poznań Archaeological Museum 1989,
pp. 295–301.

Lewis BINFORD: Mortuary Practices: Their Study and Their Potential. In: J. A.
Brown (ed.), Approaches to the Social Dimensions of Mortuary Practices, Memoirs
of the Society for American Archaeology No. 25, 1971, pp. 6–29.

Georges BOILEAU: Wu and Shaman. "Bulletin of the School of Oriental and African
Studies of the University of London" 65/2, 2002, pp. 350–376.

Paolo BRUSASCO: The Archaeology of Verbal and Nonverbal Meaning, Mesopotamian Domestic Architecture and Its Textual Dimension. BAR International Series
1631, Oxford, Archaeo-press 2007.

Elizabeth CARTER: The Piedmont and the Pusht-i-Kuh in the Early Third Millenium
B.C. In: Col-loques Internationaux du CNRS: Préhistoire de la Mésopotamia,
17–18–19 décembre 1984, Paris, Editions du CNRS 1986, pp. 73–83.

Serge CLEUZIOU – Giorgio GUDI – Charles ROBIN – Maurizio TOSI: Cachets in-
scrits de la fin du IIIe millénaire avant notre ére à Ras' al-Junayz, sultanat d'Oman.
"Académie des Inscriptions et de Belles-Letters, Comptes-rendus des séances de
l'année 1994", avril-juin, Paris, de Boccard 1994, pp. 453–468.

Andrew C. COHEN: Death Rituals, Ideology, and the Development of Early Mesopotamian King-ship - Toward a New Understanding of Iraq's Royal Cemetery
of Ur. (Ancient Magic and Divination VII), Leiden – Boston, Brill – Styx 2005.

Cynthia S. COLBURN: Exotica and the Early Minoan Elite: Eastern Imports in
Prepalatial Crete. "American Journal of Archaeology" 112, 2008, pp. 203–224.

Roger CRIBB: Nomads in Archeology. Cambridge, Cambridge University Press 1991.

Françoise DEMANGE: No. 303 – Cylinder seal of Shu-ilishu, Interpreter for Meluhha.
In: Jonathan Kenoyer, The Indus Civilization, in Joan Aruz, Ronald Wallenfels
(ed.), Art of the First Cities – The Third millenium B.C. from the Mediterranean
to the Indus, New York – New Haven and London, The Metropolitan Museum
of Art, Yale University Press 2003, pp. 377–413, on p. 413.

Dossiers d'Archéologie: No. 307, octobre 2005: L'Egypte prédynastique. Dijon, Edi-
tions Faton S. A. S. 2005, with contributions by Béatrix Midant-Reynes, Yann
Tristrant, Krzysztof Cialowicz, Sylvie Duchesne, Luc Staniaszek, Eric Crubézy,
Nathalie Baduel, Dominique Farout, Renée Friedman, Marcella Campagna and
Stan Hendricks.

Christopher EYRE – John BAINES: Interactions between Orality and Literacy in
Ancient Egypt. In: K. Schousboe and M. T. Larsen (ed.), Literacy and Society,
Center for Research in the Humanities, Copenhagen University, Kjabenhavn,
Akademisk Forlag 1989, pp. 91–119.

Gabriele FAHR-BECKER (ed.): The Art of East Asia. Tandem Verlag 2006, p. l.

Walter A. FAIRSERVIS, Jr: G. L. Possehl's and M. H. Raval's 'Harappan Civilization
and Rojdi'. "Journal of the American Oriental Society" 111/1, 1991, pp. 108–114.

Walter FARBER: Die Vergöttlichung Narâm-Sîns. "Orientalia" N. S. 52, 1983,
pp. 67–72.

Steve FARMER – Richard SPROAT – Michael WITZEL: The Collapse of the Indus-Script Thesis: The Myth of a Literate Harappan Civilization. "Electronic Journal of Vedic Studies" 11–2, 2004, pp. 19–57, on pp. 22 and 35–36 (cited on June 24, 2008 from http://www.safarmer.com/ fsw2.pdf).

Jan FILIPSKÝ: Zrození indické civilizace (The birth of the Indian civilization). In: Jaroslav Strnad – Jan Filipský – Jaroslav Holman – Stanislava Vavroušková, Dějiny Indie (The History of India), Prague, Nakladatelství Lidové noviny 2008, pp. 23–123.

Jean-Daniel FOREST: Les pratiques funéraires en Mésopotamie au début du 3e millénaire avant Jésus Christ, étude de cas, Paris, ERC 1983 (chapter Ur cimetiěre Jemdet Nasr).

Jean-Jacques GLASSNER: Écrire a Sumer – L'invention du cunéiforme. Editions du Seuil 2000, p. l.

Jean-Jacques GLASSNER: The Invention of Cuneiform. Tr. Zainab Bahrani, Marc van de Mieroop, Baltimore and London, The Johns Hopkins University Press 2003 (The English translation of this book).

Jean GUILAINE (ed.): Le Chalcolithique et la construction des inégalités. I. II., Paris, Editions Errance 2007.

Hao JITAO: Peasant and State in Classical Athens and Zhou China: A Comparative Survey. "Journal of Ancient Civilizations" 8, 1993, pp. 78-104.

Stefan R. HAUSER (ed.): Die Sichtbarkeit von Nomaden und Saisonaler Besiedlung in der Archeologie. Multidisziplinäre Annäherungen an ein methodisches Problem, Mitteilung des SFB "Differenz und Integration" 9, Orientwissenschaftliche Hefte herausge-geben vom Orientwissenschaftlichen Zentrum der Martin-Luther Universität Halle-Wittenberg Heft 21/2006, Halle (Saale), OWZ 2006.

Jane A. HILL: Cylinder Seal Glyptic in Predynastic Egypt and Neighboring Regions. Oxford, Archaeopress 2004.

Wayne HOROWITZ: Mesopotamian Cosmic Geography. Winona Lake, Indiana, Eisenbrauns 1998.

Michael HUDSON: How Interest Rates Were Set, 2500 BC – 1000 AD. "Journal of the Economic and Social History of the Orient" 43/2, 2000, pp. 132–161.

Petr CHARVÁT: On People, Signs and States – Spotlights on Sumerian Society, c. 3500–2500 B.C. Prague, The Oriental Institute, Academy of Sciences of the Czech Republic 1997.

Petr CHARVÁT: Mesopotamia Before History. London and New York, Routledge – Taylor and Francis Group 2002.

Petr CHARVÁT: The Iconography of Pristine Statehood – Painted Pottery and Seal Impressions from Susa, Southwestern Iran. Prague, Karolinum Press 2005.

Petr CHARVÁT: The Backs of Some Sealings from Nineveh 5, "Iraq". LXVII Part 1, Spring 2005 (Papers of the XLIXe Rencontre Assyriologique Internationale London, 7–11 July 2003, Part Two), pp. 391-397.

Petr CHARVÁT: Review of Jane A. Hill, Cylinder Seal Glyptic in Predynastic Egypt and Neighboring Regions. Oxford, Archaeopress 2004, in "Bibliotheca Orientalis" LXIII/5-6, September–December 2006, pp. 519–522.

Petr CHARVÁT: Social configurations in Early Dynastic Babylonia (c. 2500-2334 B.C.).

In: Gwendolyn Leick (ed.), The Babylonian World, New York and London, Rout-
ledge, Taylor and Francis Group 2007, pp. 251–264.
Joan CHING: Son of Heaven: Sacral Kingship in Ancient China. "T'oung pao"
83/1–3,1997, pp. 3–41.
Jiří JANÁK: 105. kapitola Knihy mrtvých v období Nové říše – Staroegyptské pojetí
vzkříšení (Chapter 105 of the book of the dead during the New Empire – the
Ancient Egyptian concept of resurrection). doctoral dissertation, Charles Uni-
versity in Prague, the Hussite Theological Faculty, Religious Studies Department
Prague, 2002.
Jinhua JIA – Kwok DANG-FEI: From Clan Manners to Ethical Obligation and
Righteousness: A New Interpretation of the Term yi. "Journal of the Royal Asiatic
Society", 3rd Series, vol. 17, Part I, 2007, pp. 33–41.
Peter KAPLONY: "Rollsiegel" entry. In: Lexikon der Ägyptologie V, Wiesbaden,
Harrassowitz Verlag 1983, pp. 294–300.
Peter KAPLONY: Der Schreiber, das Gotteswort und die Papyruspflanze. "Zeitschrift
für ägyptische Sprache und Literatur" 110, 1983, pp. 143–173.
David N. KEIGHTLEY (ed.): The Origins of Chinese Civilization. Berkeley – Los
Angeles – London, University of California Press 1983.
David N. KEIGHTLEY: The Late Shang State: When, Where, and What? In: David
N. Keightley (ed.): The Origins of Chinese Civilization, Berkeley – Los Angeles
– London, University of California Press 1983, pp. 523–564.
Jonathan KENOYER: The Indus Civilization. In: Joan Aruz, Ronald Wallenfels (ed.),
Art of the First Cities – The Third Millenium B.C. from the Mediterranean to the
Indus, New York – New Haven and London, The Metropolitan Museum of Art,
Yale University Press 2003, pp. 377–413.
Lech KRZYZANIAK: Trends in the Socio-Economic Development of Egyptian Predy-
nastic Societies. In: Acts of the First International Congress of Egyptology, Cairo,
October 2–10, 1976, Berlin, Akademie-Verlag 1979, pp. 407–412.
Marc LEBEAU – Thierry de PUTER: Un fragment de vase en pierre égyptien
vraisemblablement d'époque protodynastique découvert à Tell Beydar, Syrie. In:
"Baghdader Mitteilungen" 37, 2006, pp. 279–294.
Alan LUPTON: Stability and Change – Socio-Political Development in Northern
Mesopotamia and Southeastern Anatolia. 4000–2700 BC. (BAR International
Series 627), p. l.: Tempvs reparatum 1996.
Charles K. MAISELS: Early Civilizations of the Old World. London and New York,
Routledge – Taylor and Francis Group 2001.
Jakub MARŠÁLEK: Sociální analýza pohřebišť pozdního neolitu (cca 3000–2000
př. n. l.) na území provincie Shandong. (A social analysis of late Neolithic burial
grounds in the Shandong province (3000–2000 BC)), doctoral dissertation, Charles
University in Prague, Faculty of Arts, Institute of the Far East (specialization: The
History and Culture of Asia and Africa, supervisor: Prof. Oldřich Král, PhD.),
June 2003.
Eric M. MEYERS (ed.), The Oxford Encyclopaedia of Archeology in the Near East
I–IV, Oxford etc., Oxford University Press 1996.
Ian MORRIS: Gift and commodity in archaic Greece. "Man" 21/1, 1986, pp. 1–17.

Asko PARPOLA: Special lecture: Study of the Indus Script, paper read at the 50th ICES. Tokyo Session, 19th May 2005 (cited on June 24, 2008 from http://www.harappa.com/script/indusscript.pdf).

John PEOPLES – George BAILEY: Humanity – An Introduction to Cultural Anthropology. Saint Paul – New York – Los Angeles – San Francisco, West Publishing Company 1988.

Susan POLLOCK: Ancient Mesopotamia – The Eden that Never Was. Cambridge, Cambridge University Press 1999.

Gregory POSSEHL – Vasant SHINDE: Excavations at Gilund 2001–2003: The seal impressions and other finds, South Asian Archeology 2003. My gratitude to Professor Gregory Possehl for providing access to the manuscript.

Kateřina POSTUPOVÁ: Počátky kontaktu Egypta a Předního Východu (Early contact between Egypt and the Near East), B.A. thesis, West Bohemian University in Plzeň – Faculty of Arts, Plzeň, 2007.

Jiří PROSECKÝ et al.: Encyklopedie starověkého Předního Východu (Encyclopedia of the Ancient Near East). Prague, LIBRI 1999.

Marshall SAHLINS: Stone Age Economics. Chicago, Aldine 1972.

Benjamin Adam SAIDEL – Eveline J. Van der STEEN (eds.): On the Fringe of Society: Archaeological and Ethnoarchaeological Perspectives on Pastoral and Agricultural Societies. BAR International Series 1657, Oxford, Archaeopress 2007.

Walther SALLABERGER: Nachrichten an den Palast von Ebla: Eine Deutung von níg-mul(-an). In: Semitic and Assyriological Studies Presented to Pelio Fronzaroli by Pupils and Colleagues, Wiesbaden, Harrassowitz Verlag 2003, pp. 600–625.

Andrew SHERRATT: Plough and pastoralism: aspects of the secondary products revolution. In: I. Hodder – G. Isaac – N. Hammond (eds.), Pattern of the Past: Studies in Honour of David Clarke, Cambridge, Cambridge University Press 1981, pp. 261–305.

Denise SCHMANDT-BESSERAT: The Interface Between Writing and Art – The Seals of Tepe Gawra. In: "Syria" 83, 2006 (Hommage á Henri Contenson), pp. 183–193.

Robert SCHMITT: Dumézilsche Dreifunktionentheorie. In: H. Beck et al. (eds.), Reallexikon der germanischen Altertumskunde, Band 6, Lieferung 3–4, Berlin – New York, Walter de Gruyter 1985, pp. 276–280.

Jaroslav STRNAD – Jan FILIPSKÝ – Jaroslav HOLMAN – Stanislava VAVROUŠKOVÁ: Dějiny Indie (The History of India). Prague, Nakladatelství Lidové noviny 2008.

Elizabeth C. STONE: Texts, Architecture and Ethnographic Analogy: Patterns of Residence in Old Babylonian Nippur. "Iraq" 43/1, 1981, pp. 1–18.

Elizabeth C. STONE: Nippur Neighborhoods. Chicago, The Oriental Institute 1987.

Taťjana A. ŠERKOVA: "Oko Chora": simvolika glaza v dodinastičeskom Jegipete. "Vestnik drevnej istorii" 1996/4, pp. 96–115.

Giuseppe VISICATO: Archéologie et documents écrits: Les "silos" et les textes sur l'orge de Fara. "Revue d'Assyriologie" 87/1, 1993, pp. 83–85.

Petra VLČKOVÁ: Kamenné nádoby s nápisy – Pramey k poznání správního systému Raně Dynastického Egypta (Stone vessels bearing inscriptions – sources providing an understanding of the Administrative System of Early Dynastic Egypt). In:

/346/

Ľubica Obuchová – Petr Charvát (eds.), Stát a státnost ve starém Orientu, soubor studií pracovní skupiny (The state and statehood in the ancient Orient), a series of studies by the "People and the Land in History" work group, Prague, The Czech Society for Oriental Studies 2006, pp. 8–25.

Wang TAO: Shang ritual animals: colour and meaning (Part 1). In: "Bulletin of the School of Oriental and African Studies of the University of London" 70/2, 2007, pp. 305–372.

Wang TAO: Shang ritual animals: colour and meaning (Part 2). In: "Bulletin of the School of Oriental and African Studies of the University of London" 70/3, 2007, pp. 539–567.

David WENGROW: The Archaeology of Early Egypt – Social Transformations in North-East Africa, 10,000 to 2650 BC. Cambridge – New York – Melbourne – Madrid – Cape Town – Singapore – Sao Paulo, Cambridge University Press 2006.

Alwo von WICKEDE: Die Ornamentik der Tell Halaf-Keramik, Ein Beitrag zu ihrer Typologie. "Acta Praehistorica et Archaeologica" 18, 1986, pp. 7–32.

Claus WILCKE: Literatur um 2000 vor Christus. In: J. W. Meyer – W. Sommerfeld (eds.), 2000 v. Chr., Politische, wirtschaftliche und kulturelle Entwicklung im Zeichen einer Jahrtausendwende, Berlin, DOG in Kommission bei Saarbrücker Druckerei und Verlag 2004, pp. 205–218.

Yang YANG – Zhao GUSHAN: Culture de la Chine – L'archéologie. Beijing, Editions en Langues étrangeres 2003.

Norman YOFFEE: Myths of the Archaic State. Cambridge, Cambridge University Press 2005.

Richard ZETTLER: The Ur III Temple of Inanna at Nippur. The Operation and Organization of Urban Religious Institutions in Mesopotamia in the Late Third Millenium B.C. (Berliner Beiträge zum Vorderen Orient 11), Berlin, Dietrich Reimer Verlag 1992.

# INDEX

PETR CHARVÁT

THE BIRTH OF THE STATE
Ancient Egypt, Mesopotamia, India and China

translated by Daniel Morgan

Published by Charles University in Prague
Karolinum Press
Ovocný trh 3–5, 116 36 Prague 1
Prague 2013
Editor vice-rector Prof. PhDr. Ivan Jakubec, CSc.
Edited by Martin Janeček
Graphic design by Zdeněk Ziegler
Illustrations Dagmar Hamsíková and Kateřina Řezáčová
Typeset by DTP Karolinum Press
Printed by Karolinum Press
First English edition

ISBN 978-80-246-2214-9